WALL STREET'S PICKS FOR

2000

KIRK KAZANJIAN

DEARBORN™

A **Kaplan Professional** Company

Associate Publisher: Cynthia A. Zigmund
Managing Editor: Jack Kiburz
Interior Design: the dotted i
Cover Design: Design Alliance, Inc.
Typesetting: the dotted i

Charts and some financial data reprinted with permission of IDD Information Services. All information contained in this book was gathered from sources believed to be reliable, but accuracy is not guaranteed.

© 2000 by Kirk Kazanjian

Published by Dearborn, a Kaplan Professional Company

Printed in the United States of America

00 01 10 9 8 7 6 5 4 3 2 1

ISBN 0-7931-3395-5

Dearborn books are available at special quantity discounts to use as premiums and sales promotions, or for use in corporate training programs. For more information, please call the Special Sales Manager at 800-621-9621, ext. 4514, or write to Dearborn Financial Publishing, Inc., 155 North Wacker Drive, Chicago, IL 60606-1719.

DEDICATION

To my aunt, Dr. Janet D. Kazanjian, with thanks for instilling in me an entrepreneurial spirit.

C ONTENTS

INTERNATIONAL FUNDS

PREFACE

It's not easy gaining access to Wall Street's top minds. After all, most manage multi-billion-dollar portfolios and won't even consider taking you on as a private client unless you have $1 million or more to invest. It's even harder to convince these folks to let you pick their brains for a while, maybe over lunch or dinner, to learn their investment secrets and favorite stock or fund ideas for the coming months.

Fortunately, I have come to know many of the investment world's biggest stars personally. I'm privileged to enjoy the kind of access to these luminaries that few have. And now, for the fourth year in a row, I'm pleased to let you in on their investment insights and strategies for the new millennium in *Wall Street's Picks for 2000*.

This is by far one of the most timely and user-friendly investment guides on the market today. Instead of focusing on a bunch of abstract theories or listing hundreds of possible investment choices (like many other publications), *Wall Street's Picks for 2000* cuts through the financial jargon to bring you specific and current recommendations from the very best minds in the business.

In Part 1 of this new edition, you will learn the number-one favorite stock ideas for the year ahead, according to such gurus as Louis Navellier, Elizabeth Bramwell, David Dreman, Seth Glickenhaus, Elizabeth Dater, Martin Whitman, James O'Shaughnessy, L. Roy Papp, Robert Sanborn, Joseph Battipaglia, Alan Bond, and many more. These are all successful investment managers who are at the top of their profession and consistently generate outstanding returns for their clients.

In essence, I asked each panelist to name the single stock he or she would own in the year 2000 if only one could be chosen. The answers are revealed in the form of in-depth reports on each selection, including background information on the company, reasons for the recommendation, financial figures and charts, and a discussion of what kind of performance to expect as the year unfolds.

Because many readers are more interested in mutual funds, I have interviewed some of the country's leading fund analysts for Part 2. Following a general discussion about how funds work and why they are such great investment vehicles, you will find promising recommendations in various categories from such renowned fund authorities as Don Phillips, Sheldon Jacobs, Harold Evensky, Michael Hirsch, Paul Merriman, Janet Brown, and Bob Markman.

As I've said before, the idea behind this book is to bring together an investment dream team to help you develop a first-rate portfolio. It's the kind of inside information that used to be reserved exclusively for Wall Street's heavy hitters.

This collective knowledge can't be found in any other book or magazine on the market today.

Of course, no pick is guaranteed to go up, and some may fall dramatically in price, despite my panel's optimistic expectations. That's all part of the risk you take when you become part-owner of a company through purchasing stock. However, judging from the past performance of those featured on my panel, most of these choices should be very rewarding.

As usual, Part 3 features a complete biography of each adviser, describing his or her background, investment philosophy, and market outlook, along with other bits of advice you can use to make more money in the market. I want to thank nationally syndicated personal finance columnist Humberto Cruz for calling *Wall Street's Picks* one of only three investment books available today that survives the marketing hype. Humberto agreed with me that Part 3 is perhaps the most valuable part of the book because the insights these living investment legends share can help make you richer for many years to come.

In addition, even though this book is written in reader-friendly language, if you're ever confused by financial verbiage that seems like gobbledygook, simply turn to the back where you'll find a glossary that provides definitions of some of the more commonly used investment terms and phrases you will encounter in the pages that follow.

By the way, if you want to know how last year's contributors feel about the prospects for their investment ideas going into 2000, their latest buy, sell, and hold ratings can be found at the end of Part 3.

For now, sit back, relax, and enjoy what I trust will be a very prosperous journey into the world of Wall Street's best advice on how to invest your money over the next 12 months.

—Kirk Kazanjian

part

1

THE
TOP
STOCKS
FOR 2000

STOCK PICKS—
AN INTRODUCTION

Before we discuss this year's stock selections, it makes sense to review some of the important principles that should guide all of your investment decisions. To begin with, as all smart investors know, basing portfolio decisions solely on the economy, specific items in the news, or the direction of the Dow is a recipe for disaster. In fact, the richest and most successful investors understand the key to great profits is finding individual companies with stories and valuations so compelling that their share prices are bound to go up, regardless of what happens in the overall economy or underlying indexes.

Those who try to time the market usually end up making the least amount of money. That's because no one has created a foolproof system for predicting where stocks are headed. Though some look back and boast about how accurate they were at calling certain tops, bottoms, and crashes, they rarely mention the number of times their advice was wrong.

Investors versus Traders

It has often been said that *investors,* those who buy quality companies and stay in the market regardless of outside influences, drive Cadillacs, while *traders,* people who jump in and out on a regular basis, ride around in Chevys. History suggests this is true. Statistics show that the majority of all market gains are made on only a handful of trading sessions each year. Therefore, if you are out on those days, you can expect nothing more than mediocre returns or even losses.

An often-cited study shows that during the 1980s, the Standard & Poor's 500 index produced an average annual return of 17.6 percent. However, if you were in cash on the top-ten trading days during that period, the figure dropped to 12.6 percent. Had you been on the sidelines for the 20 best days, you would have earned a mere 9.3 percent. And if you missed the 30 biggest advancing sessions, your return would have plummeted to just 6.5 percent, less than the amount you would have earned in a money market fund. Once the research is in on the 1990s, I'm confident the numbers will look very similar. Clearly, not being fully invested is costly because stocks tend to move in "lumps." They rise or fall, and then remain stagnant for a while, before rallying up or sliding down again. This is further proof that market timing rarely makes sense.

Sure, it would be great to avoid every correction and bear market. But that's impossible to do. Those who make the right calls often owe their success to luck more than to anything else. It's a point driven home by the great investor Sir John Templeton. When I asked for his market outlook a few years ago, he replied, "In the 52 years I was in the investment industry, I was never able to answer that question. I just searched for those stocks whose prices were lowest in relation to earnings." In other words, he had a strategy and stuck with it, regardless of what was happening with the "market."

Take it from Sir John: The secret to investment riches is finding the right stocks to be in at any given time. After all, though the major indexes may fall or go nowhere, some individual issues always manage to skyrocket. For example, back in 1994 the S&P 500 and Nasdaq each squeezed out a mere 1 percent gain, including dividends. Yet Microtouch Systems soared 555 percent, Cooper Companies leaped 227 percent, LSI Logic rose 154 percent, and Rock Bottom Restaurants jumped a full 128 percent for the year, proving that even though the overall market may be stagnant, it's possible to make a lot of money through superior stock selection. More recently, we've seen that the huge gains in both the S&P 500 and Nasdaq were primarily due to the stellar performance of just a handful of stocks. The broad market has actually been treading water during this time, and many individual stocks have suffered huge losses.

Uncle Sam Likes Investors Too

Another reason to avoid running in and out of stocks is that you'll save on the profits you have to share with the government. As part of the Taxpayers Relief Act of 1997, Congress decided to cap all long-term capital gains for positions held more than 12 months at a maximum rate of 20 percent. This contrasts with the 30 percent-plus rate you could be forced to pay for short-term trades.

Building Wealth with Equities

By now you've figured out that growing rich from stocks requires you to construct a stable of spectacular companies with bright future prospects. But how can you, as an individual investor far removed from the inner workings of Wall Street, find these jewels for yourself? That's what Part 1 of this book is all about.

Over the past several months, I personally spoke with dozens of the world's top investment experts and asked, "If you could choose only one stock to hold in the year 2000, what would it be and why?" The panelists represent leading portfolio managers, investment advisers, newsletter editors, and market strategists, all of whom have a slightly different style or area of expertise, giving you a truly diversified list of potential holdings.

Next, I followed up on these responses by analyzing the selections, such as culling through annual reports, financial statements, and historical price charts. This provided perspective on where the stocks have been and where they might be going. Additional insight came from talking with corporate officers about any developments that might make the picks either more or less compelling.

All of this revealing information was then put together in the form of an easy-to-read research report. There are a total of 25 different companies, which are listed in alphabetical order. This isn't a beauty contest to see who can pick the best performer, nor are these stocks you should buy in January and sell in December. Instead, they are quality companies that each expert considers to have great prospects for the new century.

Dissecting the Information

Each discussion starts off with a table showing the company's ticker symbol, trading exchange, and industry, along with such data as current price, PE ratio, book value, and earnings per share. Next is a profile of the company that includes specific reasons why it was selected. You'll also find IDD/Tradeline graphs showing the stock's daily price patterns for the past 12 months, total return versus the S&P 500, and performance compared with its peer index. There's even a box containing important balance sheet numbers (like current assets, liabilities, and shareholders' equity) going back two years. You should also pay attention to each stock's estimated beta factor, which is included in the statistical box at the bottom of every profile. Beta measures a stock's price volatility compared to the S&P 500, which has a beta of 1. Simply put, a stock with a beta of 0.8 is less volatile than the market overall, while a stock with a beta of 1.3 is much riskier. At the end of each profile, you'll find the address and phone number you can use to request more information from the company. In addition, I have included each company's Web site address, where applicable.

Please understand that these reports present predominately positive comments about the various companies. This stands to reason, because the recommending advisers are very upbeat about these stocks and their future prospects. However, there are always negatives to every story, and I have taken care to bring some of them to your attention. Make sure you evaluate the potential downfalls of each idea before investing. Remember, not every optimistic expectation by my panel of experts will come to fruition.

When choosing equities, it usually makes sense to stick with companies that report steady annual earnings growth, a characteristic shared by most of the stocks in this book. Sizable ownership by inside management is another bullish sign. It indicates that those in the know have enough faith in the firm to put their own money on the line. You'll learn much more about many different successful stock-picking strategies by reading the biographies in Part 3. In many respects, this is one of the most important sections of the book because the insights and advice these market masters provide are invaluable.

Stock Selection

Each stock has been chosen for a different reason, from low valuation to high future earnings potential, based on the adviser's particular style. In fact, every panelist has a unique process for selecting stocks. This information is spelled out for you in every discussion and should be an important consideration as you decide which ideas make the most sense for you, given your risk tolerance and overall objectives.

You'll notice the recommendations cover the gamut in terms of market capitalizations, industry groups, and geographic locations. There are some very big blue chips, namely IBM and Goodyear; smaller high-tech outfits with more risk, such as Uniphase and Pervasive Software; and international concerns, among them Administradora de Fondos ADS and LaSalle Re Holdings.

Asset Allocation

As you peruse these pages, keep in mind the principles of asset allocation. You need to consider whether you even belong in stocks in the first place and, if so, to what extent.

Let me first make it clear that only *investment capital* should be put into the market. In essence, this is money above and beyond what you need to live on. Think of it as funds you could afford to lose without dramatically altering your lifestyle. Granted, no one invests to lose. But because the stock market is inherently risky, knowing you can afford to lose your investment capital won't scare you out just when you should be jumping in.

After you've identified your investment capital, you must outline your goals. If you're saving for retirement or a similar long-term objective that's at least five to ten years away, stocks should make up a significant amount of your portfolio. They are the only investment class to consistently stay ahead of inflation while providing the highest rates of return throughout history. (We'll delve deeper into the subject of asset allocation in Parts 2 and 3.)

Once you determine what percentage to devote to stocks, you should understand that smaller and international issues generally carry more risk than those that are larger and better known. Keep this in mind as you evaluate which companies to purchase. If you consider yourself to be conservative, you might want to stick with only blue chips. If you're more moderate, perhaps several large companies sprinkled with a few small-caps and an international issue or two make sense. The brave, those shooting for huge gains and willing to take a potential roller-coaster ride, could concentrate almost entirely on smaller names with big prospects.

How many stocks do you need in your portfolio? Ask ten different people and you'll get ten different answers. An important rule of thumb is you should never put more than 5 percent of your total assets into any single investment. Therefore, to really reduce your downside exposure, you need at least 20 different issues. Some say you need upwards of 40 or more companies in your portfolio for proper diversification. Then there's Warren Buffett, who is among the greatest investors ever. He only holds a handful of stocks and has racked up enormous gains by concentrating on a select group of companies he knows well.

Just make sure you don't buy too many stocks in the same sector. If you simply own 30 high-technology stocks, your diversification is virtually nil. Spread your choices over many different sectors, so when one is out of favor, you can profit from another. Fortunately, the selections in this book are highly diversified in terms of size, industry, and even geographic location.

A good technique for developing a nice mix involves constructing your portfolio around a core. In other words, you choose a handful of great, mostly blue chip, companies that you plan to hold for the long haul and build some speculative names around them.

Remember, you will have to pay a commission for each stock you buy or sell. These charges can add up quickly and eat into your profits. You can save money by using a quality discount broker. Some brokers now execute trades on the Internet for as little as $5, so be certain to shop around. I'm sure you'll agree there's no use paying those high full-service brokerage fees when you're acting on your own investment advice (with the help of a few well-connected friends).

Limit or Market Orders?

Another decision you will face is whether to place market or limit orders for your stock selections. When you place a market order, you agree to pay whatever the prevailing price is at the time your order is executed, which may be more or less than the amount quoted by your broker.

On the other hand, limit orders allow you to set the terms. In today's crazy markets, limit orders make a lot of sense, even though some of the low-cost Internet brokers charge a bit more (usually $5) to execute them. Here's why: All stocks trade at a spread, which is the difference between the bid price and offer price. If a stock is trading at a bid of $15 and offered at $15.50, the spread is 50¢. With a limit order, you can specify that you will buy the stock only at $15. Otherwise, it would likely clear at market, or $15.50. It could be much higher, especially for a volatile Internet stock. Be advised, however, that while limit orders can save you money, they may take longer to execute, especially for thinly traded issues.

Limit orders are also used to set much lower price targets. For example, if you like a stock today that trades at $20 but only want to get in if it drops to $16, you can place a good-till-canceled (GTC) limit order for $16, which means the trade won't clear unless the issue hits your price point of $16. This may not ever happen, so be realistic if you place such an order.

Conversely, you can set stop loss limit orders once you've purchased a stock on the New York or American Stock Exchange to cushion your potential loss. Let's say you buy a stock for 20 and want to sell if it falls more than 10 percent. You can place a stop loss order for 18, which means the stock will automatically be sold if it reaches that level. (This technique should be used with caution, given that the market has never been more volatile and many stocks today tend to bounce around by several points during each trading session. If you're not careful, you could be sold out of a position even though the stock closes the day at a much higher price.)

When You Should Buy or Sell

Unfortunately, when writing about the stock market, whether for a book such as this or for a daily Internet site, information and valuations can change dramatically in a matter of seconds. That's why I have tried to include each analyst's price target for the year 2000 when available. If a stock has already reached this target by the time you read about it, you may want to determine whether this enthusiasm is sustainable or simply move on to another pick that appears to be a better bargain. If the company has just introduced a new product or acquisition that will make a significant contribution to earnings, it may merit the higher valuation. (As I mentioned earlier, it's wise to favor companies with rapidly growing earnings.) If nothing has changed, however, perhaps the price has moved ahead of itself or reached full value. On the other hand, if a stock is trading well below its target price, it may be an even more compelling buy, assuming nothing catastrophic or scandalous has happened to change the fundamentals in the interim.

The question of when to sell is more difficult. Some feel you should never get rid of a quality company. Others suggest you let go when the price appreciates or depreciates to some arbitrary level, such as 20 or 30 percent above or below cost. You'll find plenty of advice on this subject in Part 3.

Needless to say, if something happens to cloud both the company's future prospects and your reasons for buying in the first place, this too may be a good reason to get out.

Before You Begin

A few final notes: Please don't invest in any stock just because a person you admire in this book likes it. Simply use that validation as a starting point. Then call or write the company (the location, phone numbers, and addresses are provided for each stock); request an annual report and form 10-K or view it on the Net; check out available research reports at your library, on the Web, or in your broker's office; talk with an investor relations representative; check out the company's Internet site; and ultimately make a decision as to whether the recommendation makes sense for *you*. Just because it's right for David Dreman, Louis Navellier, Elizabeth Dater, Martin Whitman, or anyone else doesn't necessarily mean it belongs in your portfolio. Use these suggestions as a launching pad, but do a little legwork to confirm everything in your own mind and, for heaven's sake, make sure you understand what you're buying. If a company is engaged in some exotic technology and you have no clue what it does, stay away. Keep an eye on how your ultimate stock selections perform, and remain informed about any new positive and negative developments surrounding them.

Be sure to read quarterly and annual reports, and keep good records. This will make your life easier when it comes time to pay Uncle Sam for capital gains and dividend interest. It's also smart to periodically examine and calculate your total return figures to see how you're doing, especially compared with the S&P 500, which is the industry's standard benchmark. In essence, you should run your investment portfolio like a business. Once you make a purchase, you become a part-owner in the company and have a duty to run your affairs accordingly.

Finally, always remember: There are no guarantees. Although the following stocks truly represent the best ideas of some wonderful investors, the market never goes straight up. All equities carry a significant amount of risk. Also be aware that the various experts may own positions in the equities they recommend, either in personal and/or managed accounts. This is not necessarily a bad thing, but it's just something you should know. With that in mind, let's begin naming names of companies that could make you rich as we enter the new millennium.

ADMINISTRADORA DE FONDOS ADS

Vivian Lewis
Global Investing

Company Profile

Those who advocate privatizing the Social Security system in the United States often point to the success of another country that has done just that—Chile. "Everywhere you look in the world, the number of workers to support the number of retirees is going down," observes Vivian Lewis, publisher of *Global Investing*. "That shortage is what has caused the U.S. Social Security crisis. But this is a global phenomenon. Chile is the only country that has come up with a solution."

Under Chile's system, which has been in place for 19 years, a percentage of each worker's paycheck is taken out and put into a private pension account. Although several companies manage these assets, the largest is Administradora de Fondos de Pensiones Provida SA. We'll call it AFP for short. AFP has 82 branch offices in Chile. The company collects and administers worker contributions. It then manages the money and pays out benefits to investors. The company also offers life and disability benefits in Chile. Total assets under management are the equivalent of about U.S. $24 billion.

Although workers in America would presumably like most of their retirement money invested in equities, the Chilean government regulates the amount of money that pension providers like AFP can put into stocks. "The government is afraid these managers will lose the people's money so they have limited the portfolio's total equity exposure to 16 percent," Lewis explains. "The remaining 84 percent must be in bonds." These percentages were only recently increased from 12 percent and 88 percent, respectively.

Lewis specializes in finding promising international companies that U.S. investors can buy on one of the major American stock exchanges. She especially likes AFP. The company's American depositary receipts became available in November 1994, meaning you can now invest in the company on the New York Stock Exchange (NYSE). The stock trades under the symbol PVD.

In addition to Chile, AFP provides investment services in other parts of Latin America and Central America, including Ecuador, Peru, El Salvador, Columbia, and Mexico. It also is creating a pension plan for Poland. The company's variable fees are quite high by U.S. standards, totaling 2.6 percent of assets as of the most recent report. The company has a team of affiliates and in-house salespeople who peddle the AFP product. An array of technology is used to manage the various administrative functions. Pension owners even have the ability to check on their balances and make changes through both a Touch-Tone phone service and the Internet.

Reason for Recommendation

There are several reasons Lewis singles out this stock as her favorite for 2000. First, she is upbeat about the prospects for Chile overall and thinks money management is a great business to be in. "Beyond that, this is a good industry and the stock sells for a PE ratio of less than 4," she says. Lewis also notes that the stock has a 9.5 percent yield, which helps to cushion the risks associated with it. And there are plenty of risks. To begin with, the pension industry is highly regulated by the Chilean government. The government owns part of AFP, and the company is at the mercy of new policies set by lawmakers. Among other things, the Chilean government is putting pressure on pension administrators like AFP to lower management fees. It's also easy for residents to switch from one pension administrator to another with the flip of a switch, just as it's a simple task to transfer from one fund to another in your 401(k) plan at work. "The company's profits are in Chilean pesos, so there is the additional risk involved with currency translations," Lewis adds.

Interestingly enough, one of the major risks with foreign investing in general is that you can't always trust the financial figures given by overseas companies because regulations are often lax. Lewis insists that's not a problem for AFP as it is so closely regulated by the government. "I think you can trust the numbers here," she says. Other things to consider: The stock isn't very liquid, normally trading under 20,000 shares a day, although it is available on the NYSE.

"I think this company will continue to be a major player in Chile, and it is expanding into other markets," Lewis says. She hasn't set a price target for the stock but feels the potential upside is considerable, especially since the stock has such a generous yield. Spain's number-two bank, Banco Bilbao Vizcaya, apparently agrees. The institution recently bought a controlling interest in AFP.

It's not always easy getting information about foreign companies. AFP doesn't have a U.S. contact, but you can write to company headquarters in Chile at the address below. You also can find an English version of its annual report at www. provida.cl. The stock itself shouldn't be difficult to trade, even through one of the major discount brokers.

Contact Information: Administradora de Fondos de Pensiones Provida ADS
Avenida Pedro de Valdivia
100 Torre Provida
Santiago, Chile
011 562 697-0040
www.provida.cl

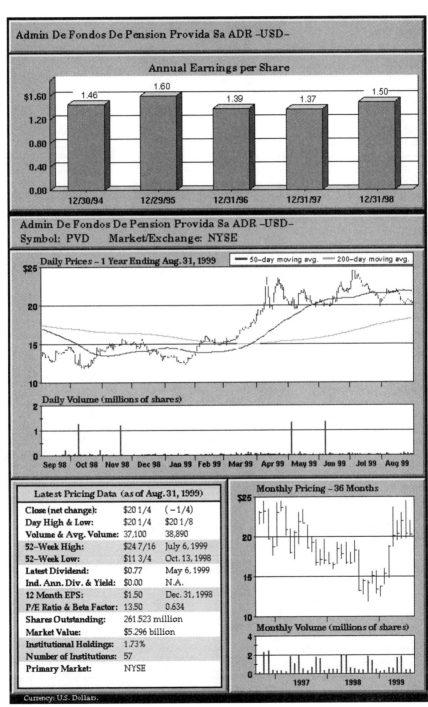

Admin De Fondos De Pension Provida Sa ADR –USD–

Annual Earnings per Share

1.46	1.60	1.39	1.37	1.50
12/30/94	12/29/95	12/31/96	12/31/97	12/31/98

Admin De Fondos De Pension Provida Sa ADR –USD–
Symbol: PVD   Market/Exchange: NYSE

Daily Prices – 1 Year Ending Aug. 31, 1999   ▬ 50–day moving avg. ▬ 200–day moving avg.

Daily Volume (millions of shares)

Sep 98 Oct 98 Nov 98 Dec 98 Jan 99 Feb 99 Mar 99 Apr 99 May 99 Jun 99 Jul 99 Aug 99

Latest Pricing Data (as of Aug. 31, 1999)

Close (net change):	$20 1/4	(–1/4)
Day High & Low:	$20 1/4	$20 1/8
Volume & Avg. Volume:	37,100	38,890
52–Week High:	$24 7/16	July 6, 1999
52–Week Low:	$11 3/4	Oct. 13, 1998
Latest Dividend:	$0.77	May 6, 1999
Ind. Ann. Div. & Yield:	$0.00	N.A.
12 Month EPS:	$1.50	Dec. 31, 1998
P/E Ratio & Beta Factor:	13.50	0.634
Shares Outstanding:	261.523 million	
Market Value:	$5.296 billion	
Institutional Holdings:	1.73%	
Number of Institutions:	57	
Primary Market:	NYSE	

Monthly Pricing – 36 Months

Monthly Volume (millions of shares)

1997 1998 1999

Currency: U.S. Dollars.

Source: IDD Information Services

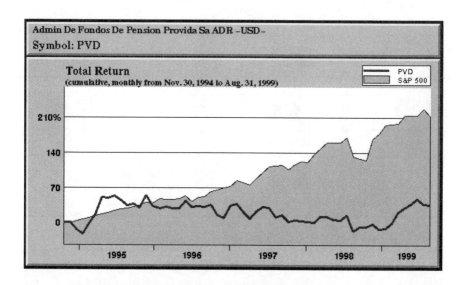

SELECTED INCOME STATEMENT AND BALANCE SHEET ITEMS

INCOME STATEMENT	12/30/94	12/29/95	12/31/96	12/31/97	12/31/98	1 Year
Sales/Revenues	115.90	144.30	133.70	143.40	145.70	145.70
Cost of Goods Sold	47.700	56.000	52.200	54.700	59.900	N.A.
Pre-tax Margin (%)	21.80	21.60	20.30	20.70	24.10	N.A.
Operating Income	29.900	36.700	29.600	32.100	35.400	N.A.
Net Income before Extras	22.200	26.800	23.800	25.300	31.100	31.100
Reported Net Income	22.200	26.800	23.800	25.300	31.100	31.100
Depreciation & Amortization	2.700	4.200	4.500	6.200	3.600	N.A.
EPS from Net Income (Primary)	1.460	1.600	1.390	1.370	1.500	1.500
EPS from Net Income (Fully Diluted)	1.460	1.600	1.390	1.370	1.500	1.500
Dividend per Common Share	0.000	0.898	0.923	0.900	0.903	0.903
Dividend Yield (%)	N.A.	3.25	4.92	5.27	6.72	6.72
Payout Ratio	N.A.	0.56	0.66	0.66	0.60	0.60
BALANCE SHEET						
ASSETS						
Cash & Cash Equivalents	1.000	2.000	8.400	0.800	4.500	
Inventories	0.000	0.000	0.000	0.000	0.000	
Total Current Assets	28.600	27.700	29.800	12.200	11.200	
Total Assets	125.10	144.30	148.90	137.40	178.90	
LIABILITIES & EQUITY						
Short Term Debt	5.600	0.100	7.700	4.700	8.100	
Long Term Debt	0.000	0.000	0.000	0.000	0.000	
Total Liabilities	21.000	17.100	23.800	21.100	51.400	
Shares Outstanding	15.242	16.673	16.734	16.734	16.734	
Common Stockholder Equity	104.10	127.20	125.20	116.30	127.50	
Total Stockholder Equity	104.10	127.20	125.20	116.30	127.50	

Note: Figures in Millions of $ except: per share items, margins, yields, and ratios.

Source: IDD Information Services

AT HOME

Elizabeth Dater
Warburg Pincus Asset Management

Company Profile

If there is one complaint that people have about the Internet these days, it's that access is too slow. At Home Corporation is doing something about that. At Home, or @Home as it is often called, provides an integrated system for delivering high-speed Internet service to your home through your cable TV. The technology allows you to connect at speeds that are hundreds of times faster than those currently possible using traditional telephone modems. It also merges your TV and the Internet into one unit. It's clear to see that the possibilities of this combination are endless.

"At Home delivers this high-speed service to both residences and businesses using its own network architecture," says Elizabeth Dater, who manages several mutual funds for Warburg Pincus. "It provides what we call an 'always on' attribute of cable. I think this is going to allow significant multimedia applications opportunities that go far beyond what people are currently able to get on the Web." The company's mission is to provide a high-speed, fully integrated multimedia service that revolutionizes the way people interact with information and each other. Although At Home service is still not available in many areas, the company is expanding rapidly.

It's no surprise that the major owners of At Home are the cable companies themselves. The largest owner is Tele-Communications, Inc. (now a division of AT&T). "I think what AT&T is saying is that it wants to outsource this high-speed Internet function to At Home, which is very interesting," Dater says. "The other important thing to note is that building a networking business can be very capital intensive. In effect, this alliance gives the company access to a huge number of cable subscribers and allows it to achieve returns using someone else's capital infrastructure. In other words, the capital spending for getting this service into customer homes has already been done by the cable companies, which means the costs for expanding the system will be very minimal to At Home." Other cable powerhouses that have invested in At Home include Comcast Corporation, Cox Communications, Rogers Cablesystems Limited, and Shaw Communications. Since its founding in 1995, At Home has reached affiliate agreements with a total of 15 leading cable companies in North America. It also has an arrangement with Teleport Communications Group for its commercial product, @Work, in several major metropolitan centers, including Los Angeles, New York, and Boston. The one major cable holdout thus far has been Time-Warner, which has its own access company called Road Runner. "I wouldn't be surprised to see At Home and Road Runner merge at some point," Dater predicts.

In 1999 the company branched out even further by acquiring search engine company Excite. "This will further help At Home to reach millions of people with very low acquisition costs," Dater says. "It now has a database of 20 million registered users whom it can inform when its cable access becomes available in their marketplace." In fact, as this book went to press, the company was in the process of changing its corporate name to Excite@Home.

Reason for Recommendation

Without doubt, the online industry is booming. Analysts estimate the number of Web users will grow from 35 million in 1996 to more than 163 million in 2000. In the future, Dater expects that most people will use this high-broadband service to access the Internet instead of dialing up with their much slower personal computers. This means tremendous potential for At Home. Like most Internet companies, At Home doesn't have any earnings at this point, so it's hard to value. That hasn't stopped the share price from zooming higher and higher since its initial public offering. "What you have to say is that this is a rapidly growing business," she says. "While it may be close to being fully valued on a short-term basis, I'm interested in what's going to happen over the next two or three years. It's my strong view that investors should view any major pullbacks in this stock as a dramatic buying opportunity."

Of course, the field for delivering this service is not without competition. In addition to Road Runner, America Online is looking at how to get into this competitive field, and there are other competitors emerging all the time. But Dater isn't too concerned. She also points out that At Home has other business units, including Excite and At Media, both of which develop content and negotiates partnerships with content providers such as Bloomberg and CNN. "The major risk I see is the company's inability to establish itself as the standard provider in the marketplace," she maintains. "But the company has excellent management and was founded by veterans of Silicon Valley. At Home is not as capital intensive as one might expect, which will add to future profitability." She also notes that the Internet is largely unregulated right now, but a change to more regulation could impact the company.

Dater expects At Home to start making money around 2002 and thinks 2003 will mark a major turnaround that will be followed by many years of incredible growth. "I'm convinced At Home will be a very dynamic growth company in the new millennium," she adds.

Contact Information: At Home Corporation
425 Broadway Street
Redwood City, CA 94063
650-569-5000
www.home.net

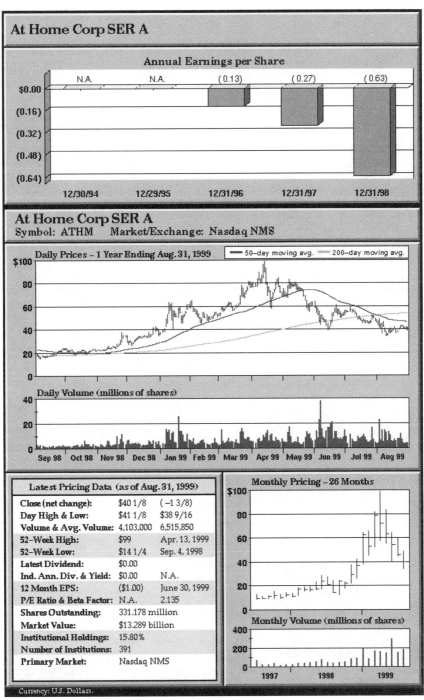

Source: IDD Information Services

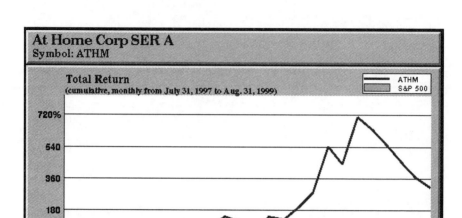

At Home Corp SER A
Symbol: ATHM

Total Return
(cumulative, monthly from July 31, 1997 to Aug. 31, 1999)

— ATHM
S&P 500

SELECTED INCOME STATEMENT AND BALANCE SHEET ITEMS						
INCOME STATEMENT	**12/30/94**	**12/29/95**	**12/31/96**	**12/31/97**	**12/31/98**	**1 Year**
Sales/Revenues	N.A.	N.A.	0.700	7.400	48.000	128.60
Cost of Goods Sold	N.A.	N.A.	5.100	13.500	32.000	N.A.
Pre–tax Margin (%)	N.A.	N.A.	N.A.	N.A.	N.A.	N.A.
Operating Income	N.A.	N.A.	(25.000)	(49.500)	(46.500)	N.A.
Net Income before Extras	N.A.	N.A.	(24.500)	(219.10)	(144.20)	(274.10)
Reported Net Income	N.A.	N.A.	(24.500)	(219.10)	(144.20)	(274.10)
Depreciation & Amortization	N.A.	N.A.	1.900	8.900	15.000	N.A.
EPS from Net Income (Primary)	N.A.	N.A.	(0.130)	(0.270)	(0.630)	(1.000)
EPS from Net Income (Fully Diluted)	N.A.	N.A.	(0.130)	(0.270)	(0.630)	(1.000)
Dividend per Common Share	0.000	0.000	0.000	0.000	0.000	0.000
Dividend Yield (%)	N.A.	N.A.	N.A.	N.A.	N.A.	N.A.
Payout Ratio	N.A.	N.A.	N.A.	N.A.	N.A.	N.A.
BALANCE SHEET						
ASSETS						
Cash & Cash Equivalents	N.A.	N.A.	9.700	44.200	300.70	
Inventories	N.A.	N.A.	0.000	0.000	0.000	
Total Current Assets	N.A.	N.A.	18.300	125.40	433.30	
Total Assets	N.A.	N.A.	33.400	160.60	780.60	
LIABILITIES & EQUITY						
Short Term Debt	N.A.	N.A.	3.200	10.000	12.000	
Long Term Debt	N.A.	N.A.	5.700	15.700	243.70	
Total Liabilities	N.A.	N.A.	15.100	41.500	286.80	
Shares Outstanding	N.A.	N.A.	23.710	237.206	246.546	
Common Stockholder Equity	N.A.	N.A.	(26.700)	119.10	493.90	
Total Stockholder Equity	N.A.	N.A.	18.300	119.10	493.90	

Note: Figures in Millions of $ except: per share items, margins, yields, and ratios.

Source: IDD Information Services

ATS MEDICAL

Larry Jeddeloh
The Institutional Strategist

Company Profile

Larry Jeddeloh doesn't have to travel very far to visit his top pick for 2000. The corporate headquarters of ATS Medical are located about five miles from his home in Minneapolis. The company manufactures a device known as the ATS Open Pivot Valve, which is an artificial heart valve with at least one unusual twist. "It is quieter," says Jeddeloh, president of The Institutional Strategist. "It has a unique design that allows the valve to swing like a door instead of in the traditional way, which creates a lot of turbulence in the blood. This turbulence can cause blood clots. But because the Pivot Valve swings like a door, the amount of turbulence is significantly reduced. That prevents people from developing clots or having strokes." The other downside to traditional heart valves, Jeddeloh reports, is that patients can hear them pumping all the time, especially when they're lying in bed. "People find the noise very disconcerting," he observes.

Unfortunately, the Pivot Valve is not yet approved for use in the United States. (As this book went to press, the company was still waiting for FDA approval.) Nevertheless, ATS has been implanting the device in patients overseas for several years, and it has achieved great acceptance from surgeons around the globe. Since its founding in 1991, ATS has implanted some 28,000 Pivot Valves. Among the regions in which it is most prominent are Europe, northern Africa, and the Pacific region of Asia. The company has also entered the Australian market. Testing continues in the United States, and FDA approval is expected near the summer of 2000. Approval may come a bit sooner, thanks to a ruling by the FDA allowing the company to submit results from its international studies to fulfill part of the requirements for its U.S. trials.

ATS Medical is managed by Manuel Villafaña, a man Jeddeloh insists is more than qualified for the position. "He was the founder and lead manager at both St. Jude Medical and Cardiac Pacemakers (now Guidant)," Jeddeloh explains. "Both of these stocks went up 10 to 20 times under his care. I think ATS looks exactly like these other companies. He runs all of his businesses with a pristine balance sheet. ATS has no debt and plenty of cash sitting in the bank. Right now, ATS has the equivalent of $3 a share in cash." What's more impressive is that Villafaña has been able to steer the company to a profit, even though its only product still hasn't been approved by regulators in what could be its biggest market yet—the United States.

ATS reported record sales and earnings for 1998 despite the fact that a strong U.S. dollar overseas caused the company to make some price concessions to offset the effects of negative currency translations. Villafaña admits that 1999 was a major transition year for the company. It was faced with growing its share in existing markets while waiting for permission to do business in the United States. That put earnings under serious pressure. There is also the issue of distribution. At present, ATS doesn't have much of a sales force in the United States, so once FDA approval comes, it will have to beef up its domestic distribution channel quickly.

Reason for Recommendation

Without question, ATS has plenty of competition. Many other companies are selling artificial heart valves today, including Villafaña's former company, St. Jude (with about 60 percent of the market), and CarboMedics. But Jeddeloh insists the Open Pivot Valve is the best thing on the market. "Villafaña has definitely built a better mousetrap," Jeddeloh maintains. "The other thing about him is that when he goes to sell this valve, he'll personally walk into the operating room with the surgeon and show him how to implant it. And keep in mind that Villafaña is not a doctor."

It's important to note that ATS is a one-product company. As all investors know, diversification is important for long-term success as you spread your risk around. If something happens to derail the prospects for the Open Pivot Valve or the FDA approval process hits a snag, ATS will certainly be in trouble. There is also a risk that someone else will come out with a better valve technology, making the Open Pivot less attractive.

But Jeddeloh isn't worried. Not only does he expect the FDA to clear the way for the product to enter the U.S. market, but he also feels Villafaña is hard to beat. In addition, some analysts have noted that ATS could be an attractive buyout candidate by a larger manufacturer with an established distribution channel. Regardless of what happens, Jeddeloh predicts shares of ATS will trade for at least $15 by the end of 2000, perhaps much higher depending on the outcome of current FDA clinical trials.

Contact Information: ATS Medical, Inc.
3905 Annapolis Lane
Minneapolis, MN 55447
612-553-2736
www.atsmedical.com

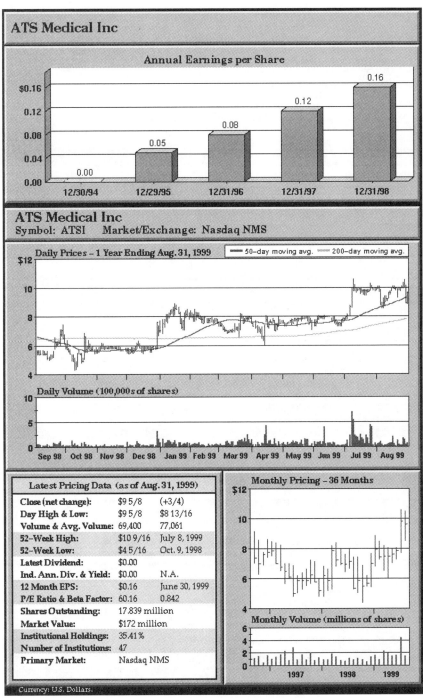

Source: IDD Information Services

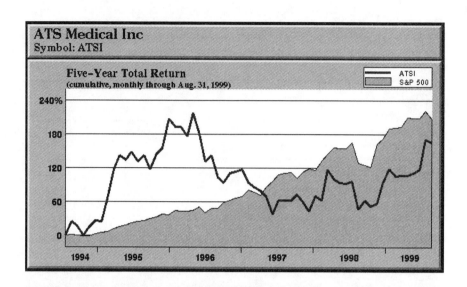

ATS Medical Inc
Symbol: ATSI

Five-Year Total Return
(cumulative, monthly through Aug. 31, 1999)

Legend: ATSI, S&P 500

SELECTED INCOME STATEMENT AND BALANCE SHEET ITEMS

INCOME STATEMENT	12/30/94	12/29/95	12/31/96	12/31/97	12/31/98	1 Year
Sales/Revenues	6.800	9.300	11.900	14.500	18.000	18.000
Cost of Goods Sold	4.000	5.800	7.300	9.200	11.100	N.A.
Pre-tax Margin (%)	0.00	7.50	10.90	14.50	16.10	N.A.
Operating Income	0.000	0.100	0.700	0.700	1.500	N.A.
Net Income before Extras	0.000	0.700	1.300	2.100	2.800	2.800
Reported Net Income	0.000	0.700	1.300	2.100	2.800	2.800
Depreciation & Amortization	0.200	0.200	0.200	0.200	0.300	N.A.
EPS from Net Income (Primary)	0.000	0.050	0.080	0.120	0.160	0.160
EPS from Net Income (Fully Diluted)	0.000	0.050	0.080	0.120	0.160	0.160
Dividend per Common Share	N.A.	N.A.	N.A.	N.A.	N.A.	N.A.
Dividend Yield (%)	N.A.	N.A.	N.A.	N.A.	N.A.	N.A.
Payout Ratio	N.A.	N.A.	N.A.	N.A.	N.A.	N.A.

BALANCE SHEET						
ASSETS						
Cash & Cash Equivalents	0.600	2.200	2.300	4.600	7.800	
Inventories	9.300	13.400	18.200	22.700	30.000	
Total Current Assets	13.000	30.100	32.000	53.200	56.800	
Total Assets	14.600	31.300	33.300	54.400	58.400	
LIABILITIES & EQUITY						
Short Term Debt	1.300	0.000	0.000	0.000	0.000	
Long Term Debt	0.000	0.000	0.000	0.000	0.000	
Total Liabilities	1.800	2.300	1.400	0.800	2.700	
Shares Outstanding	11.178	14.964	15.288	17.589	17.824	
Common Stockholder Equity	12.800	29.100	31.900	53.500	55.800	
Total Stockholder Equity	12.800	29.100	31.900	53.500	55.800	

Note: Figures in Millions of $ except: per share items, margins, yields, and ratios.

Source: IDD Information Services

BORDERS GROUP

David Dreman
Dreman Value Management

Company Profile

David Dreman feels the future for Borders Group reads like a thrilling best-seller. Borders is the world's second largest retailer of books and music, behind Barnes and Noble. The chain began as a single location in Ann Arbor in 1971, specializing in academic and more serious subjects, such as African poetry. It quickly became known as one of the finest book shops around. Founders Tom and Louis Borders transformed that success into a string of additional stores. There are now more than 1,100 locations in all 50 states, including almost 250 Borders super-stores and 900 Waldenbooks in malls, shopping centers, and airports nationwide. The superstores contain thousands of books plus a full selection of music, maga-zines, and a cafe. The first overseas location opened in Singapore in 1997.

The growing company was acquired by Kmart Corporation in 1992. Three years later, Borders bought its stock back and raised new capital through an initial pub-lic offering, becoming independent again. "The company is opening up a lot of new stores," observes David Dreman, president of Dreman Value Management.

Predictably, Borders also has its own Web site, www.borders.com, to com-pete with the likes of Barnes and Noble and Amazon.com. The trouble is that Bor-ders was the last of the big three book retailers to develop a Web presence and remains a distant third in cyberspace. "Web sales are expected to go up fourfold in 1999 and even more in 2000," Dreman notes. "But the company's CEO was dumb enough to say publicly that the company didn't think the Web was that important. I think he was probably right, but it would have been better not to say that." Coin-cidentally or not, that CEO, Philip Pfeffer, resigned just days after making this bold pronouncement.

Following Pfeffer's departure, the company reiterated its future goals: to open a number of additional stores, introduce a new line of stationery and lifestyle side-lines, integrate Web technology into its physical locations, develop an affiliates program for Borders.com, create more effective cross-promotions for its Internet site, and improve its special order service.

Dreman maintains that Borders's stock has been punished because of fears the Internet will put it out of business. The stock, after making it all the way up to the mid-$40 range, fell back down well into the low teens on fears that Amazon. com would eventually eat it for lunch. "The funny thing is that Amazon has not become a category killer at all," Dremain notes. "The company has been around about four years and still has less than 6 percent of the overall market." Dreman contends that the Internet can't replace the experience of being in a bookstore, and Borders excels at providing this experience. It's one thing to type a title on your keyboard and watch the information pop up on your screen. It's another to walk into a clean store, greeted by the smell of fresh paper and coffee with the ability to actually hold the book in your hands and thumb through its contents while browsing and interacting with other shoppers. "Most people who go into a bookstore don't buy just one book," Dreman adds. "They look at a lot of different things. Many are there to browse. Others are on the prowl for closeouts. I'm speaking from experience. When I go to a Borders store, I may be looking for one particular title, but I look at a lot of other things too. You can't really do that at Amazon or any of the other Internet sites. At some point people are going to realize this experience is worth something and that this is still a growth business."

Reason for Recommendation

Dreman insists Borders has been unfairly punished for being so far behind in building its Internet presence. He chalks it up to the whole "dot-com" mania, in which investors believe that Internet retailers are going to swallow up all of the storefront retailers. In fact, one Wall Street analyst recently went so far as to proclaim, "Borders is toast," predicting Amazon.com would eventually drive it out of business. Dreman thinks that is hogwash. "This is a big, powerful chain," he maintains. "The truth is, Amazon is almost certainly going to continue to gain market share. But Borders will remain a very profitable company." Dreman predicts the company will grow by 10 to 15 percent a year and believes Borders stock is worth at least double what it currently trades for. If the market doesn't realize this value on its own, Dreman expects the company to be bought out at a much higher price. In either case, he looks for the shares to at least double in 2000. "Here's a company that I think is down for all the wrong reasons. It's a growth company trading at a value price. It's really cheap. And it has the possibility of either being taken over or just going up on its own."

Contact Information: Borders Group, Inc.
100 Phoenix Drive
Ann Arbor, MI 48108
734-477-1100
www.bordersgroupinc.com

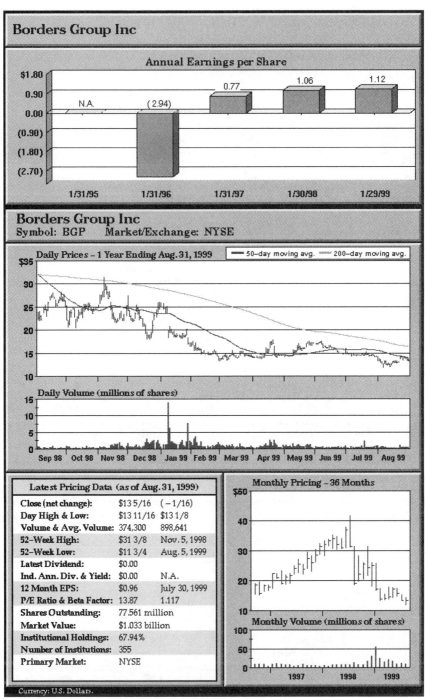

Borders Group Inc

Annual Earnings per Share

	1/31/95	1/31/96	1/31/97	1/30/98	1/29/99
	N.A.	(2.94)	0.77	1.06	1.12

Borders Group Inc
Symbol: BGP   Market/Exchange: NYSE

Daily Prices – 1 Year Ending Aug. 31, 1999   ▬ 50-day moving avg. ▬ 200-day moving avg.

Daily Volume (millions of shares)

Sep 98 Oct 98 Nov 98 Dec 98 Jan 99 Feb 99 Mar 99 Apr 99 May 99 Jun 99 Jul 99 Aug 99

Latest Pricing Data (as of Aug. 31, 1999)		
Close (net change):	$13 5/16	(–1/16)
Day High & Low:	$13 11/16	$13 1/8
Volume & Avg. Volume:	374,300	898,641
52-Week High:	$31 3/8	Nov. 5, 1998
52-Week Low:	$11 3/4	Aug. 5, 1999
Latest Dividend:	$0.00	
Ind. Ann. Div. & Yield:	$0.00	N.A.
12 Month EPS:	$0.96	July 30, 1999
P/E Ratio & Beta Factor:	13.87	1.117
Shares Outstanding:	77.561 million	
Market Value:	$1.033 billion	
Institutional Holdings:	67.94%	
Number of Institutions:	355	
Primary Market:	NYSE	

Monthly Pricing – 36 Months

Monthly Volume (millions of shares)

1997   1998   1999

Currency: U.S. Dollars.

Source: IDD Information Services

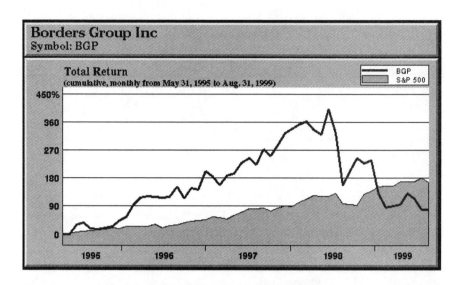

SELECTED INCOME STATEMENT AND BALANCE SHEET ITEMS

INCOME STATEMENT	1/31/95	1/31/96	1/31/97	1/30/98	1/29/99	1 Year
Sales/Revenues	N.A.	1,749.0	1,958.8	2,266.0	2,595.0	2,753.5
Cost of Goods Sold	N.A.	1,260.3	1,394.9	1,581.1	1,795.6	N.A.
Pre-tax Margin (%)	N.A.	(11.70)	4.90	5.80	5.80	N.A.
Operating Income	N.A.	(200.40)	103.10	138.00	167.30	N.A.
Net Income before Extras	N.A.	(211.10)	57.900	80.200	92.100	79.200
Reported Net Income	N.A.	(211.10)	57.900	80.200	92.100	79.200
Depreciation & Amortization	N.A.	42.000	42.900	54.800	66.700	N.A.
EPS from Net Income (Primary)	N.A.	(2.940)	0.770	1.060	1.120	0.960
EPS from Net Income (Fully Diluted)	N.A.	(2.940)	0.700	0.980	1.120	0.960
Dividend per Common Share	0.000	0.000	0.000	0.000	0.000	0.000
Dividend Yield (%)	N.A.	N.A.	N.A.	N.A.	N.A.	N.A.
Payout Ratio	N.A.	N.A.	N.A.	N.A.	N.A.	N.A.
BALANCE SHEET						
ASSETS						
Cash & Cash Equivalents	N.A.	36.500	42.600	65.100	42.800	
Inventories	N.A.	637.50	737.50	879.10	1,019.6	
Total Current Assets	N.A.	740.20	846.40	1,018.4	1,133.3	
Total Assets	N.A.	1,052.3	1,211.0	1,534.9	1,766.6	
LIABILITIES & EQUITY						
Short Term Debt	N.A.	60.500	30.500	127.30	134.10	
Long Term Debt	N.A.	8.100	6.200	5.200	6.300	
Total Liabilities	N.A.	580.30	699.60	936.80	1,051.5	
Shares Outstanding	N.A.	75.318	75.858	75.396	77.695	
Common Stockholder Equity	N.A.	472.00	511.40	598.10	715.10	
Total Stockholder Equity	N.A.	472.00	511.40	598.10	715.10	

Note: Figures in Millions of $ except: per share items, margins, yields, and ratios.

Source: IDD Information Services

CNF TRANSPORTATION

David Williams
U.S. Trust

Company Profile

If you need something shipped across the street or around the world, CNF Transportation has a way to get it there. The company has three operating segments encompassing both trucking and air freight. Its Con-Way Transportation Services group provides time-specific motor carrier delivery to destinations in all 50 states plus Canada, Puerto Rico, and parts of Mexico. This division employs some 15,000 workers and specializes in one-day and two-day deliveries. Emery Worldwide is responsible for all domestic and international air freight services. CNF added Emery to its list of holdings in April 1989. While Emery's freight system is designed to primarily handle parcels, packages of all weights and sizes are handled. Of the major overnight delivery services, Emery is perhaps the least known. The division's hub-and-spoke system is based at the Dayton, Ohio airport. Its hub is currently being upgraded to increase capacity by some 30 percent. Emery also has a ten-year contract to provide Express Mail (overnight) and Priority Mail (two- to three-day) delivery services for the U.S. Postal Service. Finally, CNF's Menlo Logistics segment helps companies plan shipping strategies.

"This is a shipping company that's involved in all aspects of the business," says David Williams, a portfolio manager with U.S. Trust. CNF has more than 300,000 customers and 30,000 employees worldwide. It moves about 30 billion pounds worth of shipments each year. The company has operations in more than 200 countries. CNF began in 1929, when Leland James founded a small regional trucking company in Portland, Oregon. James originally operated a successful large retail tire business and later a private intercity Portland bus company. He soon realized, however, that he could make more money moving freight instead of people. So he sold both of his existing businesses and bought several local freight companies, which became Consolidated Truck Lines. The name was changed to Consolidated Freightways in 1939.

Over time, the western United States–based company grew to the eastern part of the country and began expanding the list of items it could ship. Consolidated continued to make acquisitions and expanded into air freight in 1966. By 1990, the company had a large portfolio of air and truck freight–shipping divisions under its umbrella but realized customers needed more services than just getting packages from one point to another. That's when Menlo Logistics was born. This division provides warehouse, inventory, and transportation management. It also integrates all links in the supply chain through customized systems and software. In 1996 Consolidated Freightways spun off CF MotorFreight, its long-haul motor carrier,

27

and created two separate publicly traded companies. At that point, the parent company was renamed CNF Transportation.

Reason for Recommendation

Although all of the company's divisions are doing well, Williams is most intrigued by the growing relationship with the U.S. Postal Service. "I think eventually the post office will contract out all of its Express and Priority Mail shipments," he predicts. "The private sector could probably do it better anyway. The shipping business really isn't that exciting. It's very cyclical and highly competitive. But this company is changing its stripes and getting into the more profitable side of the business."

Williams also points out that the company is growing its non-asset-based Menlo Logistics unit well. This business doesn't involve much capital and is highly profitable. Con-Way is also making money. "The real problem child is Emery, and the company is working hard to straighten that business out," Williams admits. That's not easy as Emery competes with such better-known heavyweights as FedEx, United Parcel Service, and Airborne Express. "This is a really tough business and Emery is not doing well," Williams frets. "I wouldn't be surprised if CNF eventually sold Emery off, but at this point it probably wouldn't get a very good price for it. The company is trying to give Emery a more upscale image so it can charge more than its competitors." Emery's turnaround is important for CNF, because it accounts for about one-half of all revenues.

CNF is exactly the kind of company Williams looks for—one in the middle of a restructuring that could become very rewarding and profitable. "I expect this company to grow 13 to 14 percent a year in the future, and the stock is pretty cheap," he maintains. "The company is not undiscovered, but it has a pretty good story and this relationship with the post office is really exciting."

The biggest risk, in Williams's mind, is that the company might not get more business from the U.S. Postal Service, as he expects. "If that happens, the stock is in big trouble," he adds. However, he thinks that is highly unlikely, given that CNF has done such a good job in fulfilling its contract so far. Williams looks for the stock to rise some 50 percent in 2000, assuming the company continues to operate on all cylinders.

Contact Information: CNF Transportation, Inc.
3240 Hillview Avenue
Palo Alto, CA 94304
650-494-2900
www.cnf.com

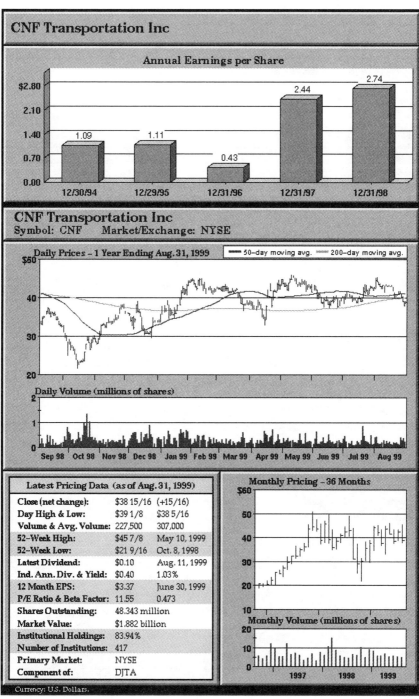

CNF Transportation Inc

Annual Earnings per Share

Date	EPS
12/30/94	1.09
12/29/95	1.11
12/31/96	0.43
12/31/97	2.44
12/31/98	2.74

CNF Transportation Inc
Symbol: CNF   Market/Exchange: NYSE

Daily Prices – 1 Year Ending Aug. 31, 1999 — 50-day moving avg. ---- 200-day moving avg.

Daily Volume (millions of shares)

Sep 98 Oct 98 Nov 98 Dec 98 Jan 99 Feb 99 Mar 99 Apr 99 May 99 Jun 99 Jul 99 Aug 99

Latest Pricing Data (as of Aug. 31, 1999)		
Close (net change):	$38 15/16	(+15/16)
Day High & Low:	$39 1/8	$38 5/16
Volume & Avg. Volume:	227,500	307,000
52–Week High:	$45 7/8	May 10, 1999
52–Week Low:	$21 9/16	Oct. 8, 1998
Latest Dividend:	$0.10	Aug. 11, 1999
Ind. Ann. Div. & Yield:	$0.40	1.03%
12 Month EPS:	$3.37	June 30, 1999
P/E Ratio & Beta Factor:	11.55	0.473
Shares Outstanding:	48.343 million	
Market Value:	$1.882 billion	
Institutional Holdings:	83.94%	
Number of Institutions:	417	
Primary Market:	NYSE	
Component of:	DJTA	

Monthly Pricing – 36 Months

Monthly Volume (millions of shares)

1997   1998   1999

Currency: U.S. Dollars.

Source: IDD Information Services

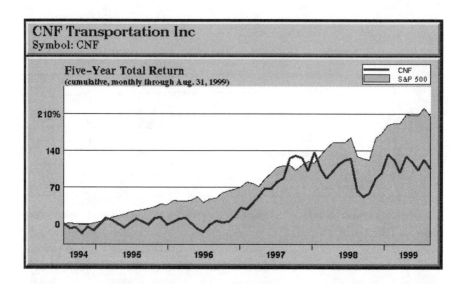

CNF Transportation Inc
Symbol: CNF

Five-Year Total Return
(cumulative, monthly through Aug. 31, 1999)

| | CNF |
| | S&P 500 |

210%

140

70

0

1994   1995   1996   1997   1998   1999

SELECTED INCOME STATEMENT AND BALANCE SHEET ITEMS

INCOME STATEMENT	12/30/94	12/29/95	12/31/96	12/31/97	12/31/98	1 Year
Sales/Revenues	4,680.5	5,281.1	3,662.2	4,266.8	4,941.5	5,268.9
Cost of Goods Sold	3,812.1	4,382.8	2,910.4	3,314.3	3,850.1	4,190.1
Pre-tax Margin (%)	2.40	2.10	4.00	5.20	5.10	5.77
Operating Income	142.20	144.00	192.20	264.90	290.60	313.20
Net Income before Extras	60.300	57.400	80.200	120.90	139.00	169.90
Reported Net Income	60.300	57.400	27.600	120.90	139.00	169.90
Depreciation & Amortization	145.80	148.10	95.700	130.50	173.20	189.20
EPS from Net Income (Primary)	1.090	1.110	0.430	2.440	2.740	3.370
EPS from Net Income (Fully Diluted)	1.810	1.640	1.480	2.190	2.450	3.000
Dividend per Common Share	0.084	0.261	0.337	0.400	0.400	0.400
Dividend Yield (%)	0.45	1.17	1.51	1.03	1.06	1.04
Payout Ratio	0.08	0.24	0.78	0.16	0.15	0.12
BALANCE SHEET						
ASSETS						
Cash & Cash Equivalents	95.700	86.300	82.100	97.600	73.900	
Inventories	41.700	45.900	32.900	36.600	41.800	
Total Current Assets	1,031.5	1,151.6	815.90	1,009.4	1,100.4	
Total Assets	2,472.7	2,750.1	2,081.9	2,421.5	2,689.4	
LIABILITIES & EQUITY						
Short Term Debt	3.700	52.400	158.20	4.900	48.300	
Long Term Debt	397.90	495.50	477.20	473.50	592.60	
Total Liabilities	1,799.1	2,027.7	1,573.6	1,638.4	1,913.1	
Shares Outstanding	36.354	43.902	44.566	47.392	47.875	
Common Stockholder Equity	530.00	692.10	483.80	658.10	741.30	
Total Stockholder Equity	673.70	722.40	508.30	783.10	776.40	

Note: Figures in Millions of $ except: per share items, margins, yields, and ratios.

Source: IDD Information Services

COMPUTER SCIENCES

Elizabeth Bramwell
Bramwell Capital Management

Company Profile

Computer Sciences Corporation uses information technology to solve various business problems for its clients. The company offers a full range of services, including management and information technology consulting, operations support and information services outsourcing, and systems consulting and integration. "It plays into the theme that companies want to focus on their core business and outsource everything else," says Elizabeth Bramwell of Bramwell Capital Management. Computer Sciences Corporation, or CSC, has 50,000 employees who work in some 600 offices nationwide. The company was the brainchild of Roy Nutt and Fletcher Jones, who were 20-something aerospace computer analysts when they got the entrepreneurial spirit back in 1959. The two formed CSC with $100 and a contract from Honeywell to develop a business-language compiler called FACT. They saw an opportunity to provide computer manufacturers with software that could increase the productivity of programmers while making it easier to use their machines. Back then, there were fewer than 3,000 computers in the entire world, compared with 200 million today.

CSC became the first software company to be listed on the New York Stock Exchange in 1968. The company initially focused on getting business from the federal government. It put more emphasis on the commercial market in the mid-1980s. "The company is well diversified, both in terms of geographic exposure and the industries to which it consults," Bramwell notes. "CSC basically has relationships with 85 percent of the Fortune 500 companies. It also has solid exposure to the U.S. government." The company now gets 75 percent of its revenue from commercial contracts, and the remaining 25 percent from the U.S. government. In all, 42 percent of its revenue stems from outsourcing, 38 percent from management consulting and professional services, and 20 percent from systems integration.

CSC most recently completed the implementation of two of its largest contracts ever. The first was with J. P. Morgan. CSC led a team that helped J. P. Morgan form Pinnacle Alliance, which supports a large portion of its worldwide information technology structure. The second contract was with DuPont. Among other things, CSC helped DuPont incorporate technology solutions such as SAP, Year 2000, supply chain, and software engineering into the company's business. In both cases, this initial work is just the start of the businesses these contracts could potentially bring to CSC.

"The three major forces driving dramatic change in the business world—globalization, deregulation, and consolidation—are creating very strong growth in demand for information technology outsourcing and systems consulting and integration services," says CSC chairman, president, and CEO Van B. Honeycutt. "This will continue as we move into the 21st century. Research groups that follow our industry expect spending for information technology services to soar from approximately $335 billion in 1997 to nearly $860 billion in 2002, a compound annual growth rate of more than 20 percent." Not wanting to be left behind, CSC is also moving rapidly to play a part in creating electronic commerce solutions for doing business on the Internet. Its global initiative in this area is called "CSC e-Wave." The company is also hard at work on updated solutions to support the financial services and health care industries.

In recent years, CSC has been on a buying spree, acquiring companies like Continuum, Planmetrics, American Practice Management, DAN Computer Management, and The Pinnacle Group. "Continuum basically has software for facilitating the processing of insurance claims, which really helps to bring down the cost of processing medical claims," Bramwell observes. "CSC integrated these various organizations into its existing structure and it seems to be working very well."

CSC has managed some of the world's toughest projects over the past three decades, from advancing the nation's air traffic control system to developing Europe's largest online tax system. It even created a private data network for the U.S. Treasury Department. Its clients come from a wide array of industries, including aerospace, automotive, banking, manufacturing, pharmaceuticals, retail, transportation, and utilities. "I think the company is well-positioned for doing systems integration on different computer systems for consulting and general outsourcing," Bramwell contends.

Reason for Recommendation

Bramwell is encouraged that not only is CSC's core business humming along but it also continues to get a steady stream of new contracts. "The company just picked up big projects from Budget Group and the Internal Revenue Service," she says. "The depth of management is strong and outsourcing is booming." Bramwell estimates CSC will continue to grow more than 20 percent a year for the foreseeable future. "It has a lot of recurring business and I think it will earn over $3 per share in the year ending March 2000," she says. "I can see this stock going above $80."

Contact Information: Computer Sciences Corporation
2100 East Grand Avenue
El Segundo, CA 90245
310-615-0311
www.csc.com

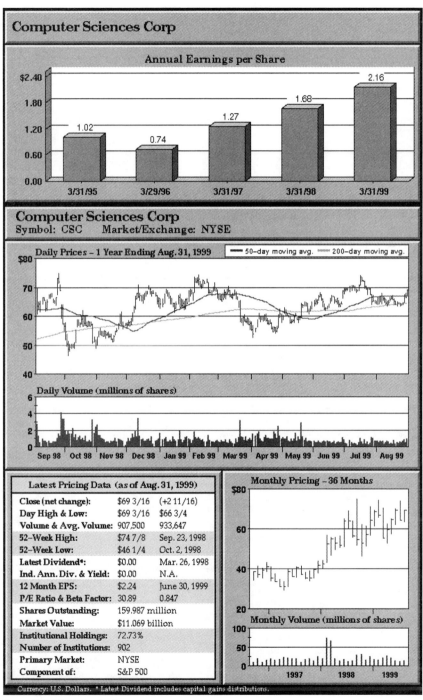

Computer Sciences Corp

Annual Earnings per Share

Date	EPS
3/31/95	1.02
3/29/96	0.74
3/31/97	1.27
3/31/98	1.68
3/31/99	2.16

Computer Sciences Corp
Symbol: CSC   Market/Exchange: NYSE

Daily Prices – 1 Year Ending Aug. 31, 1999   ▬ 50-day moving avg. ▬ 200-day moving avg.

Daily Volume (millions of shares)

Sep 98 Oct 98 Nov 98 Dec 98 Jan 99 Feb 99 Mar 99 Apr 99 May 99 Jun 99 Jul 99 Aug 99

Latest Pricing Data (as of Aug. 31, 1999)

Close (net change):	$69 3/16	(+2 11/16)
Day High & Low:	$69 3/16	$66 3/4
Volume & Avg. Volume:	907,500	933,647
52–Week High:	$74 7/8	Sep. 23, 1998
52–Week Low:	$46 1/4	Oct. 2, 1998
Latest Dividend*:	$0.00	Mar. 26, 1998
Ind. Ann. Div. & Yield:	$0.00	N.A.
12 Month EPS:	$2.24	June 30, 1999
P/E Ratio & Beta Factor:	30.89	0.847
Shares Outstanding:	159.987 million	
Market Value:	$11.069 billion	
Institutional Holdings:	72.73%	
Number of Institutions:	902	
Primary Market:	NYSE	
Component of:	S&P 500	

Monthly Pricing – 36 Months

Monthly Volume (millions of shares)

1997   1998   1999

Currency: U.S. Dollars. * Latest Dividend includes capital gains distributions.

Source: IDD Information Services

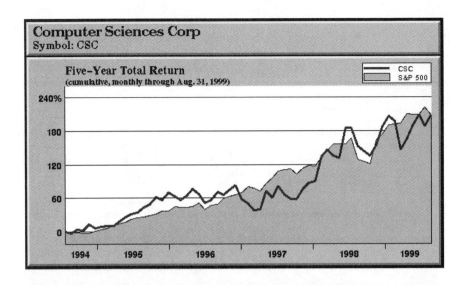

Computer Sciences Corp
Symbol: CSC

Five-Year Total Return
(cumulative, monthly through Aug. 31, 1999)

Legend: CSC, S&P 500

Y-axis: 240%, 180, 120, 60, 0
X-axis: 1994, 1995, 1996, 1997, 1998, 1999

SELECTED INCOME STATEMENT AND BALANCE SHEET ITEMS

INCOME STATEMENT	3/31/95	3/29/96	3/31/97	3/31/98	3/31/99	1 Year
Sales/Revenues	3,372.5	4,242.4	5,616.0	6,600.8	7,660.0	7,969.5
Cost of Goods Sold	2,685.6	3,349.7	4,413.2	5,149.2	5,973.8	6,227.3
Pre-tax Margin (%)	5.20	5.50	5.40	2.90	6.70	6.65
Operating Income	203.10	261.70	384.50	462.00	545.40	566.30
Net Income before Extras	110.70	141.70	192.40	260.40	341.20	355.10
Reported Net Income	110.70	141.70	192.40	260.40	341.20	355.10
Depreciation & Amortization	172.60	252.10	333.20	386.90	445.00	455.50
EPS from Net Income (Primary)	1.020	0.740	1.270	1.680	2.160	2.240
EPS from Net Income (Fully Diluted)	1.000	0.710	1.230	1.640	2.110	2.190
Dividend per Common Share	0.000	0.000	0.000	0.002	0.000	0.000
Dividend Yield (%)	N.A.	N.A.	N.A.	0.00	N.A.	N.A.
Payout Ratio	N.A.	N.A.	N.A.	0.00	N.A.	N.A.
BALANCE SHEET						
ASSETS						
Cash & Cash Equivalents	155.30	104.90	110.70	274.70	602.60	
Inventories	0.000	0.000	0.000	0.000	0.000	
Total Current Assets	1,081.5	1,144.3	1,612.4	1,982.6	2,669.0	
Total Assets	2,333.7	2,595.8	3,580.9	4,046.8	5,007.7	
LIABILITIES & EQUITY						
Short Term Debt	137.40	70.300	29.900	28.900	592.90	
Long Term Debt	310.30	405.50	630.80	736.10	397.90	
Total Liabilities	1,185.1	1,290.2	1,911.2	2,045.6	2,607.9	
Shares Outstanding	110.342	112.060	153.186	156.978	159.140	
Common Stockholder Equity	1,148.6	1,305.7	1,669.6	2,001.3	2,399.9	
Total Stockholder Equity	1,148.6	1,305.7	1,669.6	2,001.3	2,399.9	

Note: Figures in Millions of $ except: per share items, margins, yields, and ratios.

Source: IDD Information Services

CONSECO

Ronald Muhlenkamp
Muhlenkamp & Company

Company Profile

Conseco is a company with a lot of products of interest to aging baby boomers. "This is an insurance conglomerate that has been put together over the past decade or so," observes Ron Muhlenkamp of Muhlenkamp & Company. "It offers long-term care insurance; Medicare supplement insurance; universal life; fixed annuities; cancer, heart, and stroke insurance—all of the things that are important to boomers. The company also bought Green Tree Financial in 1998, which is a big financier of mobile homes and home remodeling, and has an investment management arm."

Conseco serves some 12 million customers through its headquarters in Carmel, Indiana. The company was incorporated in 1979, began operations in 1982, and went public in 1985. It has since evolved into a leading provider of insurance, investment, and lending products to middle America. Its customers are primarily among the 50 million U.S. households with annual incomes between $25,000 and $75,000, a market relatively underserved by financial services companies.

During its years as an operating company, Conseco has acquired 20 other businesses. Green Tree was by far the largest. "Green Tree is a perfect fit with Conseco," insists Conseco president and CEO Stephen Hilbert. "Both cultures are entrepreneurial and success oriented. Both organizations are lean. Both companies embrace nontraditional channels for distributing their products. And both companies are experienced and knowledgeable in serving middle America." Hilbert claims the acquisition gave Conseco earnings diversity, stability, and growth potential.

Nevertheless, Wall Street did not greet the acquisition with much enthusiasm. Quite the contrary. "Green Tree got lumped in with a group of subprime lenders. These are companies that, for instance, might finance a used car to the tune of $4,000 to $10,000," Muhlenkamp explains. "A couple of years ago, a few subprime lenders went bankrupt. That killed the stocks of the whole industry, including Green Tree, even though Green Tree didn't lend on a subprime basis." Green Tree's reduced share price made it an attractive acquisition target for Conseco. But Muhlenkamp maintains investors are still painting Conseco with the same brush as Green Tree. "This doesn't make sense because the company has a consistent 20 percent return on equity," he says. "Once people find out that Conseco's assets and businesses are good, and separate the good guys from the bad guys, these fears will dissipate. Until then, you are able to buy a great company at a cheap price."

Conseco's business model is pretty simple. It gathers assets, funds them with various forms of liabilities, invests those assets to earn a spread over its funding cost, and then manages the related risks. "In our insurance business, we gather

35

'bonds' or 'mortgages' and fund them with 'policyholder liabilities' or 'deposits,'" Hilbert points out. "In our finance business, we gather 'manufactured housing mortgages' or 'home equity loans' and fund them with 'warehouse bank lines' and 'securitization debt.'" The company has been building up its distribution and cross-marketing channels while keeping a watchful eye on risk management and expense control. Total managed financial assets at the end of 1998 were $87 billion, up 24 percent over the previous year.

Reason for Recommendation

Muhlenkamp is pleased with the company CEO Stephen Hilbert has built. "He has bought only businesses that fit well with the entire product line," Muhlenkamp maintains. "I think you will continue to see consolidation in this industry." Conseco probably won't be buying anything else in the immediate future. The company has told regulators it plans to strengthen its balance sheet, which means costly purchases will have to be put on hold. And with the company's share price down, it's more difficult to make purchases with stock.

Muhlenkamp says Conseco will stay ahead of the competition through cost control. "I used to work in the insurance industry and know that's the key to success," he shares. "In the case of Conseco, management keeps a close eye on costs. For instance, it buys used computers." He also emphasizes that management owns a lot of the outstanding stock and is continuing to buy more.

As they say in the investment business, past performance is no guarantee of future results. But the historical performance of Conseco stock has been very impressive. From its initial public offering 13 years ago, Conseco shares have appreciated more than 7,300 percent, including reinvested dividends, providing for an annualized return of 39 percent. While not much has been happening lately, Muhlenkamp feels the stock is worth at least $60, possibly more. "Once Wall Street views this company for what it really is, the price will come around," he predicts.

Contact Information: Conseco, Inc.
11825 N. Pennsylvania Street
Carmel, IN 46032
800-426-6732
www.conseco.com

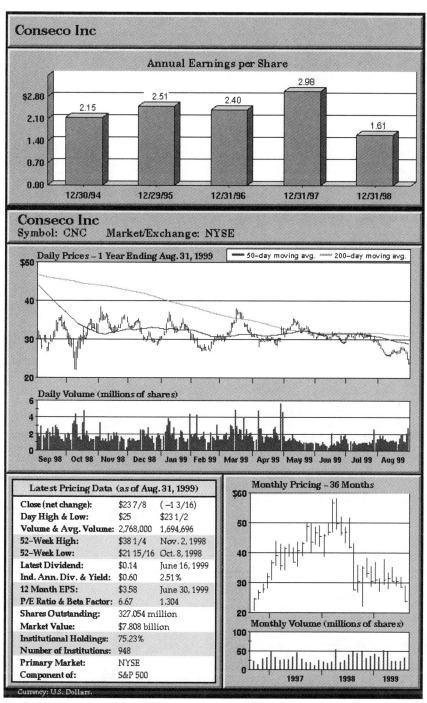

Conseco Inc

Annual Earnings per Share

Conseco Inc
Symbol: CNC   Market/Exchange: NYSE

Daily Prices – 1 Year Ending Aug. 31, 1999   ▬ 50-day moving avg. ▬ 200-day moving avg.

Daily Volume (millions of shares)

Latest Pricing Data (as of Aug. 31, 1999)		
Close (net change):	$23 7/8	(–1 3/16)
Day High & Low:	$25	$23 1/2
Volume & Avg. Volume:	2,768,000	1,694,696
52–Week High:	$38 1/4	Nov. 2, 1998
52–Week Low:	$21 15/16	Oct. 8, 1998
Latest Dividend:	$0.14	June 16, 1999
Ind. Ann. Div. & Yield:	$0.60	2.51%
12 Month EPS:	$3.58	June 30, 1999
P/E Ratio & Beta Factor:	6.67	1.304
Shares Outstanding:	327.054 million	
Market Value:	$7.808 billion	
Institutional Holdings:	75.23%	
Number of Institutions:	948	
Primary Market:	NYSE	
Component of:	S&P 500	

Monthly Pricing – 36 Months

Monthly Volume (millions of shares)

Currency: U.S. Dollars.

Source: IDD Information Services

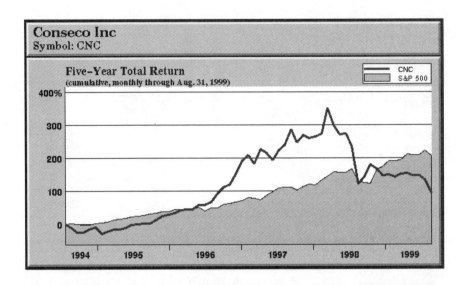

Conseco Inc
Symbol: CNC

Five-Year Total Return
(cumulative, monthly through Aug. 31, 1999)

CNC
S&P 500

SELECTED INCOME STATEMENT AND BALANCE SHEET ITEMS

INCOME STATEMENT	12/30/94	12/29/95	12/31/96	12/31/97	12/31/98	1 Year
Sales/Revenues	1,862.0	2,855.3	3,067.3	5,568.4	7,716.0	7,911.3
Cost of Goods Sold	N.A.	N.A.	N.A.	N.A.	N.A.	N.A.
Pre-tax Margin (%)	14.30	10.80	15.00	17.10	12.40	23.10
Operating Income	526.10	1,145.5	1,292.3	1,961.2	1,486.2	2,402.7
Net Income before Extras	154.40	222.50	278.90	574.20	509.70	1,141.5
Reported Net Income	154.40	222.50	278.90	574.20	509.70	1,141.5
Depreciation & Amortization	N.A.	N.A.	N.A.	N.A.	N.A.	N.A.
EPS from Net Income (Primary)	2.150	2.510	2.400	2.980	1.610	3.580
EPS from Net Income (Fully Diluted)	1.820	2.140	2.010	2.670	1.530	3.460
Dividend per Common Share	0.125	0.046	0.082	0.312	0.530	0.560
Dividend Yield (%)	1.16	0.30	0.26	0.69	1.74	1.84
Payout Ratio	0.06	0.02	0.03	0.10	0.33	0.16

BALANCE SHEET						
ASSETS						
Cash & Cash Equivalents	N.A.	N.A.	N.A.	N.A.	N.A.	
Inventories	N.A.	N.A.	N.A.	N.A.	N.A.	
Total Current Assets	N.A.	N.A.	N.A.	N.A.	N.A.	
Total Assets	10,812	17,298	25,613	35,915	43,600	
LIABILITIES & EQUITY						
Short Term Debt	0.000	298.10	0.000	0.000	956.20	
Long Term Debt	802.90	1,456.1	1,478.3	3,744.4	5,321.5	
Total Liabilities	10,065	16,186	22,527	32,025	38,326	
Shares Outstanding	88.740	104.400	167.128	186.666	315.844	
Common Stockholder Equity	463.50	828.20	2,818.2	3,774.3	5,168.1	
Total Stockholder Equity	747.00	1,111.7	3,085.3	3,890.1	5,273.6	

Note: Figures in Millions of $ except: per share items, margins, yields, and ratios.

Source: IDD Information Services

DELL COMPUTER

Cappy McGarr
McGarr Capital Management

Company Profile

What began in founder Michael Dell's dorm room at the University of Texas at Austin in 1984 has turned into one of the greatest entrepreneurial success stories of the past decade. Dell Computer pioneered the process of selling custom-built computers directly to consumers. Today, it is the world's leader in this segment of the industry, with more than 16,000 employees in 33 countries.

Dell's loyal worldwide customer base includes both individuals and companies of all sizes. The company's products include desktop and notebook systems, all of which are custom-designed based on the specific needs of each customer. Products can be purchased over the phone or through Dell's Internet site.

"I like to invest in companies that dominate their industry and Dell certainly fits the bill," says Cappy McGarr of McGarr Capital Management. "Dell's direct sales model is really the key to the company's success. Dell has leveraged its return on equity through high asset turnover, which is critical. Dell's aim is to achieve balanced profitability and rapid growth." It has certainly succeeded. Not only have all profits gone through the roof, jumping around 50 percent a quarter in recent years, but the company's share price has also rocketed an average of 140 percent annually over the past five years. "Dell is growing 3.5 times faster than the overall PC industry average of 14 to 16 percent. Dell's U.S. consumer business is growing three times faster than its nearest competitor. Dell's business in the Pacific region of Asia is growing five times faster than the overall industry. Even with Asia's recent economic slowdown, business for Dell is still up."

After resisting the move for some time, Dell recently entered the sub-$1,000 computer market, introducing a model for less than $999, including a 15-inch monitor. "The reason it was able to do that is because component costs have come down to a level where making these cheaper systems is affordable," McGarr points out. "The company originally didn't think it could make money at this price. But now that component costs are down, it can."

McGarr, who uses Dell products, notes that the company has also become a better technology proxy than fellow industry bellwethers Microsoft and Intel, which aren't growing as fast. "The government is investigating Microsoft to see if it has a 100 percent share of the market. Intel already has around an 85 percent market share for chips. But Dell has only an 8 percent worldwide market share in the personal computer segment," he says. "Microsoft and Intel have no way of doubling their market share. But Dell certainly can. I think it will easily do that. It's growing three times faster than the industry already."

Reason for Recommendation

But could the stock be ahead of itself? In early 1999, after reporting a revenue slowdown, Dell's share price fell by some 30 percent. That's not a big deal when you consider how far the stock has come in such a short period of time. Nevertheless, it has caused some analysts to question whether this rapid growth can continue going forward. McGarr is convinced it can. "Sales are as strong as ever," he says. "During 1999 Dell's Internet sales increased from $5 million to $14 million per day. That represents $5 billion a year from Web sales alone, which is equivalent to 25 percent of current earnings. Dell predicts Internet sales will make up 50 percent of earnings within the next year."

But what about the valuation? Is the stock too expensive? "Well, let's take a closer look at the business model," McGarr replies. "Dell turns its assets over two times faster than chief competitor Compaq. Under this model, Dell has negative working capital. It takes 7 days to sell its inventory versus 29 days for Compaq. Consequently, Dell has a negative collection cycle. That's key because it means Dell collects money from its customers 8 days before paying its supplier. By contrast, Compaq pays its suppliers 33 days before collecting money from customers. By virtually eliminating working capital, Dell is able to generate cash flow returns on capital of more than 2,500 percent, versus 40 percent for Compaq. These returns are driving Dell's growth rate. Therefore, I don't think the valuation is too high since I believe Dell can double its market share over the next five years. The stock could go up three or four times more during this time."

The stock is not without risks, of course. "The main risk is that management won't be able to execute its direct sales strategy as well going forward," McGarr admits. "But I also think the Y2K problem will help the company in the year 2000, as corporations increasingly upgrade their systems. You also have the release of Windows 2000 and Intel's faster chips, which will spur PC sales."

McGarr adds that Dell has an extremely loyal client base and is on target to become the industry leader. "Dell currently is the second-largest PC manufacturer behind Compaq. IBM is third," McGarr says. "In my opinion, Dell will claim the top spot within the next five years."

Contact Information: Dell Computer Corporation
One Dell Way
Round Rock, TX 78682-2244
512-338-4400
www.dell.com

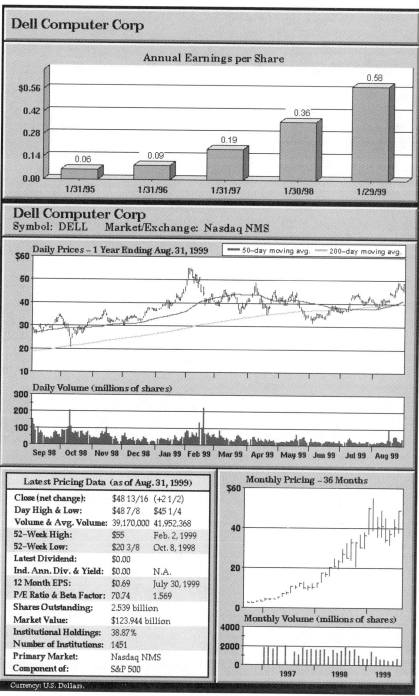

Dell Computer Corp

Annual Earnings per Share

	1/31/95	1/31/96	1/31/97	1/30/98	1/29/99
	0.06	0.09	0.19	0.36	0.58

Dell Computer Corp
Symbol: DELL   Market/Exchange: Nasdaq NMS

Daily Prices – 1 Year Ending Aug. 31, 1999   ▬ 50–day moving avg.   ▬ 200–day moving avg.

Daily Volume (millions of shares)

Sep 98 Oct 98 Nov 98 Dec 98 Jan 99 Feb 99 Mar 99 Apr 99 May 99 Jun 99 Jul 99 Aug 99

Latest Pricing Data (as of Aug. 31, 1999)

Close (net change):	$48 13/16	(+2 1/2)
Day High & Low:	$48 7/8	$45 1/4
Volume & Avg. Volume:	39,170,000	41,952,368
52–Week High:	$55	Feb. 2, 1999
52–Week Low:	$20 3/8	Oct. 8, 1998
Latest Dividend:	$0.00	
Ind. Ann. Div. & Yield:	$0.00	N.A.
12 Month EPS:	$0.69	July 30, 1999
P/E Ratio & Beta Factor:	70.74	1.569
Shares Outstanding:	2.539 billion	
Market Value:	$123.944 billion	
Institutional Holdings:	38.87%	
Number of Institutions:	1451	
Primary Market:	Nasdaq NMS	
Component of:	S&P 500	

Monthly Pricing – 36 Months

Monthly Volume (millions of shares)

1997   1998   1999

Currency: U.S. Dollars.

Source: IDD Information Services

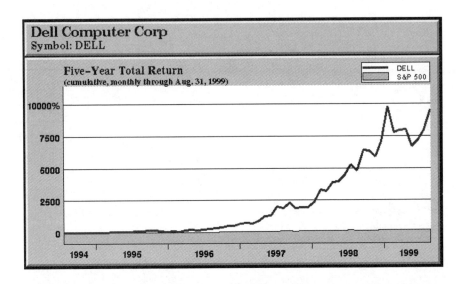

Dell Computer Corp
Symbol: DELL

Five-Year Total Return
(cumulative, monthly through Aug. 31, 1999)

DELL
S&P 500

SELECTED INCOME STATEMENT AND BALANCE SHEET ITEMS						
INCOME STATEMENT	**1/31/95**	**1/31/96**	**1/31/97**	**1/30/98**	**1/29/99**	**1 Year**
Sales/Revenues	3,475.3	5,296.0	7,759.0	12,327	18,243	21,670
Cost of Goods Sold	2,704.2	4,191.0	6,046.0	9,538.0	14,034	N.A.
Pre-tax Margin (%)	6.10	7.20	9.60	11.10	11.40	N.A.
Operating Income	249.20	377.00	714.00	1,316.0	2,046.0	N.A.
Net Income before Extras	149.20	272.00	531.00	944.00	1,460.0	1,750.0
Reported Net Income	149.20	272.00	531.00	944.00	1,460.0	1,750.0
Depreciation & Amortization	33.100	38.000	47.000	67.000	103.00	N.A.
EPS from Net Income (Primary)	0.060	0.090	0.190	0.360	0.580	0.690
EPS from Net Income (Fully Diluted)	0.050	0.090	0.180	0.320	0.530	0.650
Dividend per Common Share	0.000	0.000	0.000	0.000	0.000	0.000
Dividend Yield (%)	N.A.	N.A.	N.A.	N.A.	N.A.	N.A.
Payout Ratio	N.A.	N.A.	N.A.	N.A.	N.A.	N.A.
BALANCE SHEET						
ASSETS						
Cash & Cash Equivalents	43.000	55.000	115.00	320.00	520.00	
Inventories	292.90	429.00	251.00	233.00	273.00	
Total Current Assets	1,470.4	1,957.0	2,747.0	3,912.0	6,339.0	
Total Assets	1,594.0	2,148.0	2,993.0	4,268.0	6,877.0	
LIABILITIES & EQUITY						
Short Term Debt	0.000	0.000	0.000	0.000	0.000	
Long Term Debt	113.40	113.00	18.000	17.000	512.00	
Total Liabilities	942.20	1,175.0	2,187.0	2,975.0	4,556.0	
Shares Outstanding	2,539.520	2,990.304	2,768.752	2,561.268	2,543.000	
Common Stockholder Equity	651.70	967.00	806.00	1,293.0	2,321.0	
Total Stockholder Equity	651.70	973.00	806.00	1,293.0	2,321.0	

Note: Figures in Millions of $ except: per share items, margins, yields, and ratios.

Source: IDD Information Services

EATON CORPORATION

Robert Sanborn
The Oakmark Fund

Company Profile

Eaton Corporation is a globally diversified industrial company that is the dominant manufacturer of truck transmissions. "It also makes engine components for cars," notes Robert Sanborn, manager of The Oakmark Fund. For instance, Eaton produces the steering column switches for the new Ford Focus car, which controls turn signals, the front and rear wipers, headlight beam settings, and the trip computer. "In addition, it has a semiconductor equipment and electrical power business," Sanborn says, adding that this unit accounts for only a small portion of total revenues. The company is headquartered in Cleveland and has 155 manufacturing sites in 25 countries around the world. It serves the industrial, vehicle, construction, commercial, and semiconductor markets.

All in all, this is what Sanborn admits is a pretty "average" business. Nothing Internet-related or sexy. But the business units are all stable and the stock, in Sanborn's mind, is cheap. "This is an excellent company," Sanborn insists. "I have visited several of its plants. All are very well run. I'm impressed with the management. I've known the current chief executive officer (Stephen Hardis) since 1983 when he was the chief financial officer. This business is well managed with typical midwestern high integrity. In addition, employees own 15 percent of the company, which gives it an owner orientation. I have personally witnessed this entrepreneurial spirit during my visits to the plants." To carry its owner orientation one step further, Eaton even has an incentive program for its employees and top management.

Eaton is generally the number-one or number-two player in all of its markets. "It's not a 'me too' company," Sanborn adds. "Eaton sells no commodity products. Everything it manufactures is proprietary and value added." He further emphasizes that CEO Hardis does what's best for the company and its shareholders, not what he feels pressured to do by Wall Street. "I asked him [Hardis]," continued Sanborn, "if he would consider going through with an acquisition that would benefit the company but not Wall Street. He replied, 'Of course. I'm not going to listen to Wall Street. I'm going to do what is right.' I don't think many CEOs would say something like that." The company's latest acquisition was the $1.7 billion purchase of Aeroquip-Vickers in the first quarter of 1999.

Eaton tends to spend a lot on research and development and gets better returns and margins than its competitors. Nevertheless, it has faced some recent challenges, especially in its semiconductor unit. To make matters worse, Eaton committed to a costly new product development program for this business. "As a consequence of the sharply reduced demand [in semiconductors], we incurred substantial operating losses and one-time charges required to bring expenses in line with lower sales volumes," CEO Hardis says. "This reversal, however, has not shaken our belief that demand for semiconductor equipment will recover in the next several years." The sharp economic downturn in many developing economies also hurt the company's international expansion plans. On the positive side, earnings were bolstered by record sales of heavy-duty trucks in North America.

Reason for Recommendation

Granted, Eaton has its challenges. But Sanborn insists they are already factored into the current share price, which he believes has nowhere to go but up. In fact, although Sanborn normally buys large-cap stocks, he likes midcap Eaton because it "smells like a value stock." Hardis has publicly stated his goal is for Eaton to have $10 billion in sales and $8 in earnings per share by the end of the year 2000. Sanborn believes this is definitely possible. "Based on the current market price, that means this stock is trading for less than seven times earnings per share, which is pretty cheap," he says.

There are a few things Sanborn *doesn't* like about this company. For starters, it is highly diversified. "I think that makes it somewhat tougher to manage," he says. "If you have one product, everyone in the company can focus on it with a great intensity." As a result, Sanborn maintains there is no single driver that he sees propelling Eaton's fortunes in the year ahead. "I like all of these businesses, although I think the semiconductor unit is the source of the most volatility," he says.

Sanborn's near-term target price for the stock is $100, which is where it was a couple of years ago. "This is the quintessential example of a company that meets all of my valuation criteria," he adds. "It's not glamorous, but it's a great value and a good company."

Contact Information: Eaton Corporation
Eaton Center
Cleveland, OH 44114-2584
216-523-5000
www.eaton.com

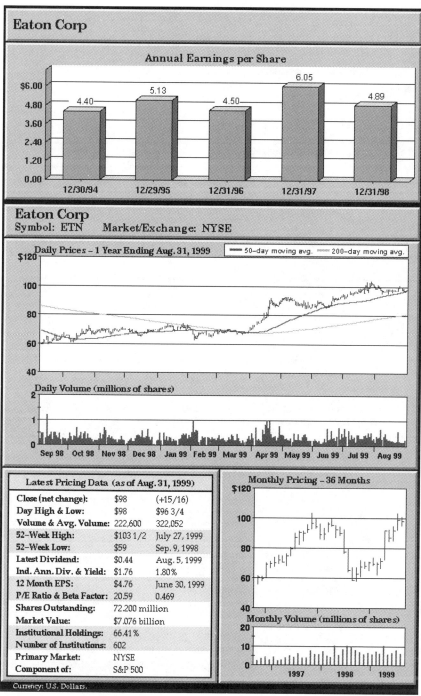

Eaton Corp

Annual Earnings per Share

4.40	5.13	4.50	6.05	4.89
12/30/94	12/29/95	12/31/96	12/31/97	12/31/98

Eaton Corp
Symbol: ETN   Market/Exchange: NYSE

Daily Prices – 1 Year Ending Aug. 31, 1999 ▬▬ 50-day moving avg. ▬▬ 200-day moving avg.

Daily Volume (millions of shares)

Sep 98 Oct 98 Nov 98 Dec 98 Jan 99 Feb 99 Mar 99 Apr 99 May 99 Jun 99 Jul 99 Aug 99

Latest Pricing Data (as of Aug. 31, 1999)		
Close (net change):	$98	(+15/16)
Day High & Low:	$98	$96 3/4
Volume & Avg. Volume:	222,600	322,052
52–Week High:	$103 1/2	July 27, 1999
52–Week Low:	$59	Sep. 9, 1998
Latest Dividend:	$0.44	Aug. 5, 1999
Ind. Ann. Div. & Yield:	$1.76	1.80%
12 Month EPS:	$4.76	June 30, 1999
P/E Ratio & Beta Factor:	20.59	0.469
Shares Outstanding:	72.200 million	
Market Value:	$7.076 billion	
Institutional Holdings:	66.41%	
Number of Institutions:	602	
Primary Market:	NYSE	
Component of:	S&P 500	

Monthly Pricing – 36 Months

Monthly Volume (millions of shares)

1997   1998   1999

Currency: U.S. Dollars.

Source: IDD Information Services

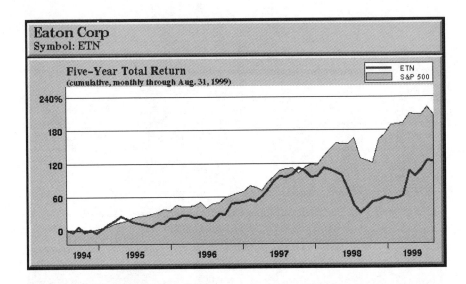

Eaton Corp
Symbol: ETN

Five-Year Total Return
(cumulative, monthly through Aug. 31, 1999)

SELECTED INCOME STATEMENT AND BALANCE SHEET ITEMS						
INCOME STATEMENT	**12/30/94**	**12/29/95**	**12/31/96**	**12/31/97**	**12/31/98**	**1 Year**
Sales/Revenues	6,052.0	6,822.0	6,961.0	7,563.0	6,625.0	7,187.0
Cost of Goods Sold	4,146.0	4,747.0	4,845.0	5,114.0	4,428.0	4,798.0
Pre-tax Margin (%)	8.10	8.70	7.00	8.80	7.30	6.50
Operating Income	560.00	640.00	534.00	700.00	482.00	550.00
Net Income before Extras	333.00	399.00	349.00	464.00	349.00	339.00
Reported Net Income	333.00	399.00	349.00	464.00	349.00	339.00
Depreciation & Amortization	251.00	281.00	320.00	342.00	331.00	369.00
EPS from Net Income (Primary)	4.400	5.130	4.500	6.050	4.890	4.760
EPS from Net Income (Fully Diluted)	4.350	5.080	4.460	5.930	4.800	4.690
Dividend per Common Share	1.200	1.500	1.600	1.720	1.760	1.760
Dividend Yield (%)	2.42	2.80	2.29	1.93	2.49	1.91
Payout Ratio	0.27	0.29	0.36	0.28	0.36	0.37
BALANCE SHEET						
ASSETS						
Cash & Cash Equivalents	18.000	56.000	22.000	53.000	80.000	
Inventories	698.00	735.00	729.00	734.00	707.00	
Total Current Assets	1,846.0	1,967.0	2,017.0	2,055.0	1,982.0	
Total Assets	4,682.0	5,053.0	5,307.0	5,465.0	5,665.0	
LIABILITIES & EQUITY						
Short Term Debt	36.000	50.000	30.000	104.00	333.00	
Long Term Debt	1,053.0	1,084.0	1,062.0	1,272.0	1,191.0	
Total Liabilities	3,002.0	3,078.0	3,147.0	3,394.0	3,608.0	
Shares Outstanding	78.000	77.600	77.100	74.700	71.700	
Common Stockholder Equity	1,680.0	1,975.0	2,160.0	2,071.0	2,057.0	
Total Stockholder Equity	1,680.0	1,975.0	2,160.0	2,071.0	2,057.0	

Note: Figures in Millions of $ except: per share items, margins, yields, and ratios.

Source: IDD Information Services

EMC CORPORATION

James Collins
Insight Capital Research & Management

Company Profile

Every time you download information from the Internet, prepare a document, or perform any other function on your computer, you create data that have to be stored somewhere. EMC is devoted to providing solutions for storing all of these data. As one analyst put it, EMC is the 800-pound gorilla in storage. But it wasn't always that way. "As recently as five years ago, if you needed more storage capacity, you would go to IBM or some other company for a solution," says Jim Collins of Insight Capital. "Now you go to EMC."

EMC began in 1979. Founders Richard Egan and Roger Marino (the E and M in EMC) initially founded a supply company for add-on memory boards. The company's fortunes began to surge in 1989, when it revised its strategy to take advantage of corporate America's growing reliance on vast and complex amounts of electronic data.

EMC's flagship Symmetrix product line of hard disk drives for the mainframe market was introduced in 1990. Since then, some 30,000 storage systems have been shipped to customers around the world. In 1994 EMC began focusing more heavily on software functionality and introduced its Symmetrix Remote Data Facility. This unique mirroring software has become the world's leading storage-based solution for business continuity and disaster recovery. The company now offers more than a dozen software solutions that allow customers to manage, protect, and share information.

In just eight short years, from 1990 to 1998, EMC's annual revenues grew from $190 million to $3.97 billion. Most of the company's engineers spend their time on new software development. The company plans to invest $1 billion in software research and development over the next three years. "The company typically spends about 8 percent of revenues on R&D," Collins points out. That's important because in today's rapidly changing environment, you have to stay on the leading edge, or someone else is bound to leapfrog you.

"EMC not only has the hardware and software but also the ability to monitor your system both cross-country and at its own headquarters," Collins notes. "That gives it a definite advantage in improving its products. If something goes down, and it sees the same thing happen repeatedly, it can make sure that all new systems going out don't have the same problem. That's important because the primary consideration when buying a storage system is reliability and data integrity." EMC's systems are manufactured in both Massachusetts and Ireland. The company opened a new state-of-the-art facility in Franklin, Massachusetts, near the company's Hopkinton headquarters, in 1998.

The company boasts the world's largest storage-dedicated direct sales and service force. "That's essential because when you are selling your storage units yourself as part of a total package, it makes it hard for an outside vendor to come in and invade your space," Collins says. "If your salespeople are always calling, customers are going to automatically turn to EMC for their storage needs." What's more, half of the world's major server makers resell EMC systems as their high-end storage solution. EMC has formed alliances with some of technology's heavy hitters, including Oracle, Microsoft, and SAP.

EMC's customer base spans a cross section of private and government agencies, from small businesses to Fortune 100 companies. All of the world's top telecommunications companies use EMC products. So do 25 percent of the largest U.S. banks and an estimated 90 percent of the world's major reservations systems.

Reason for Recommendation

Collins admits that as recently as four years ago, he was uncomfortable investing in this company. "I was concerned with how the business was being managed," he shares. "But there has been a positive change." In addition to the inherent need for storage on any mainframe system, the Internet has created an explosion of additional demand. "You're talking about a massive need for reliability 24 hours a day, 7 days a week," Collins maintains.

Collins insists that the way you make money in the high-tech area is by finding a niche player in a rapidly growing market segment. EMC fits the bill. "It has about a 35 percent share of the storage market compared with about 22 percent for second-place IBM," Collins says.

Collins isn't the first analyst to notice how well EMC is doing. The stock has skyrocketed over the past couple of years along with most other technology and Internet-related issues, so it's not cheap. Collins estimates the company will earn $2.59 per share in 2000, which represents growth of 31 percent, although he emphasizes the number could be higher. It's also important to note that many companies spent extra money on storage from 1987 to 1999 instead of facing the Y2K problem. This could stall sales for a brief period as we enter the new millennium. "Still, I'm willing to take a chance on this stock because I expect earnings to grow at least 30 percent or more annually at least over the next three years," Collins says. "There is no other company in the data storage area with the hardware, software, and service organization of EMC."

Contact Information: EMC Corporation
Corporate Headquarters
Hopkinton, MA 01748-9103
508-435-1000
www.emc.com

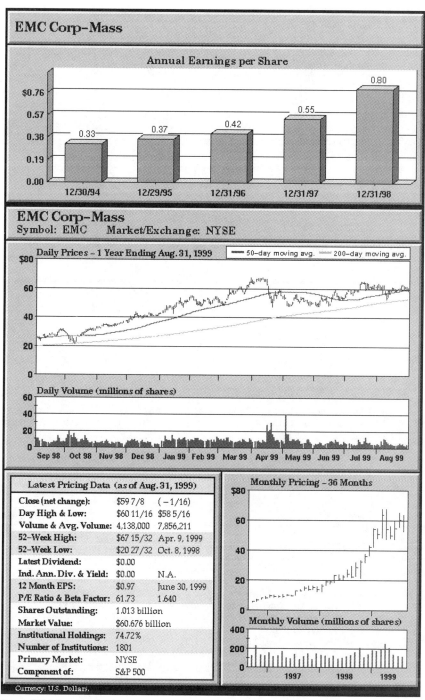

Source: IDD Information Services

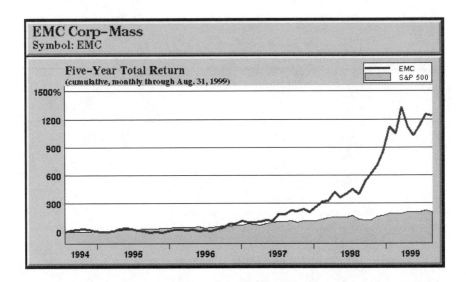

EMC Corp–Mass
Symbol: EMC

Five-Year Total Return
(cumulative, monthly through Aug. 31, 1999)

SELECTED INCOME STATEMENT AND BALANCE SHEET ITEMS

INCOME STATEMENT	12/30/94	12/29/95	12/31/96	12/31/97	12/31/98	1 Year
Sales/Revenues	1,377.5	1,921.3	2,273.7	2,937.9	3,973.7	4,613.1
Cost of Goods Sold	627.30	949.30	1,162.0	1,434.7	1,725.9	1,874.7
Pre-tax Margin (%)	25.80	23.50	22.80	24.40	26.60	27.85
Operating Income	350.60	435.80	496.60	661.90	981.80	1,211.0
Net Income before Extras	250.70	326.80	386.20	538.50	793.40	967.40
Reported Net Income	250.70	326.80	386.20	538.50	793.40	967.40
Depreciation & Amortization	32.700	53.600	86.900	136.30	203.30	254.10
EPS from Net Income (Primary)	0.330	0.370	0.420	0.550	0.800	0.970
EPS from Net Income (Fully Diluted)	0.280	0.340	0.400	0.520	0.750	0.910
Dividend per Common Share	0.000	0.000	0.000	0.000	0.000	0.000
Dividend Yield (%)	N.A.	N.A.	N.A.	N.A.	N.A.	N.A.
Payout Ratio	N.A.	N.A.	N.A.	N.A.	N.A.	N.A.
BALANCE SHEET						
ASSETS						
Cash & Cash Equivalents	240.50	379.60	496.40	954.60	705.20	
Inventories	251.10	330.20	336.60	404.70	485.80	
Total Current Assets	901.80	1,319.0	1,754.1	2,627.0	3,104.8	
Total Assets	1,317.5	1,745.7	2,293.5	3,490.1	4,568.6	
LIABILITIES & EQUITY						
Short Term Debt	9.500	0.900	7.100	7.700	29.400	
Long Term Debt	286.10	245.80	191.20	558.50	538.90	
Total Liabilities	589.90	605.30	656.80	1,113.9	1,244.6	
Shares Outstanding	795.004	919.484	952.960	993.586	1,007.266	
Common Stockholder Equity	727.60	1,140.3	1,636.8	2,376.3	3,324.1	
Total Stockholder Equity	727.60	1,140.3	1,636.8	2,376.3	3,324.1	

Note: Figures in Millions of $ except: per share items, margins, yields, and ratios.

Source: IDD Information Services

ESG RE LIMITED

Ed Walczak
Vontobel USA

Company Profile

While socialized medicine is only fodder for political rhetoric in the United States, it is a reality in many parts of the world. What many of these countries have found, however, is that such programs can be taxing on the system. "Whether it's Germany, France, Brazil, or Chile, the states are learnng that as their populations age, they are becoming overburdened," observes Ed Walczak of Vontobel USA. "You have a situation where the governments are in a deficit while their citizens are getting older and in need of more health care. As a result, they are gradually cutting back on the help they're providing, and residents are being forced to turn to private insurers. Just as we (or our employers) have to pay for insurance coverage in the United States, the same thing is happening overseas." One company poised to take advantage of that trend, according to Walczak, is ESG Re Limited.

ESG is a specialty reinsurer providing accident, life, health, and special risk coverage. It's a relatively new company that went public in December 1997. Although the company is technically based in Bermuda, the bulk of its operations are in Hamburg, Germany. "ESG's main businesses are providing medical expense, personal accident liability, and life insurance primarily to other insurers," Walczak says. "For instance, if one of the big life insurance companies has too much life insurance on its books, it might want to off-load a piece of that business to a reinsurer in order to diversify. That way the overall risk isn't concentrated in any single area. ESG is one company this risk might be off-loaded to."

What makes ESG especially attractive to Walczak is that, although the company has only been around for less than three years, its management team has been working together since 1993. "They started this company so they could become principals in their own business," Walczak notes. "ESG is run by Wolfgang Wand, who is in Germany. He is doing some very interesting things on the marketing side. ESG has a network established in Latin America, in some of the emerging markets, in Asia, and in Europe. Wand is really positioning the company to be able to reinsure certain health care risks and fill the gaps as governments in these countries recede from offering social support to individuals. If I had to oversimplify the story, I would say ESG really is a play on the increasing privatization of health care in Europe and Latin America."

ESG's growth since inception has been greater than even the founders originally expected. "The way to evaluate success is to look at how much in premiums the company has put on the books and how much is needed to have critical mass," Walczak explains. "In the latest year, ESG got up to $350 million in premiums compared with $100 million during its first year of business. Wand's original goal was to be at about $500 million in premiums by 2001."

The company is in the midst of building its international infrastructure. "ESG has made some very interesting hires," Walczak maintains. "It hired several senior people from other well-known insurance companies, including Swiss Re. A lot of the key executives have 15 to 20 years of experience."

Reason for Recommendation

As a strict value investor and Warren Buffett disciple, Walczak usually prefers buying companies with much longer histories of operations and trailing earnings. "This is a stock that normally would be an exception to all of my rules," he admits. "It is a small company with a market capitalization of around $257 million. But it's a good company with a great future that is selling for less than its initial public offering price of $20 per share." Walczak says that the company looks very cheap based on book value, which is about $17.70 per share. He looks for the company to post earnings of $2 per share in 2000. How much does he think the stock is worth? "I would say it's worth about 1.5 times book value," he insists. "But remember, book value is always changing. A year from now, book value could be up to $25 per share. Every quarter this number is going to grow as premiums and earnings increase. So my actual price target will evolve as book value increases."

Walczak also emphasizes that insiders own a lot of stock, and the company itself has been buying back 5 percent of the outstanding shares. "The books are clean because the company is relatively new," Walczak adds. "There are no odd liabilities on the balance sheet. Once Wall Street starts taking a longer-term view, this stock will do well. And I should emphasize that ESG is getting an increasing amount of analyst coverage."

There are competitors in this area, of course, but Walczak says they're not playing in ESG's specific area of the business (health care–related risks). He also notes that this company is much different from LaSalle Re (another selection in *Wall Street's Picks for 2000*) because it is involved in a completely different market segment.

Contact Information: ESG Re Limited
Skandia International House
16 Church Street
HM 11 Bermuda, Bermuda
441-295-2185

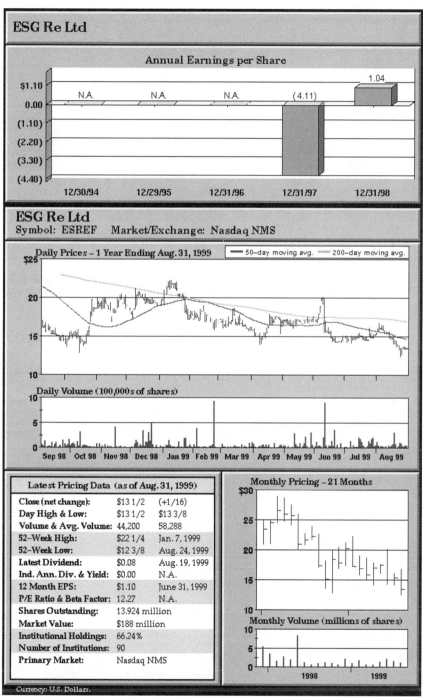

ESG Re Ltd

Annual Earnings per Share

	12/30/94	12/29/95	12/31/96	12/31/97	12/31/98
	N.A.	N.A.	N.A.	(4.11)	1.04

ESG Re Ltd
Symbol: ESREF   Market/Exchange: Nasdaq NMS

Daily Prices – 1 Year Ending Aug. 31, 1999   — 50-day moving avg. ···· 200-day moving avg.

Daily Volume (100,000s of shares)

Sep 98 Oct 98 Nov 98 Dec 98 Jan 99 Feb 99 Mar 99 Apr 99 May 99 Jun 99 Jul 99 Aug 99

Latest Pricing Data (as of Aug. 31, 1999)

Close (net change):	$13 1/2	(+1/16)
Day High & Low:	$13 1/2	$13 3/8
Volume & Avg. Volume:	44,200	58,288
52–Week High:	$22 1/4	Jan. 7, 1999
52–Week Low:	$12 3/8	Aug. 24, 1999
Latest Dividend:	$0.08	Aug. 19, 1999
Ind. Ann. Div. & Yield:	$0.00	N.A.
12 Month EPS:	$1.10	June 31, 1999
P/E Ratio & Beta Factor:	12.27	N.A.
Shares Outstanding:	13.924 million	
Market Value:	$188 million	
Institutional Holdings:	66.24%	
Number of Institutions:	90	
Primary Market:	Nasdaq NMS	

Monthly Pricing – 21 Months

Monthly Volume (millions of shares)

1998   1999

Currency: U.S. Dollars.

Source: IDD Information Services

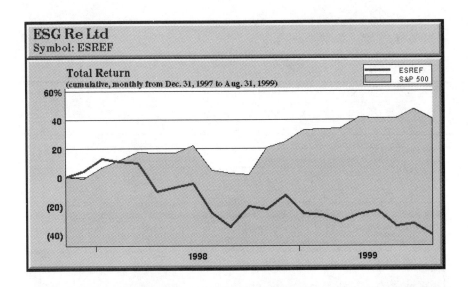

SELECTED INCOME STATEMENT AND BALANCE SHEET ITEMS						
INCOME STATEMENT	**12/30/94**	**12/29/95**	**12/31/96**	**12/31/97**	**12/31/98**	**1 Year**
Sales/Revenues	N.A.	N.A.	N.A.	17.800	115.80	149.70
Cost of Goods Sold	N.A.	N.A.	N.A.	N.A.	N.A.	N.A.
Pre-tax Margin (%)	N.A.	N.A.	N.A.	(32.00)	13.60	12.38
Operating Income	N.A.	N.A.	N.A.	(5.700)	15.800	16.400
Net Income before Extras	N.A.	N.A.	N.A.	(5.100)	14.500	15.200
Reported Net Income	N.A.	N.A.	N.A.	(5.100)	14.500	15.200
Depreciation & Amortization	N.A.	N.A.	N.A.	N.A.	N.A.	N.A.
EPS from Net Income (Primary)	N.A.	N.A.	N.A.	(4.110)	1.040	1.100
EPS from Net Income (Fully Diluted)	N.A.	N.A.	N.A.	(4.110)	1.030	1.100
Dividend per Common Share	0.000	0.000	0.000	0.000	0.300	0.305
Dividend Yield (%)	N.A.	N.A.	N.A.	N.A.	1.48	1.92
Payout Ratio	N.A.	N.A.	N.A.	N.A.	0.29	0.28
BALANCE SHEET						
ASSETS						
Cash & Cash Equivalents	N.A.	N.A.	N.A.	N.A.	N.A.	
Inventories	N.A.	N.A.	N.A.	N.A.	N.A.	
Total Current Assets	N.A.	N.A.	N.A.	N.A.	N.A.	
Total Assets	N.A.	N.A.	N.A.	273.10	466.40	
LIABILITIES & EQUITY						
Short Term Debt	N.A.	N.A.	N.A.	0.000	0.000	
Long Term Debt	N.A.	N.A.	N.A.	0.000	0.000	
Total Liabilities	N.A.	N.A.	N.A.	38.600	221.60	
Shares Outstanding	N.A.	N.A.	N.A.	13.924	13.924	
Common Stockholder Equity	N.A.	N.A.	N.A.	234.40	244.80	
Total Stockholder Equity	N.A.	N.A.	N.A.	234.40	244.80	

Note: Figures in Millions of $ except: per share items, margins, yields, and ratios.

Source: IDD Information Services

GOODYEAR

James O'Shaughnessy
O'Shaughnessy Capital Management

Company Profile

Goodyear is one of the world's leading makers of tires and rubber products. It develops and sells several product lines and manufactures many rubber-related chemicals for various applications. The company continues to expand its global distribution base. It formed a landmark alliance by joining forces with SRI/Dunlop in 1998, thus opening up additional sales channels overseas. The company operates 80 plants in 33 countries and boasts the world's largest fleet of blimps. It also has one of the best brand names in the tire business.

But that's not why James O'Shaughnessy of O'Shaughnessy Capital Management selected this company as his favorite pick for 2000. He simply chose Goodyear because it fits his strategy of buying the stock with the second lowest price of the top ten highest-yielding stocks in the Dow Jones Industrial Average—one derivative of the popular "Dogs of the Dow" investment technique. "I tested this strategy back to 1928 and found that while it is considerably more volatile than the traditional Dogs of the Dow approach [which calls for buying all ten of the highest-yielding stocks], the returns it generates are outstanding," he says. "It has averaged about 26 percent annually going back over 60 years."

The premise behind this strategy is simple. The high yield is a sign a stock is out of favor. "Essentially, you're buying well-known blue chip companies when they are in some distress and/or are unloved or misunderstood on Wall Street," he explains. "The fact is that if you were to do additional fundamental research on such companies, you would probably find a reason not to invest in them. This strategy works because it forces you to buy stock in a company that appears to be in the deepest trouble possible. If you do additional outside research, you will almost certainly conclude it's the one stock you don't want to own." In the case of Goodyear, revenues have been negatively impacted as a result of adverse currency translations, worldwide competitive pricing pressures, and lower tire sales in Latin America and Asia.

According to O'Shaughnessy's strategy, stocks as downtrodden as Goodyear can't get any worse and therefore have no where to go but up. Once conditions improve, investors should start piling back in, driving the share price up and in turn causing the yield to fall. In addition, it's not like you're buying an unproven start-up, which provides an added level of safety. "These are not brand new babies," O'Shaughnessy points out. "They're wise old guys. They've been around the block a million times and can weather virtually any downturn. If the movie *Independence Day* comes true, these companies will still be around."

Goodyear clearly is a solid company. It has been in business for more than 100 years. Despite recent economic difficulties, the company has a strong balance sheet and sound business base. Its tires are being fitted on an increasing number of cars, trucks, and airplanes. The company's stated goal is to become the best tire and rubber company in the world and the industry's lowest-cost producer among top-tier manufacturers.

Reason for Recommendation

As you know by now, O'Shaughnessy doesn't really care about a list of positives. He hasn't met with the company's CEO and has no plans to visit Goodyear headquarters in Akron, Ohio. He likes the stock only because it fit into his Dogs-of-the-Dow investment strategy at the time this book was being written. In fact, by the time you read this, there's a good chance the company's meeting the requirements of this strategy will have changed. Therefore, assuming you want to take O'Shaughnessy's advice, you should jot down the ten highest-yielding Dow stocks at the moment, which are also listed in *The Wall Street Journal* each month, and see which one has the second-lowest price. If it's still Goodyear, that's the stock to buy. If it's another company, put your money there instead.

O'Shaughnessy did share one observation about Goodyear, however, that makes him think the stock could do especially well, assuming you believe the past is predictive of the future. "The last time Goodyear fit my strategy—in 1991—it went up something like 180 percent in a year," he observes. "Right after it fit my criterion, the company cut its dividend to nothing, and everyone started to believe that management was serious about taking care of problems within the company. That sent the stock to the moon. I'm happy it's back in the place it is. Will it cut the dividend this time? I have no idea. But it has a good track record for being in the position to do it."

Recently, some have questioned whether O'Shaughnessy's strategy still works as it underperformed the Dow in 1997 and 1998. O'Shaughnessy's response? "Absolutely," he insists. "I love hearing people say it's dead. You usually hear those cries right when the strategy is about to take off. I always remind people you'll never find a strategy that works every year. You have to keep your eye on the long term. And when you do that, this approach has been absolutely marvelous. It's the ultimate contrarian strategy."

Contact Information: The Goodyear Tire & Rubber Company
1144 East Market Street
Akron, OH 44316-0001
330-796-2121
www.goodyear.com

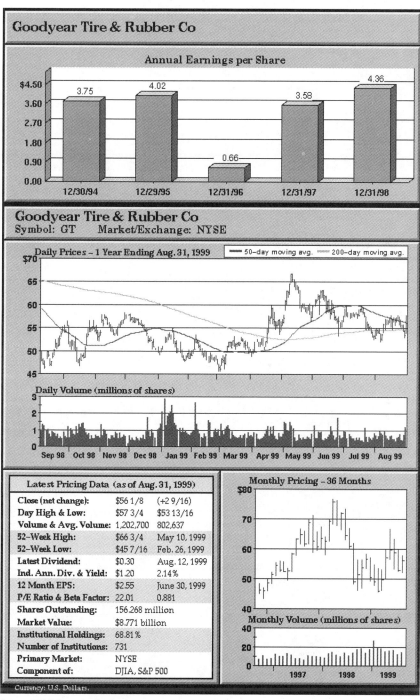

Goodyear Tire & Rubber Co

Annual Earnings per Share

Date	EPS
12/30/94	3.75
12/29/95	4.02
12/31/96	0.66
12/31/97	3.58
12/31/98	4.36

Goodyear Tire & Rubber Co
Symbol: GT   Market/Exchange: NYSE

Daily Prices – 1 Year Ending Aug. 31, 1999   ▬ 50–day moving avg. ▬ 200–day moving avg.

Daily Volume (millions of shares)

Sep 98 Oct 98 Nov 98 Dec 98 Jan 99 Feb 99 Mar 99 Apr 99 May 99 Jun 99 Jul 99 Aug 99

Latest Pricing Data (as of Aug. 31, 1999)

Close (net change):	$56 1/8	(+2 9/16)
Day High & Low:	$57 3/4	$53 13/16
Volume & Avg. Volume:	1,202,700	802,637
52–Week High:	$66 3/4	May 10, 1999
52–Week Low:	$45 7/16	Feb. 26, 1999
Latest Dividend:	$0.30	Aug. 12, 1999
Ind. Ann. Div. & Yield:	$1.20	2.14%
12 Month EPS:	$2.55	June 30, 1999
P/E Ratio & Beta Factor:	22.01	0.881
Shares Outstanding:	156.268 million	
Market Value:	$8.771 billion	
Institutional Holdings:	68.81%	
Number of Institutions:	731	
Primary Market:	NYSE	
Component of:	DJIA, S&P 500	

Monthly Pricing – 36 Months

Monthly Volume (millions of shares)

1997   1998   1999

Currency: U.S. Dollars.

Source: IDD Information Services

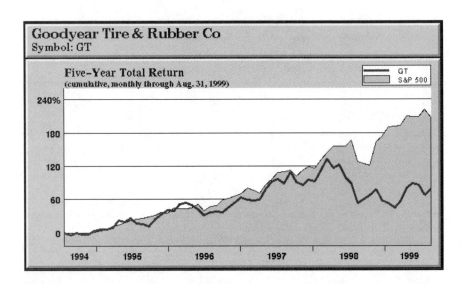

Goodyear Tire & Rubber Co
Symbol: GT

Five-Year Total Return
(cumulative, monthly through Aug. 31, 1999)

GT
S&P 500

240%
180
120
60
0

1994   1995   1996   1997   1998   1999

SELECTED INCOME STATEMENT AND BALANCE SHEET ITEMS

INCOME STATEMENT	12/30/94	12/29/95	12/31/96	12/31/97	12/31/98	1 Year
Sales/Revenues	12,288	13,166	13,113	13,155	12,626	12,435
Cost of Goods Sold	8,861.1	9,658.7	9,565.9	9,576.6	9,185.1	9,204.8
Pre-tax Margin (%)	7.00	7.00	0.90	6.10	7.90	4.30
Operating Income	1,058.6	1,135.4	1,196.0	1,219.7	1,072.3	828.90
Net Income before Extras	567.00	611.00	101.70	558.70	717.00	397.70
Reported Net Income	567.00	611.00	101.70	558.70	682.30	397.70
Depreciation & Amortization	410.30	434.90	460.80	469.30	487.80	510.80
EPS from Net Income (Primary)	3.750	4.020	0.660	3.580	4.360	2.550
EPS from Net Income (Fully Diluted)	3.750	3.970	0.650	3.530	4.310	2.520
Dividend per Common Share	0.750	0.950	1.030	1.140	1.200	1.200
Dividend Yield (%)	2.23	2.09	2.00	1.79	2.38	2.04
Payout Ratio	0.20	0.24	1.56	0.32	0.28	0.47
BALANCE SHEET						
ASSETS						
Cash & Cash Equivalents	250.90	268.30	238.50	258.60	239.00	
Inventories	1,425.1	1,765.2	1,774.2	1,835.2	2,164.5	
Total Current Assets	3,622.7	3,841.6	4,025.0	4,163.9	4,529.1	
Total Assets	9,123.3	9,789.6	9,671.8	9,917.4	10,589	
LIABILITIES & EQUITY						
Short Term Debt	226.90	226.70	244.50	506.70	789.30	
Long Term Debt	1,108.7	1,320.0	1,132.2	844.50	1,186.5	
Total Liabilities	6,320.1	6,507.9	6,392.7	6,521.9	6,843.5	
Shares Outstanding	151.407	153.524	156.050	156.589	155.944	
Common Stockholder Equity	2,803.2	3,281.7	3,279.1	3,395.5	3,745.8	
Total Stockholder Equity	2,803.2	3,281.7	3,279.1	3,395.5	3,745.8	

Note: Figures in Millions of $ except: per share items, margins, yields, and ratios.

Source: IDD Information Services

IBM

Art Bonnel
Bonnel Growth Fund

Company Profile

Big Blue is definitely back from the dead. IBM has gone from posting record losses in 1993 to record revenues and earnings per share in 1998. Much of the credit for the company's turnaround has gone to Chairman and CEO Louis Gerstner. Before joining IBM in April 1993, Gerstner had been chairman and CEO of RJR Nabisco and had spent 11 years as a top executive at American Express. Gerstner placed a new emphasis on customer satisfaction and realized the company's future was dependent on its ability to be competitive in the networking area.

IBM's dramatic turnaround has not gone unnoticed by Wall Street. The company's market capitalization ballooned from $43 billion to $169 million from 1994 to 1998. During this same period, the stock's share price zoomed from $37 to $184. But Art Bonnel, manager of the Bonnel Growth Fund, believes the good times have only just begun.

"I'm very optimistic about IBM's future," Bonnel says. "This is a very aggressive company. PC sales are doing well. The software business is humming right along. And IBM is moving rapidly into the area of e-commerce." Bonnel admits the company could have gone out of business in 1993. "I think the key was that it lost money that year," he shares. "It wasn't much, but it made IBM realize it had to get its act together. The company moved away from big computers and began to concentrate on personal computers. It also reduced its workforce and became a much healthier company."

IBM's stated mission is to lead in the creation, development, and manufacture of the industry's most advanced information technologies, including computer systems, software, networking systems, storage devices, and microelectronics. The company prospered in 1998 despite a number of challenges throughout the year, including weakness in Asia and ongoing softness in memory chip prices. The strongest growth has come from the company's software, hard disk drives, and global services segments. IBM's AS/400 product line is also doing well. But going forward, Gerstner agrees with Bonnel that the driving force for the company will be its ability to be a major part of the Internet, which he believes is here to stay. "One school of thought says a new mass medium has been born when it's used by 50 million people," Gerstner offers. "Radio took nearly 40 years to hit that threshold. TV took 13 years. Cable TV, 10 years. The Internet did it in less than 5." While the Internet is largely a U.S. phenomenon, Gerstner doesn't expect that to last long. "Since 1995 we have been saying that the Net is about mainstream business, not browsing," Gerstner adds. "At IBM, we call this 'e-business,' and it represents an enormous opportunity. We expect the overall information technology industry to grow at an annual rate of 10 percent to $1.6 trillion by 2002. Of that, the e-business segment will grow to $600 billion, and it will grow twice as fast as the industry overall." Gerstner intends to capture a good bit of that business.

In essence, IBM has come to realize that the PC era is over. It's not that Gerstner or anyone else believes personal computers will disappear completely. "But the PC's reign as the driver of customer-buying decisions and the primary platform for application development is over," Gerstner predicts. "In all those respects, it has been supplanted by the network."

IBM has invested heavily to reinvent its server and enterprise software lines. To speed this process along, the company has acquired a number of related businesses in recent years, including Lotus, Tivoli Systems, NetObjects, Footprint Software, Edmark, and Software Artistry. "And to keep better focused, IBM sold its Internet service to AT&T, which means it can focus on providing the hardware and software instead of just being a service provider," Bonnel adds.

Reason for Recommendation

Bonnel admits this company is unlikely to grow as fast as it has in the past five years. But he calls IBM in 2000 "an almost sure bet." Why? "This company is so diversified," he insists. "Sure, it's an older company. But when you think of computers, what do you think of? IBM." There are also a number of drivers that make Bonnel especially upbeat about IBM's prospects for the upcoming year. "For one thing, a lot of people have been putting off major computer purchases until after the year 2000," he says. "What's more, Intel keeps coming up with new and faster chips. Everyone is going to need the Pentium III before long. I maintain that machines with this chip are going to be very popular in 2000. People are going to want IBM's new computers."

Despite the company's rapid growth thus far, Bonnel believes it has much further to go. He expects the company to earn at least $2.50 per share in 2000, jumping to $3.50 in 2001. "The stock has the momentum, and the industry itself is going to show prodigious gains that are hard to forecast," he insists. "This company could see earnings growth of 30 to 40 percent annually for the next couple of years." The biggest risk, Bonnel cautions, is that if the company misses its numbers for a couple of quarters, the stock could get hammered. "But I would be buying on any pullbacks because I have faith it will come back," he says.

Contact Information: International Business Machines Corporation
New Orchard Road
Armonk, NY 10504
914-499-1900
www.ibm.com

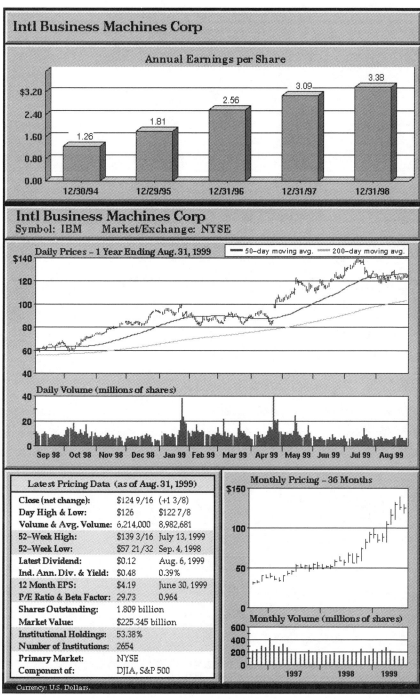

Intl Business Machines Corp

Annual Earnings per Share

				3.38
			3.09	
		2.56		
	1.81			
1.26				
12/30/94	12/29/95	12/31/96	12/31/97	12/31/98

$3.20
2.40
1.60
0.80
0.00

Intl Business Machines Corp
Symbol: IBM   Market/Exchange: NYSE

Daily Prices – 1 Year Ending Aug. 31, 1999

━━ 50-day moving avg.   ▦▦▦ 200-day moving avg.

$140
120
100
80
60
40

Daily Volume (millions of shares)

40
20
0

Sep 98 Oct 98 Nov 98 Dec 98 Jan 99 Feb 99 Mar 99 Apr 99 May 99 Jun 99 Jul 99 Aug 99

Latest Pricing Data (as of Aug. 31, 1999)

Close (net change):	$124 9/16	(+1 3/8)
Day High & Low:	$126	$122 7/8
Volume & Avg. Volume:	6,214,000	8,982,681
52-Week High:	$139 3/16	July 13, 1999
52-Week Low:	$57 21/32	Sep. 4, 1998
Latest Dividend:	$0.12	Aug. 6, 1999
Ind. Ann. Div. & Yield:	$0.48	0.39%
12 Month EPS:	$4.19	June 30, 1999
P/E Ratio & Beta Factor:	29.73	0.964
Shares Outstanding:	1.809 billion	
Market Value:	$225.345 billion	
Institutional Holdings:	53.38%	
Number of Institutions:	2654	
Primary Market:	NYSE	
Component of:	DJIA, S&P 500	

Monthly Pricing – 36 Months

$150
100
50
0

1997 1998 1999

Monthly Volume (millions of shares)

600
400
200
0

Currency: U.S. Dollars.

Source: IDD Information Services

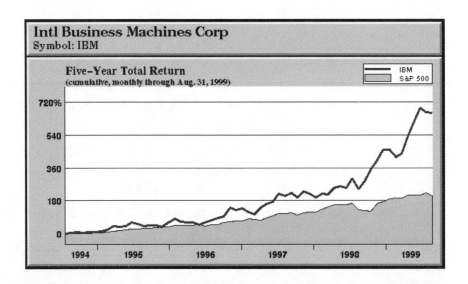

Intl Business Machines Corp
Symbol: IBM

Five-Year Total Return
(cumulative, monthly through Aug. 31, 1999)

IBM
S&P 500

720%
540
360
180
0

1994   1995   1996   1997   1998   1999

SELECTED INCOME STATEMENT AND BALANCE SHEET ITEMS

INCOME STATEMENT	12/30/94	12/29/95	12/31/96	12/31/97	12/31/98	1 Year
Sales/Revenues	64,052	71,940	75,947	78,508	81,667	87,448
Cost of Goods Sold	34,571	35,971	40,396	42,898	45,803	49,096
Pre–tax Margin (%)	8.00	10.90	11.30	11.50	11.10	13.12
Operating Income	5,005.0	7,591.0	8,596.0	9,098.0	9,164.0	11,723
Net Income before Extras	3,021.0	4,178.0	5,429.0	6,093.0	6,328.0	7,701.0
Reported Net Income	3,021.0	4,178.0	5,429.0	6,093.0	6,328.0	7,701.0
Depreciation & Amortization	4,197.0	5,602.0	5,012.0	5,001.0	4,992.0	5,594.0
EPS from Net Income (Primary)	1.260	1.810	2.560	3.090	3.380	4.190
EPS from Net Income (Fully Diluted)	1.240	1.770	2.510	3.010	3.290	4.070
Dividend per Common Share	0.250	0.250	0.325	0.388	0.430	0.450
Dividend Yield (%)	1.36	1.09	0.86	0.74	0.47	0.35
Payout Ratio	0.20	0.14	0.13	0.13	0.13	0.11

BALANCE SHEET						
ASSETS						
Cash & Cash Equivalents	7,922.0	7,259.0	7,687.0	7,106.0	5,375.0	
Inventories	6,334.0	6,323.0	5,870.0	5,139.0	5,200.0	
Total Current Assets	41,338	40,691	40,695	40,418	42,360	
Total Assets	81,091	80,292	81,132	81,499	86,100	
LIABILITIES & EQUITY						
Short Term Debt	9,570.0	11,569	12,957	13,230	13,905	
Long Term Debt	12,548	10,060	9,872.0	13,696	15,508	
Total Liabilities	57,678	57,869	59,504	61,683	66,667	
Shares Outstanding	2,350.844	2,191.096	2,031.924	1,936.182	1,851.814	
Common Stockholder Equity	22,332	22,170	21,375	19,564	19,186	
Total Stockholder Equity	23,413	22,423	21,628	19,816	19,433	

Note: Figures in Millions of $ except: per share items, margins, yields, and ratios.

Source: IDD Information Services

INTERNATIONAL GAME TECHNOLOGY

John Rogers

Ariel Capital Management

Company Profile

If you like to gamble, chances are you spend a lot of time in front of the slot machines when you visit a casino. And these days, casinos are everywhere. Of course, they are on every street corner in places like Las Vegas, Reno, and Atlantic City. But today you can probably find them close to your neighborhood too, especially on protected Indian reservations.

There's something magical about feeding our hard-earned money to these colorful machines. It's thrilling to pull the lever and watch with excitement to see if Lady Luck will give us a winning combination of the spinning reels, prompting a waterfall of coins to come flowing out below. Although the odds are clearly stacked against us, we still are intrigued by the possibilities.

One company that profits from this fascination is International Game Technology. IGT makes many of the slot machines you find in casinos everywhere. "IGT is the world's leading manufacturer of slot machines," notes John Rogers, manager of the Ariel Growth Fund. "It is very good at what it does. I was recently meeting with the management team in Las Vegas and got a clear sense that the company is in the right place at the right time as gaming continues to proliferate around the world."

IGT has about a 70 percent share of the traditional slot machine market. It is licensed in more than 100 legal gaming jurisdictions worldwide. Perhaps most important, it dominates the progressive games business. "That's where you have a chance to win a megajackpot by playing on slot machines at several different locations," Rogers explains. "These progressives are becoming more and more popular in Las Vegas and around the country. When I was last in Vegas, the progressive jackpot was worth $14 million, so this is a big deal."

The way the progressive jackpots work is that IGT gets a cut of every dollar that goes into these machines. That money is used to build up the jackpot, develop new games, and build overhead profits for the company. "Of course, IGT has to follow the gaming rules in the states it operates in," Rogers observes. "For example, in Las Vegas the rules say a certain percentage of all that money going into the slot machine must be returned to the players to make sure tourists aren't being taken advantage of."

Casino owners in Las Vegas have never been happy about IGT getting a cut of the profits. They recently tried to enact legislation in Nevada that would both force IGT to pay gaming taxes and outlaw progressive jackpots altogether. "The fear that such legislation will eventually be passed has hurt the shares of IGT,"

Rogers maintains. "This revenue is nice and consistent, and it would be hard to see it suddenly stop coming in."

Reason for Recommendation

But being a contrarian at heart, Rogers finds that this threat makes IGT stock all the more attractive. He thinks the best time to buy a company is when other investors are afraid of it, because that's when it can be had for a cheap price. "I think that over time two things are going to happen," he reasons. "First, the Nevada legislature has always been probusiness. So I don't think they'll ever meddle in a war between a manufacturer and an end user of a product. I expect that rationality will prevail. Second, I think that the proposed legislation is nothing but posturing on the part of the casinos to get a bigger split of the revenue. Let's face it. The casinos love these progressive games because they bring people into the casinos. They don't want to bite the hand that feeds them."

Some have also voiced concern that the gambling industry has reached a peak. Construction of new megacasinos is beginning to slow down and one has to wonder whether the demand for slot machines will follow. "I think the exact opposite will happen," Rogers insists. "There is currently a proliferation of new slot machine gaming concepts. You can play Wheel of Fortune, Elvis, and Monopoly, just to name a few. There are all kinds of new technological video-based games that players are very excited about." In fact, it was IGT's video poker machines that started the video gaming revolution in the 1970s. "You're going to see a rapid obsolescence of the games that are currently out there, which will create a high demand for new machines," Rogers adds. "With the intense competition among casinos in Vegas in particular, I think you'll see them turning over the machines on the floors rather quickly to one-up the competition. Therefore, demand to replace those machines with newer ones should be terrific for IGT." The company estimates that the replacement cycle for slot machines will go from five to seven years today to as short as two years in the future.

The only thing Rogers is a little concerned about is that IGT will lose its patent on the progressive games concept in Nevada in about three years. "That will create more competition in the marketplace," Rogers notes. "It's not a major concern right now, but it's something I'm going to keep my eye on."

Rogers estimates that IGT's private market value is around $30 per share, which is where he expects the stock to trade in 2000.

Contact Information: International Game Technology
9295 Prototype Drive
Reno, NV 89510
725-448-1137
www.igtgame.com

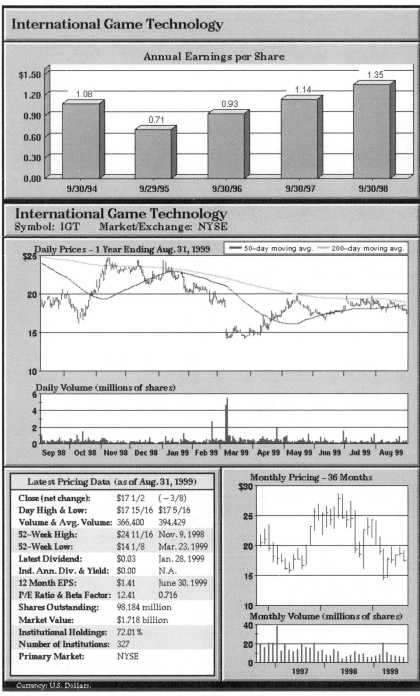

International Game Technology

Annual Earnings per Share

	9/30/94	9/29/95	9/30/96	9/30/97	9/30/98
	1.08	0.71	0.93	1.14	1.35

International Game Technology
Symbol: IGT   Market/Exchange: NYSE

Daily Prices – 1 Year Ending Aug. 31, 1999

━━ 50-day moving avg.   ▨▨▨ 200-day moving avg.

Daily Volume (millions of shares)

Sep 98 Oct 98 Nov 98 Dec 98 Jan 99 Feb 99 Mar 99 Apr 99 May 99 Jun 99 Jul 99 Aug 99

Latest Pricing Data (as of Aug. 31, 1999)

Close (net change):	$17 1/2	(– 3/8)
Day High & Low:	$17 15/16	$17 5/16
Volume & Avg. Volume:	366,400	394,429
52–Week High:	$24 11/16	Nov. 9, 1998
52–Week Low:	$14 1/8	Mar. 23, 1999
Latest Dividend:	$0.03	Jan. 28, 1999
Ind. Ann. Div. & Yield:	$0.00	N.A.
12 Month EPS:	$1.41	June 30, 1999
P/E Ratio & Beta Factor:	12.41	0.716
Shares Outstanding:	98.184 million	
Market Value:	$1.718 billion	
Institutional Holdings:	72.01%	
Number of Institutions:	327	
Primary Market:	NYSE	

Monthly Pricing – 36 Months

Monthly Volume (millions of shares)

1997   1998   1999

Currency: U.S. Dollars.

Source: IDD Information Services

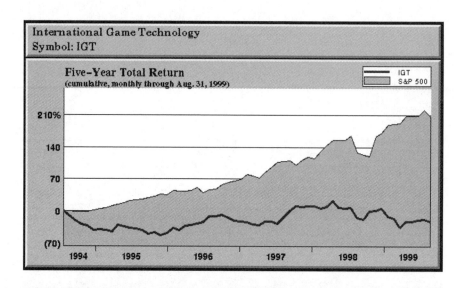

International Game Technology
Symbol: IGT

Five-Year Total Return
(cumulative, monthly through Aug. 31, 1999)

SELECTED INCOME STATEMENT AND BALANCE SHEET ITEMS						
INCOME STATEMENT	**9/30/94**	**9/29/95**	**9/30/96**	**9/30/97**	**9/30/98**	**1 Year**
Sales/Revenues	674.50	620.80	733.50	744.00	824.10	955.50
Cost of Goods Sold	341.50	330.60	387.40	378.50	415.00	N.A.
Pre-tax Margin (%)	31.80	23.30	25.10	28.60	28.50	N.A.
Operating Income	205.20	145.20	181.40	191.50	218.80	N.A.
Net Income before Extras	140.40	92.600	118.00	137.20	152.40	147.30
Reported Net Income	140.40	92.600	118.00	137.20	152.40	147.30
Depreciation & Amortization	20.600	27.900	30.500	35.000	41.500	N.A.
EPS from Net Income (Primary)	1.080	0.710	0.930	1.140	1.350	1.410
EPS from Net Income (Fully Diluted)	1.050	0.710	0.930	1.130	1.330	1.390
Dividend per Common Share	0.120	0.120	0.120	0.120	0.120	0.090
Dividend Yield (%)	0.58	0.89	0.59	0.52	0.65	N.A.
Payout Ratio	0.11	0.17	0.13	0.11	0.09	0.06
BALANCE SHEET						
ASSETS						
Cash & Cash Equivalents	142.70	241.60	169.90	151.80	175.40	
Inventories	104.00	73.800	100.30	92.400	133.20	
Total Current Assets	559.10	606.60	615.60	571.50	670.50	
Total Assets	868.00	971.70	1,154.2	1,215.1	1,543.6	
LIABILITIES & EQUITY						
Short Term Debt	2.600	7.400	8.100	25.400	30.300	
Long Term Debt	111.50	107.50	107.20	140.70	322.50	
Total Liabilities	347.20	417.60	531.10	695.10	1,002.4	
Shares Outstanding	135.394	128.850	125.576	113.708	108.162	
Common Stockholder Equity	520.90	554.10	623.20	519.80	541.30	
Total Stockholder Equity	520.90	554.10	623.20	519.80	541.30	

Note: Figures in Millions of $ except: per share items, margins, yields, and ratios.

Source: IDD Information Services

LaSALLE RE HOLDINGS

Martin Whitman
Third Avenue Funds

Company Profile

The past couple of years haven't been very good for insurance companies, especially those that write policies for catastrophes. In addition to strong competitive pricing pressures, a number of weather-related events have caused major damage around the world. "You've had many severe and frequent catastrophes of late, including Hurricane George, floods and tornadoes in the Midwest, freezes and hailstorms in the Southeast, and we haven't even begun to talk about events in other countries," says Martin Whitman of the Third Avenue Funds. LaSalle Re Holdings has felt the pain of these disasters as much as any insurer, perhaps a bit more as disasters are its primary area of specialty. Losses from catastrophes in the United States during the first nine months of 1998 alone totaled more than $8.3 billion, which is more than three times the sum for all of 1997.

Through its operating subsidiary, LaSalle Re Limited, this Bermuda-based company writes property and casualty reinsurance with an emphasis on catastrophe coverage. Such reinsurance covers damage from unpredictable events like hurricanes, windstorms, hailstorms, earthquakes, fires, industrial explosions, freezes, riots, floods, and other man-made or natural disasters. These are the kinds of events no one ever expects to fall victim to. But when they occur, damage can be significant.

LaSalle Re began operations in 1993. Majority shareholders of the company include Aon and CNA, each of which owns about 15 percent of the outstanding shares. LaSalle is rated A by both A. M. Best and Standard & Poor's—a testament to its strong balance sheet. Despite lower premiums and high loss payouts, 1998 was profitable for the company even though earnings per share were down significantly from the previous year. The company tries to control its risks through geographic diversification and by gradually adding to lines of business outside its core property catastrophe specialization.

"Managing risk in a changing environment is, by necessity, a central part of a successful long-term strategy," says LaSalle Chairman, President, and CEO Victor H. Blake. "Our business is to absorb a share of catastrophe losses, which would otherwise fall on primary insurers. Our ability to meet these obligations during times of uncertainty is what substantiates the value of our product and the service we provide to our clients."

LaSalle markets its policies through reinsurance brokers around the world. Around 49 percent of its business is in the United States, and much of the rest is in Europe (20 percent), Japan (2.4 percent), and Australasia (2.5 percent). In light of recent events, the company took a charge against earnings of approximately

$35 million, or $1.68 per share, in 1999 to strengthen its reserve. "We have been part of an industry caught in a prolonged soft insurance cycle that has created excessive competition and oversupply of capital," Blake said. "In diversifying our portfolio, certain lines of business have proven to be unprofitable. We have identified the unprofitable lines of business and have discontinued them. We have reaffirmed our underwriting strategy as a specialty catastrophe reinsurer, emphasizing low-frequency and high-severity business. We believe that LaSalle Re's reserve position will be among the strongest in the reinsurance industry with the action we have taken."

Reason for Recommendation

As you might guess given all of the challenges LaSalle faces right now, there has been little interest in the company's stock. In fact, shares have been trading far below their book value of $23.39 per share. So what's it going to take for investors to once again get interested and drive the share price higher? Frankly, Whitman admits, he has no clue. "What I can tell you is this company has a good financial position, extremely strong management, and is very well run," he says. "When the current outlook is not great (which it obviously isn't right now), nobody wants to own stocks like this at any price." But Whitman is what's known as a vulture investor. In other words, he relies on picking up shares precisely when everyone wants out. That way he gets them cheap and after all of the sellers have fled. At least if his timing is right!

Whether LaSalle has seen its lows and is poised to rebound is impossible to guarantee. But Whitman sees nothing but an upside for this stock. "This is a blue chip business where the short-term outlook is quite dismal," he maintains. "I'm looking beyond today. The company sells for a big discount from book, has huge future earnings power, and even if it takes a while for things to get moving again, I'm not paying that much for the stock, so my risk is very low." LaSalle also pays a $3 annual dividend, and Whitman admits it would also be a strong takeover candidate at current levels.

(Because this company is based in Bermuda, with no U.S. contact, one of the most efficient ways to request additional investor information is by visiting the company's Web site. The investor relations department is very quick to respond to requests from potential shareholders.)

Contact Information: LaSalle Re Holdings Limited
Continental Building, 25 Church Street
Hamilton HM 12, Bermuda
441-292-3339
www.lasallere.com

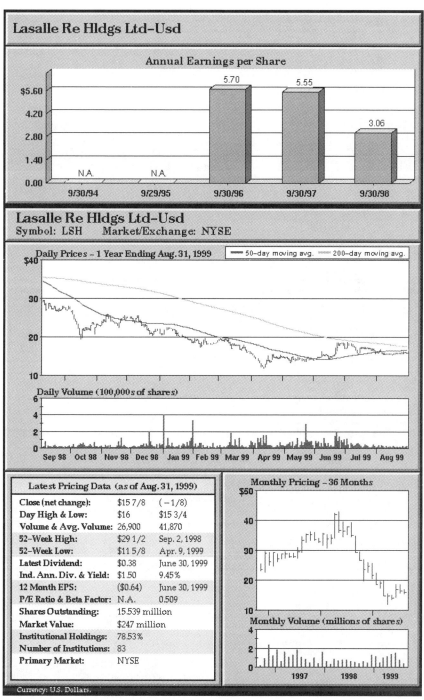

Lasalle Re Hldgs Ltd–Usd

Annual Earnings per Share

	9/30/94	9/29/95	9/30/96	9/30/97	9/30/98
EPS	N.A.	N.A.	5.70	5.55	3.06

Lasalle Re Hldgs Ltd–Usd
Symbol: LSH   Market/Exchange: NYSE

Daily Prices – 1 Year Ending Aug. 31, 1999

— 50-day moving avg.   ▬ 200-day moving avg.

Daily Volume (100,000s of shares)

Sep 98 Oct 98 Nov 98 Dec 98 Jan 99 Feb 99 Mar 99 Apr 99 May 99 Jun 99 Jul 99 Aug 99

Latest Pricing Data (as of Aug. 31, 1999)

Close (net change):	$15 7/8	(–1/8)
Day High & Low:	$16	$15 3/4
Volume & Avg. Volume:	26,900	41,870
52-Week High:	$29 1/2	Sep. 2, 1998
52-Week Low:	$11 5/8	Apr. 9, 1999
Latest Dividend:	$0.38	June 30, 1999
Ind. Ann. Div. & Yield:	$1.50	9.45%
12 Month EPS:	($0.64)	June 30, 1999
P/E Ratio & Beta Factor:	N.A.	0.509
Shares Outstanding:	15.539 million	
Market Value:	$247 million	
Institutional Holdings:	78.53%	
Number of Institutions:	83	
Primary Market:	NYSE	

Monthly Pricing – 36 Months

Monthly Volume (millions of shares)

1997   1998   1999

Currency: U.S. Dollars.

Source: IDD Information Services

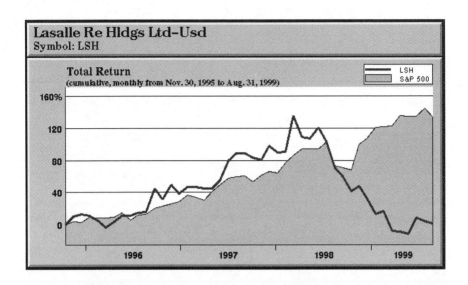

Lasalle Re Hldgs Ltd–Usd
Symbol: LSH

Total Return
(cumulative, monthly from Nov. 30, 1995 to Aug. 31, 1999)

LSH
S&P 500

SELECTED INCOME STATEMENT AND BALANCE SHEET ITEMS

INCOME STATEMENT	9/30/94	9/29/95	9/30/96	9/30/97	9/30/98	1 Year
Sales/Revenues	N.A.	N.A.	221.60	197.80	194.50	176.70
Cost of Goods Sold	N.A.	N.A.	N.A.	N.A.	N.A.	N.A.
Pre-tax Margin (%)	N.A.	N.A.	36.80	49.10	26.60	N.A.
Operating Income	N.A.	N.A.	129.70	123.20	67.100	N.A.
Net Income before Extras	N.A.	N.A.	81.500	97.100	51.800	(4.400)
Reported Net Income	N.A.	N.A.	81.500	97.100	51.800	(4.400)
Depreciation & Amortization	N.A.	N.A.	N.A.	N.A.	N.A.	N.A.
EPS from Net Income (Primary)	N.A.	N.A.	5.700	5.550	3.060	(0.640)
EPS from Net Income (Fully Diluted)	N.A.	N.A.	5.400	5.140	2.800	(0.610)
Dividend per Common Share	0.000	0.000	0.500	2.380	3.710	1.875
Dividend Yield (%)	N.A.	N.A.	2.13	6.78	13.93	11.03
Payout Ratio	N.A.	N.A.	0.09	0.43	1.21	N.A.
BALANCE SHEET						
ASSETS						
Cash & Cash Equivalents	N.A.	N.A.	N.A.	N.A.	N.A.	
Inventories	N.A.	N.A.	N.A.	N.A.	N.A.	
Total Current Assets	N.A.	N.A.	N.A.	N.A.	N.A.	
Total Assets	N.A.	N.A.	634.40	686.10	757.30	
LIABILITIES & EQUITY						
Short Term Debt	N.A.	N.A.	0.000	0.000	0.000	
Long Term Debt	N.A.	N.A.	0.000	0.000	0.000	
Total Liabilities	N.A.	N.A.	327.00	260.90	327.20	
Shares Outstanding	N.A.	N.A.	14.398	15.074	15.179	
Common Stockholder Equity	N.A.	N.A.	307.40	422.20	427.10	
Total Stockholder Equity	N.A.	N.A.	307.40	425.20	430.10	

Note: Figures in Millions of $ except: per share items, margins, yields, and ratios.

Source: IDD Information Services

THE LIMITED

Susan Byrne
Westwood Management

Company Profile

The Limited believes that branding is the key to its long-term success. The company has built a portfolio of the best-known brand names in fashion retailing today: Victoria's Secret, Bath & Body Works, Lane Bryant, Express, Lerner New York, The Limited, Structure, Limited Too, Galyan's, and Henri Bendel. "I think investors would be wise to think of The Limited as a retail holding company," says Susan Byrne of Westwood Management.

Over the years, The Limited has spun off some of its biggest crown jewels. Most notably, in 1998 former holding Abercrombie & Fitch Co. became a wholly independent company. Previously, The Limited sold off 15 percent of Victoria's Secret and Bath & Body Works as a holding company known as Intimate Brands, which trades under the symbol IBI on the New York Stock Exchange. Most recently, the company announced plans to spin off 100 percent of its Limited Too chain, which sells apparel for fashion-aware young girls from 7 to 14. In 1999 it also sold a majority interest in its Galyan's Trading Co. division to a private investment firm.

Leslie H. Wexner, chairman and CEO of The Limited, claims he's never been more excited about the prospects for his company's brands. "Not in the first phase of our growth, from 1963 to 1981, when we went from a single Limited store with just a few employees to hundreds of Limited stores with thousands of associate partners," he says. "Not in our second phase of growth, which ended around 1992, when we, at the center of the enterprise, operated essentially as venture capitalists." During this time, the company used its leverage and financial strength to expand its roster of specialty businesses. But Wexner admits that back then the company hadn't created the competencies to lead the large enterprise that soon blossomed. "In the early to mid-1990s, it became apparent that simply working harder at the same things was not going to allow us to reach our goals," he reflects. "We had to change."

As a result, the company brought a team of experienced managers to its executive team, added expertise in planning and information technology, and formalized the process of building and sustaining brands. Now each retail chain has its own CEO, marketing efforts have become tighter, and the company is working hard to build strong names for its various brands. "We have more resources, more talent, and more intellect in our business now than at any point in our history," Wexner insists. "And I am determined to mobilize our assets [to support] the brands that offer the greatest growth potential."

Reason for Recommendation

What Byrne likes more than anything else is The Limited's 85 percent ownership of Intimate Brands. "There are 250 million shares outstanding of Intimate Brands, and The Limited owns more than 210 million of them," she says. Because each share of The Limited represents 85 percent of Intimate Brands based on current valuations, Byrne notes that you're getting all of the retailer's other brands for next to nothing.

"Buying The Limited is a way with much lower risk to get Intimate Brands," Byrne says. You might think of its as a backdoor approach to owning the other stock. She's also excited that the company has a history of spinning off its other brands with huge success. "Abercrombie & Fitch has been an absolutely fantastic stock," she notes.

Remember, Intimate Brands owns both Victoria's Secret and Bath & Body Works. Intimate Brands's newest venture, The White Barn Candle Co., is growing rapidly. Still, Victoria's Secret is clearly the standout performer. This leading retailer of lingerie not only has a chain of stores across the country but also a very successful Web site. In fact, the launch of the Victoria's Secret Internet site at the end of 1998 was a huge media event that attracted record crowds who came to view a real-time fashion show featuring the store's merchandise. "Many people have said that people won't buy soft goods on the Internet," Byrne observes. "For the most part, I agree. But I think Victoria's Secret has hit a real bull's-eye. It is marketing to men through the Internet, whereas the stores appeal more to women."

Byrne is also encouraged by what she sees happening with The Limited's other brands, which she feels you're getting for next to nothing given the current stock price. "That's not to say I expect Express, Limited, or Lane Bryant to become as exciting a merchandising concept as Abercrombie & Fitch or Victoria's Secret, but I think you're looking at some great values here." The company itself apparently agrees. It has announced plans to repurchase up to 15 million shares at between $50 and $55 a share, which is still much less than Byrne thinks the stock is worth, especially given its potential breakup value.

Contact Information: The Limited, Inc.
Three Limited Parkway
Columbus, OH 43230
614-415-7000
www.limited.com

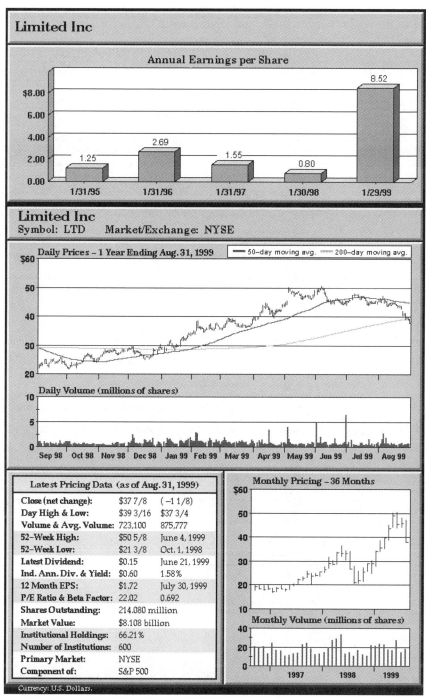

Limited Inc

Annual Earnings per Share

1/31/95	1/31/96	1/31/97	1/30/98	1/29/99
1.25	2.69	1.55	0.80	8.52

Limited Inc
Symbol: LTD   Market/Exchange: NYSE

Daily Prices – 1 Year Ending Aug. 31, 1999   ▬ 50-day moving avg.   ▬ 200-day moving avg.

Daily Volume (millions of shares)

Sep 98   Oct 98   Nov 98   Dec 98   Jan 99   Feb 99   Mar 99   Apr 99   May 99   Jun 99   Jul 99   Aug 99

Latest Pricing Data (as of Aug. 31, 1999)

Close (net change):	$37 7/8	(−1 1/8)
Day High & Low:	$39 3/16	$37 3/4
Volume & Avg. Volume:	723,100	875,777
52–Week High:	$50 5/8	June 4, 1999
52–Week Low:	$21 3/8	Oct. 1, 1998
Latest Dividend:	$0.15	June 21, 1999
Ind. Ann. Div. & Yield:	$0.60	1.58%
12 Month EPS:	$1.72	July 30, 1999
P/E Ratio & Beta Factor:	22.02	0.692
Shares Outstanding:	214.080 million	
Market Value:	$8.108 billion	
Institutional Holdings:	66.21%	
Number of Institutions:	600	
Primary Market:	NYSE	
Component of:	S&P 500	

Monthly Pricing – 36 Months

Monthly Volume (millions of shares)

1997   1998   1999

Currency: U.S. Dollars.

Source: IDD Information Services

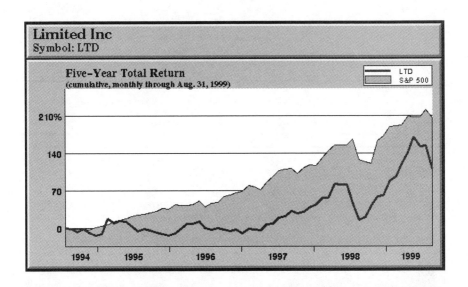

Limited Inc
Symbol: LTD

SELECTED INCOME STATEMENT AND BALANCE SHEET ITEMS

INCOME STATEMENT	1/31/95	1/31/96	1/31/97	1/30/98	1/29/99	1 Year
Sales/Revenues	7,320.8	7,881.4	8,644.8	9,188.8	9,346.9	9,628.4
Cost of Goods Sold	4,938.6	5,508.0	5,858.6	6,057.5	6,062.9	N.A.
Pre-tax Margin (%)	10.20	15.00	7.80	4.40	25.30	N.A.
Operating Income	799.00	612.00	648.10	693.30	697.50	N.A.
Net Income before Extras	448.30	961.50	434.20	217.40	2,053.6	375.70
Reported Net Income	448.30	961.50	434.20	217.40	2,053.6	375.70
Depreciation & Amortization	267.80	285.90	289.60	313.30	286.00	N.A.
EPS from Net Income (Primary)	1.250	2.690	1.550	0.800	8.520	1.720
EPS from Net Income (Fully Diluted)	1.250	2.680	1.540	0.790	8.320	1.670
Dividend per Common Share	0.360	0.400	0.400	0.480	0.520	0.560
Dividend Yield (%)	2.13	2.39	2.34	1.81	1.52	1.23
Payout Ratio	0.29	0.15	0.26	0.60	0.06	0.33
BALANCE SHEET						
ASSETS						
Cash & Cash Equivalents	242.80	1,645.7	312.80	746.40	870.30	
Inventories	870.40	959.00	1,007.3	1,101.9	1,218.5	
Total Current Assets	2,547.7	2,800.0	1,545.1	2,031.2	2,318.2	
Total Assets	4,570.1	5,266.6	4,120.0	4,300.8	4,549.7	
LIABILITIES & EQUITY						
Short Term Debt	0.000	0.000	0.000	0.000	100.00	
Long Term Debt	650.00	650.00	650.00	650.00	550.00	
Total Liabilities	1,809.1	2,065.6	2,197.3	2,255.8	2,316.4	
Shares Outstanding	358.325	355.366	271.291	272.800	226.572	
Common Stockholder Equity	2,761.0	3,201.0	1,922.6	2,045.0	2,233.3	
Total Stockholder Equity	2,761.0	3,201.0	1,922.6	2,045.0	2,233.3	

Note: Figures in Millions of $ except: per share items, margins, yields, and ratios.

Source: IDD Information Services

PERVASIVE SOFTWARE

Kevin Landis
Firsthand Funds

Company Profile

If you have a lot of complex information that you want to put on the Internet, you'll need to do the "tango." Specifically, you'll need Tango software, which is manufactured by Pervasive Software. Kevin Landis of Firsthand Funds not only likes the stock but he's a customer of the company and uses Tango on his own Web site. "Tango allows you to build exciting Web applications and is an integral part of our site," he says. "We can take all of our data and turn them into information-rich Web-based charts and tables, both on our internal and external networks."

Landis claims Tango is so good that the information systems experts at his office tell him they don't know what they would do without it. "I asked them which other product they could use if Tango weren't available," he shares. "They basically turned their hands palms up and said, 'We aren't sure, since a lot of what we want to accomplish is impossible without this software."

You don't have to be in the business of generating complex data, as Landis is, to use Tango. "You simply need to be presenting information in a Web-based format in such a way that you need to take cuts of a database," he says. "Most e-commerce today is very much driven by databases. It's pretty much impossible to put up such a site without a powerful database running it. So you can see there's a big demand for this product."

Pervasive Software doesn't live on Tango alone. The company has a number of other software products that help to manage information easily, including its high-performance zero-administration Pervasive.SQL database and a series of reporting and data transformation tools.

"At Pervasive Software, we are riding the wave of an emerging market with unique technologies—technologies that will reshape the way distributed and Web-based applications are developed and deployed," says Ron Harris, the company's chief executive officer. "Today, thousands of developers around the world depend on our information management solutions for applications in everything from health care to accounting, manufacturing to retail, Web appliances to smart cards, and more."

Reason for Recommendation

Landis says you should simply think of Pervasive as a company that will give you all of the tools you need for Web-based applications. He predicts the demand for these tools will be explosive in the future. Nevertheless, he admits Tango is really the driver of Prevasive's fortunes. "The thing to remember is that if you're going to impart any kind of meaningful information, which is what the Internet is all about, you need a database," he says. "If you're going to personalize those data, you must be able to generate reports on the fly. In most cases, you would be running a program like Tango on top of your database that will allow you to click on some buttons to customize your search."

Like most companies involved in the Internet, Pervasive Software hasn't been around very long. As a result, so far it really doesn't have much competition, according to Landis. "This is an extremely important program and Pervasive has a clear head start," he says. "But you'd be naive to think it has the whole field to itself. Certainly, others are looking at developing these same kinds of technologies."

This may be the biggest risk to the stock—that another up-and-coming company will create a better program. "When you look at a young company like this that doesn't have much competition, it's usually because it's early in the game or it has picked a niche so narrow and limited that it's uninteresting to others," Landis observes. With Pervasive, it's much more likely that the company was fortunate enough to be first in its field.

Landis points out that Pervasive's management is aware of the competitive pressures and is meeting the challenge. "These guys know how to run fast, and they realize they must keep building the next generation of products," he says. "Whether it's future versions of Tango or other complimentary products, they are working on all of these things." CEO Ron Harris has vowed to keep growing Pervasive's international channel, aggressively invest in sales and research and development, and expand into new products and markets.

The company is actually making money, albeit not much. And while it hasn't enjoyed the high-flying stock price growth of some other Internet companies, it's certainly not a cheap stock. "The market is clearly looking ahead and pricing this as a growth stock," Landis says. "But if you look at the company's revenues, which are showing year-over-year growth above 50 percent, I don't think it's unreasonable. Of course, the great thing about software is that the cost of goods is just about nil. Once you've written the software and everybody's using it, you're looking good as long as you can profitably support your existing customers."

Contact Information: Pervasive Software
12365 Riata Trace Parkway, Building II
Austin, TX 78727
512-231-6000
www.pervasive.com

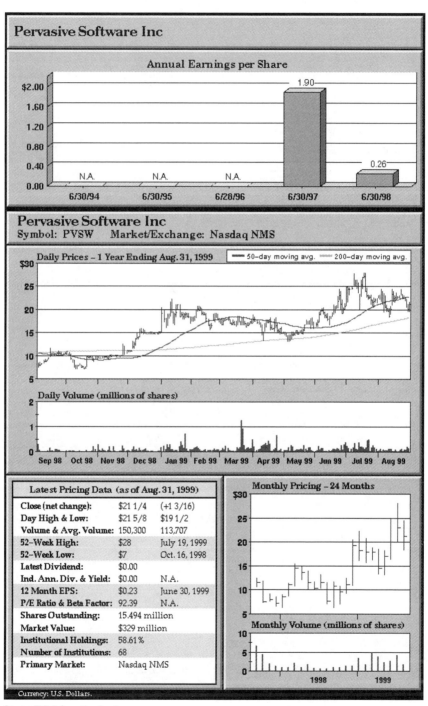

Pervasive Software Inc

Annual Earnings per Share

	6/30/94	6/30/95	6/28/96	6/30/97	6/30/98
	N.A.	N.A.	N.A.	1.90	0.26

Pervasive Software Inc
Symbol: PVSW   Market/Exchange: Nasdaq NMS

Daily Prices – 1 Year Ending Aug. 31, 1999

— 50-day moving avg.   — 200-day moving avg.

Daily Volume (millions of shares)

Sep 98 Oct 98 Nov 98 Dec 98 Jan 99 Feb 99 Mar 99 Apr 99 May 99 Jun 99 Jul 99 Aug 99

Latest Pricing Data (as of Aug. 31, 1999)

Close (net change):	$21 1/4	(+1 3/16)
Day High & Low:	$21 5/8	$19 1/2
Volume & Avg. Volume:	150,300	113,707
52–Week High:	$28	July 19, 1999
52–Week Low:	$7	Oct. 16, 1998
Latest Dividend:	$0.00	
Ind. Ann. Div. & Yield:	$0.00	N.A.
12 Month EPS:	$0.23	June 30, 1999
P/E Ratio & Beta Factor:	92.39	N.A.
Shares Outstanding:	15.494 million	
Market Value:	$329 million	
Institutional Holdings:	58.61%	
Number of Institutions:	68	
Primary Market:	Nasdaq NMS	

Monthly Pricing – 24 Months

Monthly Volume (millions of shares)

1998   1999

Currency: U.S. Dollars.

Source: IDD Information Services

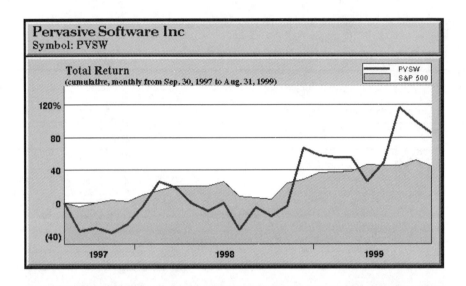

SELECTED INCOME STATEMENT AND BALANCE SHEET ITEMS						
INCOME STATEMENT	**6/30/94**	**6/30/95**	**6/28/96**	**6/30/97**	**6/30/98**	**1 Year**
Sales/Revenues	N.A.	N.A.	N.A.	24.500	36.700	59.400
Cost of Goods Sold	N.A.	N.A.	N.A.	2.600	3.900	N.A.
Pre-tax Margin (%)	N.A.	N.A.	N.A.	9.00	10.40	N.A.
Operating Income	N.A.	N.A.	N.A.	2.300	3.300	N.A.
Net Income before Extras	N.A.	N.A.	N.A.	1.600	2.700	3.600
Reported Net Income	N.A.	N.A.	N.A.	1.600	2.700	3.600
Depreciation & Amortization	N.A.	N.A.	N.A.	0.700	1.400	N.A.
EPS from Net Income (Primary)	N.A.	N.A.	N.A.	1.900	0.260	0.230
EPS from Net Income (Fully Diluted)	N.A.	N.A.	N.A.	0.120	0.180	0.210
Dividend per Common Share	N.A.	N.A.	N.A.	N.A.	N.A.	N.A.
Dividend Yield (%)	N.A.	N.A.	N.A.	N.A.	N.A.	N.A.
Payout Ratio	N.A.	N.A.	N.A.	N.A.	N.A.	N.A.
BALANCE SHEET						
ASSETS						
Cash & Cash Equivalents	N.A.	N.A.	N.A.	4.100	15.600	
Inventories	N.A.	N.A.	N.A.	0.100	0.400	
Total Current Assets	N.A.	N.A.	N.A.	7.700	28.100	
Total Assets	N.A.	N.A.	N.A.	10.400	32.600	
LIABILITIES & EQUITY						
Short Term Debt	N.A.	N.A.	N.A.	0.000	0.000	
Long Term Debt	N.A.	N.A.	N.A.	0.000	0.000	
Total Liabilities	N.A.	N.A.	N.A.	6.800	8.700	
Shares Outstanding	N.A.	N.A.	N.A.	13.105	13.347	
Common Stockholder Equity	N.A.	N.A.	N.A.	(4.300)	24.000	
Total Stockholder Equity	N.A.	N.A.	N.A.	3.600	24.000	

Note: Figures in Millions of $ except: per share items, margins, yields, and ratios.

Source: IDD Information Services

RITE AID

Vita Nelson
The Moneypaper

Company Profile

From its humble beginnings in 1962 in Scranton, Pennsylvania, Rite Aid has become one of the nation's largest drugstore chains, with more than 4,000 stores in 30 states across the country. Rite Aid Chairman and CEO Martin L. Grass called 1998 "the most challenging, exciting, and profitable year in the history of our company." It was a year in which the company's largest acquisition ever, Thrifty Payless, was fully integrated into the Rite Aid system. The company also purchased the two largest privately held drugstore chains in the nation, Harco and K&B, and saw its stock continue to zoom higher as Wall Street expressed its approval of all the company's actions.

Then came the shocker. On March 12, 1999, Rite Aid announced that because of its acquisitions, earnings for the quarter would be around 30¢ to 32¢ per share, well below analysts' estimates of 52¢. That announcement caused the chain's stock to plummet almost 40 percent in a single day. In return, some shareholders filed a class action lawsuit, alleging Rite Aid and Grass "issued a series of materially false and misleading statements concerning Rite Aid's operating results and business prospects."

These clouds of controversy have created an excellent buying opportunity, according to Vita Nelson, publisher of *The Moneypaper*. "This is a decent company that always seems to be looking forward," she says. "It appears to be a great value, especially in relation to all of the other stocks we follow." In fact, the revelation that charges and other expenses would lower short-term earnings pleased Nelson. "Management is planning ahead, buying things, fixing facilities, updating the infrastructure, and getting ready for the next 100 years," she maintains. "This is an aggressive company. I loved it when it's stock price was much higher, so I love it even more now."

Rite Aid's future plans call for opening 200 stores on both coasts, relocating another 250 to 300 locations, and remodeling at least 200 acquired pharmacies each year. It has developed a prototype store that will eventually be phased in systemwide and features easy access, expanded parking, a full-service and drive-up pharmacy, one-hour photo finishing, express mail, convenience foods, and an expanded cosmetics department. In fact, cosmetics has become one of the company's fastest-growing categories, thanks to an innovative marketing campaign that promises to give customers their money back if they don't like any makeup product after trying it. What's more, some 200 Rite Aid stores are now open 24 hours a day.

Vitamins are another area of strong growth for the company. "Rite Aid recently formed a marketing alliance with General Nutrition [Centers (GNC)], which will make GNC's full line of vitamins and dietary supplements available in 1,500 of its stores within three years," Nelson adds. "Rite Aid has also announced plans to acquire Edgehill Drugs, which operates 25 stores in Delaware and Maryland with $75 million in annual sales."

Prescription revenue accounts for around 53 percent of store sales. In most locations the chain has installed voice response units that allow customers to order prescription refills by using a Touch-Tone phone 24 hours a day. Also, in an interesting strategic alliance, the company owns Eagle Managed Care, which markets prescription benefit plans and other managed care services to employers. "In addition, Rite Aid bought pharmacy benefits management company PCH Health Systems from Eli Lilly for $1.5 billion in late 1998, well below the $4.1 billion Lilly paid for the unit five years ago," Nelson adds.

"There are many areas we want to focus on to improve the performance of our company," CEO Grass states. "First, we are mounting a full-scale push to reduce working capital through the reduction of inventory invested in our business. Now that the dust has settled from the integration of [the most recent] acquisitions, we anticipate that more than $150 million of inventory can be eliminated during the current year. The second [area of focus] is the major job of teaching and training . . . the thousands of new associates who joined us in recent acquisitions."

Reason for Recommendation

Grass claims Rite Aid is in the midst of the greatest growth period in the company's history. "We are extremely confident in the direction we are taking the business," Grass says. Nelson is too. She's also fond of Rite Aid's dividend reinvestment program, or DRIP, which allows shareholders to reinvest dividends and buy additional shares of stock directly through the company without paying any brokerage commissions. "I like companies that invite broad participation by the public," she insists. "It means that if you own stock in Rite Aid and there are two pharmacies next to each other, you're going to use Rite Aid because you're an owner of the company." Incidentally, Nelson says she enjoys shopping at Rite Aid herself, which is in the tradition of Peter Lynch who advises that you "buy what you know." Nelson emphasizes that she considers this stock to be a long-term hold that investors can easily continue to invest in through the DRIP program for many years to come.

Contact Information: Rite Aid Corporation
30 Hunter Lane
Camp Hill, PA 17011-2404
717-761-2633
www.RiteAid.com

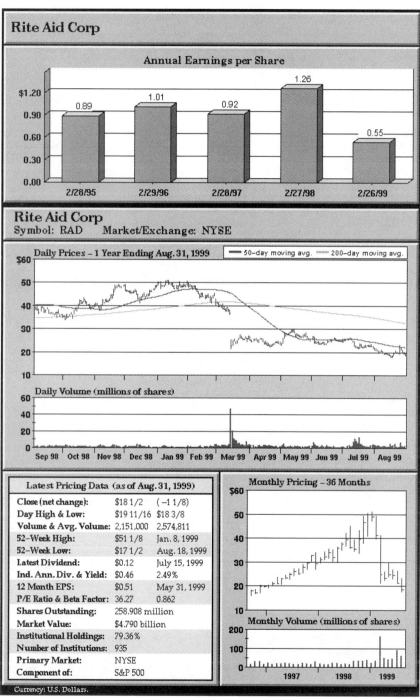

Rite Aid Corp

Annual Earnings per Share

2/28/95	2/29/96	2/28/97	2/27/98	2/26/99
0.89	1.01	0.92	1.26	0.55

Rite Aid Corp

Symbol: RAD   Market/Exchange: NYSE

Daily Prices – 1 Year Ending Aug. 31, 1999   ▬ 50-day moving avg.   ▬ 200-day moving avg.

Daily Volume (millions of shares)

Sep 98 Oct 98 Nov 98 Dec 98 Jan 99 Feb 99 Mar 99 Apr 99 May 99 Jun 99 Jul 99 Aug 99

Latest Pricing Data (as of Aug. 31, 1999)

Close (net change):	$18 1/2	(–1 1/8)
Day High & Low:	$19 11/16	$18 3/8
Volume & Avg. Volume:	2,151,000	2,574,811
52–Week High:	$51 1/8	Jan. 8, 1999
52–Week Low:	$17 1/2	Aug. 18, 1999
Latest Dividend:	$0.12	July 15, 1999
Ind. Ann. Div. & Yield:	$0.46	2.49%
12 Month EPS:	$0.51	May 31, 1999
P/E Ratio & Beta Factor:	36.27	0.862
Shares Outstanding:	258.908 million	
Market Value:	$4.790 billion	
Institutional Holdings:	79.36%	
Number of Institutions:	935	
Primary Market:	NYSE	
Component of:	S&P 500	

Monthly Pricing – 36 Months

Monthly Volume (millions of shares)

1997   1998   1999

Currency: U.S. Dollars.

Source: IDD Information Services

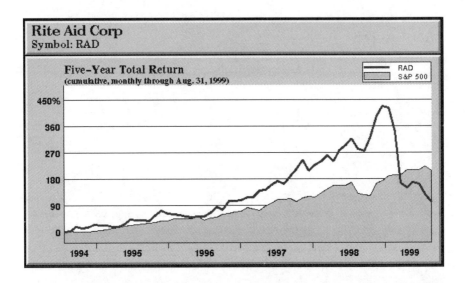

Rite Aid Corp
Symbol: RAD

Five-Year Total Return
(cumulative, monthly through Aug. 31, 1999)

RAD
S&P 500

SELECTED INCOME STATEMENT AND BALANCE SHEET ITEMS

INCOME STATEMENT	2/28/95	2/29/96	2/28/97	2/27/98	2/26/99	1 Year
Sales/Revenues	4,533.9	5,446.0	6,970.2	11,375	12,732	13,324
Cost of Goods Sold	3,229.3	3,898.7	4,944.9	8,016.7	9,137.9	9,602.2
Pre-tax Margin (%)	5.10	4.70	3.70	4.70	1.60	1.25
Operating Income	273.80	324.50	423.50	689.80	651.70	673.80
Net Income before Extras	141.30	158.90	160.50	316.40	143.70	133.90
Reported Net Income	141.30	158.90	160.50	316.40	143.70	133.90
Depreciation & Amortization	98.600	118.70	168.10	274.20	302.60	319.80
EPS from Net Income (Primary)	0.890	1.010	0.920	1.260	0.550	0.510
EPS from Net Income (Fully Diluted)	0.860	0.980	0.900	1.220	0.540	0.500
Dividend per Common Share	0.310	0.348	0.383	0.407	0.438	0.445
Dividend Yield (%)	2.51	2.21	1.82	1.26	1.06	1.78
Payout Ratio	0.35	0.34	0.42	0.32	0.80	0.87
BALANCE SHEET						
ASSETS						
Cash & Cash Equivalents	7.100	3.100	7.000	91.000	82.900	
Inventories	1,070.3	1,170.7	2,336.7	3,061.2	2,893.1	
Total Current Assets	1,373.2	1,465.0	2,771.5	3,378.3	3,802.4	
Total Assets	2,472.6	2,842.0	6,417.0	7,655.3	10,422	
LIABILITIES & EQUITY						
Short Term Debt	137.60	232.80	44.300	47.500	1,550.2	
Long Term Debt	806.00	994.30	2,415.7	2,551.4	3,304.2	
Total Liabilities	1,460.8	1,738.5	3,928.5	4,738.8	7,444.4	
Shares Outstanding	168.330	167.696	245.620	258.215	258.862	
Common Stockholder Equity	1,011.8	1,103.6	2,488.7	2,916.5	2,953.7	
Total Stockholder Equity	1,011.8	1,103.6	2,488.7	2,916.5	2,977.3	

Note: Figures in Millions of $ except: per share items, margins, yields, and ratios.

Source: IDD Information Services

ROUGE INDUSTRIES

Al Frank
The Prudent Speculator

Company Profile

In an age when investors seem enamored of sexy Internet start-ups and fast-growing technology firms, why would anyone be interested in a seemingly boring company like Rouge Industries? "Because it's undervalued and no one wants to own it," insists Al Frank, publisher of *The Prudent Speculator*. "Investors have been selling shares of this company even though it's not going bankrupt, has a lot of assets, and shows good potential for future growth."

Rouge is the eighth largest integrated steel manufacturer in the United States. It has two wholly owned subsidiaries, QS Steel and Eveleth Taconite Company. Eveleth also has a 45 percent interest in Eveleth Mines. The company and its subsidiaries produce a variety of rolled steel products, including hot rolled (which accounts for about 45 percent of total business); cold rolled (hot rolled steel that is cooled and reduced in thickness to enhance ductility and surface characteristics); electrogalvanized (cold rolled steel that is coated on one or both sides with either pure zinc or a zinc/iron combination to make it more resistant); and hot dip galvanized (cold rolled steel coated on both sides with zinc or a zinc/iron combination to make it more corrosion resistant.) Most of Rouge's products are sold to the automotive market, although other end users buy steel to manufacture such items as roof decking, grating, guard rails, pipes, lighting fixtures, and doors. Ford Motor and DaimlerChrysler are the company's two biggest customers, accounting for approximately 37 percent and 10 percent of total 1998 sales, respectively.

Frank points out a few reasons people don't like Rouge right now. "To begin with, steel prices have been under pressure due to dumping from Japan, Germany, Brazil, Russia and other countries," he says. These countries were dumping steel into the U.S. market at prices far below Rouge's cost of production. "The company also hasn't been growing very much and its profits have been under pressure." Granted, Rouge was profitable in 1998, but total sales were down $178 million from the previous year. Slowing demand from the automotive industry was another factor along with the company's significant capital outlays for various expansion projects.

Rouge's Chairman and CEO Carl Valdiserri expands on what has caused the company's recent woes. "Over 16 million tons of imported steel—more than five times the annual production of Rouge Steel Company and 34 percent of the steel consumed during the period—found its way to the United States in a four-month period in mid-1998," he says. "In addition, a 54-day strike at General Motors and increasing domestic production from minimills caused spot market steel prices to plummet and order placements to drop precipitously in the second half of the year. In all my years in the steel industry, I have never seen a strong market turn soft so fast." In return, Rouge lowered production levels, curtailed discretionary spending, and reduced operating schedules.

A final setback came in February 1999, when the company's original Rouge Complex powerhouse, which is jointly owned by Rouge and Ford Motor Company, exploded. Several people lost their life, and many more were seriously injured. The accident caused significant disruption to the company.

Reason for Recommendation

It sounds like a pretty bleak story, but Frank insists the situation is starting to turn around. "Even with the accident, management has still been able to earn a profit," he maintains. "And I think current earnings are set to double soon."

Why? Steel demand is on the increase and prices are firming. In addition, Rouge is continually working to expand its product mix. One recent example is the expansion of Spartan Steel Coating, a $110 million joint venture. Spartan is a dipped galvanizing and galvannealing company in Monroe, Michigan. The Spartan facility has a projected annual capacity of more than 450,000 tons and is capable of coating a variety of steel products. This is one of the company's five Michigan-based joint ventures. The company has also formed an agreement with CMS Energy to build and operate a 710 megawatt cogeneration power plant to provide electricity and steam at more competitive prices. The company expects operation costs to be reduced by up to $30 million per year once this facility is fully operational.

Frank sees little risk to the stock at its current price level, which he feels is artificially low. "Steel demand is expected to remain strong with the automakers recently announcing product increases," he says. "Rouge's balance sheet is in relatively good shape and the stock is trading at near multiyear low levels." Frank expects earnings per share to hit $2 in 2000, driven by good sales and production. If that happens, he predicts the stock will double during the year. "This stock has been as high as $34 in the past," he adds. "In the next three to five years, I think it should trade in the area of $27."

Contact Information: Rouge Industries, Inc.
3001 Miller Road
Dearborn, MI 48121-1699
313-317-8900

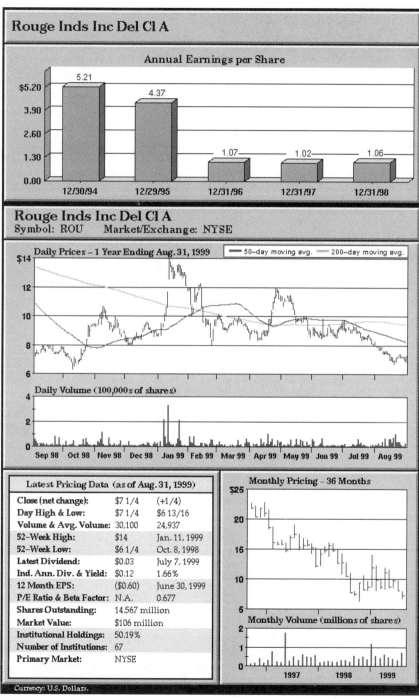

Rouge Inds Inc Del Cl A

Annual Earnings per Share

	5.21	4.37	1.07	1.02	1.06
	12/30/94	12/29/95	12/31/96	12/31/97	12/31/98

Rouge Inds Inc Del Cl A
Symbol: ROU   Market/Exchange: NYSE

Daily Prices – 1 Year Ending Aug. 31, 1999   — 50-day moving avg.   — 200-day moving avg.

Daily Volume (100,000s of shares)

Sep 98   Oct 98   Nov 98   Dec 98   Jan 99   Feb 99   Mar 99   Apr 99   May 99   Jun 99   Jul 99   Aug 99

Latest Pricing Data (as of Aug. 31, 1999)

Close (net change):	$7 1/4	(+1/4)
Day High & Low:	$7 1/4	$6 13/16
Volume & Avg. Volume:	30,100	24,937
52–Week High:	$14	Jan. 11, 1999
52–Week Low:	$6 1/4	Oct. 8, 1998
Latest Dividend:	$0.03	July 7, 1999
Ind. Ann. Div. & Yield:	$0.12	1.66%
12 Month EPS:	($0.60)	June 30, 1999
P/E Ratio & Beta Factor:	N.A.	0.677
Shares Outstanding:	14.567 million	
Market Value:	$106 million	
Institutional Holdings:	50.19%	
Number of Institutions:	67	
Primary Market:	NYSE	

Monthly Pricing – 36 Months

Monthly Volume (millions of shares)

1997   1998   1999

Currency: U.S. Dollars.

Source: IDD Information Services

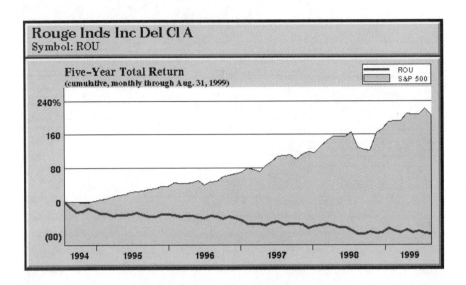

Rouge Inds Inc Del Cl A
Symbol: ROU

Five-Year Total Return
(cumulative, monthly through Aug. 31, 1999)

Legend: ROU, S&P 500

Y-axis: 240%, 160, 80, 0, (80)

X-axis: 1994, 1995, 1996, 1997, 1998, 1999

SELECTED INCOME STATEMENT AND BALANCE SHEET ITEMS

INCOME STATEMENT	12/30/94	12/29/95	12/31/96	12/31/97	12/31/98	1 Year
Sales/Revenues	1,236.1	1,206.6	1,307.4	1,341.6	1,163.2	945.40
Cost of Goods Sold	1,101.3	1,082.1	1,251.1	1,278.4	1,090.0	1,038.6
Pre-tax Margin (%)	7.90	10.60	2.30	2.30	2.80	(4.03)
Operating Income	103.00	91.600	18.900	25.800	35.100	(145.10)
Net Income before Extras	105.60	94.700	23.400	22.400	23.400	(13.300)
Reported Net Income	105.60	94.700	23.400	22.400	23.400	(13.300)
Depreciation & Amortization	5.700	5.300	13.100	15.600	14.200	25.800
EPS from Net Income (Primary)	5.210	4.370	1.070	1.020	1.060	(0.600)
EPS from Net Income (Fully Diluted)	5.210	4.370	1.070	1.020	1.060	(0.600)
Dividend per Common Share	0.040	0.090	0.120	0.120	0.120	0.120
Dividend Yield (%)	0.14	0.38	0.57	0.99	1.37	1.23
Payout Ratio	0.01	0.02	0.11	0.12	0.11	N.A.
BALANCE SHEET						
ASSETS						
Cash & Cash Equivalents	60.600	57.000	24.900	12.600	2.400	
Inventories	248.10	237.10	267.90	248.30	275.80	
Total Current Assets	486.70	483.60	414.90	380.90	421.60	
Total Assets	616.80	672.50	682.00	728.50	768.90	
LIABILITIES & EQUITY						
Short Term Debt	0.000	0.000	0.000	0.000	0.000	
Long Term Debt	0.000	0.000	0.000	17.900	29.000	
Total Liabilities	321.10	278.60	264.60	289.80	309.30	
Shares Outstanding	24.690	21.715	21.903	23.118	23.212	
Common Stockholder Equity	295.70	393.90	417.30	438.60	459.60	
Total Stockholder Equity	295.70	393.90	417.30	438.60	459.60	

Note: Figures in Millions of $ except: per share items, margins, yields, and ratios.

Source: IDD Information Services

SIMULA

Marcus Robins
The Red Chip Review

Company Profile

Whether by air, sea, or land, Simula is in the business of keeping people safe while they travel. "It really has two main businesses," says Marcus Robins, publisher and editor of *The Red Chip Review*. "First, it creates safety technology for the military. Specifically, Simula makes helicopter seats that can withstand traumatic collisions. These seats absorb the energy of a crash and therefore save the pilot's life. Second, it has come up with an airbag system that doesn't require you to press up against a steering wheel or dashboard for it to deploy."

Simula is the world's largest supplier of helicopter seating. It also makes opaque and transparent ballistic armor for the military's land vehicles, aircraft, and ships. Despite government cutbacks, Simula has been able to grow its government and defense business. It also benefits from government-funded research money, which seeds product development for the company's other business units.

Simula's automobile airbag system traces its roots back to this research. "Simula has created nonaggressive airbags for the BMW 3, 5, and 7 series models," Robins notes. These innovative head-protection systems deploy during side impacts. "The airbag lies flat when it's not inflated but turns into a huge, long tubular pillow on impact that restrains the body. It keeps your head from whipping and breaking. In addition, it keeps your body inside the car, whether the door is still intact or not." This is unlike some of the more controversial side airbags that pop out of chairs or side doors and have been blamed for killing small children by being too aggressive. "These other devices push against the person, exacerbating the pressure on the neck," Robins explains. "Simula's pillow airbag is tucked up flat above the headliner. When there's an impact, it snaps down diagonally across the opening, poufs up into a huge pillow, and keeps the driver and passengers inside."

Robins views this airbag technology as Simula's biggest future growth driver. That's because front impact airbags do a good job of keeping you from going through the front window or shoving your chest into the steering column, but they won't keep you from knocking back in your seat, which can cause a lot of harm. "Simula's airbag technology came from the idea of nestling inflatable strapping around the helicopter pilot so it would nestle him into his chair rather than allowing him to flail around," Robins adds. "This same technology could be used in automobiles, especially since around 80 percent of Americans wear seat belts anyway."

In terms of the aircraft business, there isn't much growth expected to come from supplying seats for military helicopters. What is exciting to Robins is the company's commercial possibilities. "There has not been a new manufacturer of aircraft seats in 25 years," he says. "The problem now is that commercial airlines employ seats that can withstand the stresses of a 16-G collision. Most collisions happen on landing or takeoff and fall below that level. The problem is that all of the aircraft out there have 9-G floors. So you have seats that get ripped off from the floor on impact, sandwiching people together like an accordion box." Simula has developed a technology to withstand these accidents. The company's seats stay attached to the floor, are lighter, and don't cost much more than models currently being used. Robins admits Simula still has to get FAA certification for its seats. "One reason the stock has been beaten up is because it costs at least $250,000 to make every seat alteration required to get it through the FAA process," he says. "There have also been a lot of delays in manufacturing new planes, which has caused huge losses." Nevertheless, Robins expects Simula to make money in this business beginning in 2000.

In addition, Simula is the leading provider of rail and mass transit seating systems in North America and is about to make the first reconfigured parachute for the U.S. Army in some 30 years—unique in that it doesn't have to be repacked often and can be used by both men and women.

Reason for Recommendation

Simula is a little company with big potential in Robins's eyes. He expects more automakers to get interested in the company's airbags and thinks the innovative airline seats will soon start to really take off. "I'm excited about several things," he maintains. "The military business continues to do relatively well and has immense profit margins. The airbag system is growing and will provide nice top-line growth and profits. And the aircraft seat business should go from substantial losses in 1998 to earnings of between 5¢ and 15¢ a share or more in 2000. So we're talking about a company that should go from roughly $45 million in sales in 1999 to almost $100 million in 2000."

There are, of course, no assurances that implementation of the airbag technology will go as expected nor that the demand for airbag seats will be as great as Robins thinks. But he insists the stock is priced so low, that he sees very little downside from current levels. "Even if it doesn't get earnings going soon, I think one of the big guys will come in and buy the company out," he predicts. Robins forecasts earnings of $1 per share in 2000 and has a current target price of $15 for Simula's stock.

Contact Information: Simula, Inc.
2700 North Central Avenue, Suite 1000
Phoenix, AZ 85004
602-631-4005
www.simula.com

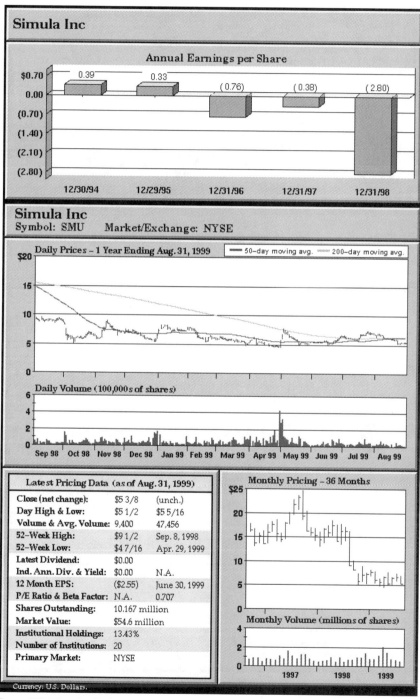

Simula Inc

Annual Earnings per Share

0.39	0.33	(0.76)	(0.38)	(2.80)
12/30/94	12/29/95	12/31/96	12/31/97	12/31/98

$0.70
0.00
(0.70)
(1.40)
(2.10)
(2.80)

Simula Inc
Symbol: SMU   Market/Exchange: NYSE

Daily Prices – 1 Year Ending Aug. 31, 1999   ▬ 50–day moving avg.   ▬ 200–day moving avg.

$20
15
10
5
0

Daily Volume (100,000s of shares)
6
4
2
0

Sep 98 Oct 98 Nov 98 Dec 98 Jan 99 Feb 99 Mar 99 Apr 99 May 99 Jun 99 Jul 99 Aug 99

Latest Pricing Data (as of Aug. 31, 1999)

Close (net change):	$5 3/8	(unch.)
Day High & Low:	$5 1/2	$5 5/16
Volume & Avg. Volume:	9,400	47,456
52–Week High:	$9 1/2	Sep. 8, 1998
52–Week Low:	$4 7/16	Apr. 29, 1999
Latest Dividend:	$0.00	
Ind. Ann. Div. & Yield:	$0.00	N.A.
12 Month EPS:	($2.55)	June 30, 1999
P/E Ratio & Beta Factor:	N.A.	0.707
Shares Outstanding:	10.167 million	
Market Value:	$54.6 million	
Institutional Holdings:	13.43%	
Number of Institutions:	20	
Primary Market:	NYSE	

Monthly Pricing – 36 Months
$25
20
15
10
5
0

Monthly Volume (millions of shares)
4
2
0
1997   1998   1999

Currency: U.S. Dollars.

Source: IDD Information Services

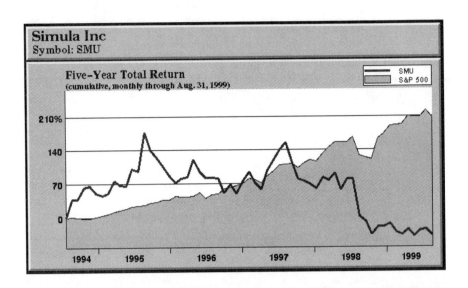

Simula Inc
Symbol: SMU

Five-Year Total Return
(cumulative, monthly through Aug. 31, 1999)

SMU
S&P 500

210%						
140						
70						
0						
1994	1995	1996	1997	1998	1999	

SELECTED INCOME STATEMENT AND BALANCE SHEET ITEMS

INCOME STATEMENT	12/30/94	12/29/95	12/31/96	12/31/97	12/31/98	1 Year
Sales/Revenues	41.200	59.100	65.800	90.400	100.60	118.20
Cost of Goods Sold	26.000	33.600	51.900	65.000	81.100	N.A.
Pre-tax Margin (%)	8.30	9.00	(17.50)	(6.40)	(10.50)	N.A.
Operating Income	5.100	6.900	(9.100)	(2.100)	(5.500)	N.A.
Net Income before Extras	2.100	4.100	(6.800)	(3.500)	(6.800)	(6.400)
Reported Net Income	2.100	4.100	(6.800)	(3.500)	(27.700)	(25.100)
Depreciation & Amortization	1.700	3.000	3.300	4.900	4.600	N.A.
EPS from Net Income (Primary)	0.390	0.330	(0.760)	(0.380)	(2.800)	(2.550)
EPS from Net Income (Fully Diluted)	0.370	0.310	(0.760)	(0.380)	(2.800)	(2.570)
Dividend per Common Share	0.000	0.000	0.000	0.000	0.000	0.000
Dividend Yield (%)	N.A.	N.A.	N.A.	N.A.	N.A.	N.A.
Payout Ratio	N.A.	N.A.	N.A.	N.A.	N.A.	N.A.

BALANCE SHEET						
ASSETS						
Cash & Cash Equivalents	1.100	3.200	1.300	9.400	0.900	
Inventories	6.700	8.100	15.600	27.500	26.000	
Total Current Assets	20.600	37.300	48.000	76.300	62.400	
Total Assets	47.700	74.700	86.700	120.30	111.00	
LIABILITIES & EQUITY						
Short Term Debt	3.100	1.400	11.400	20.100	24.400	
Long Term Debt	15.300	11.300	24.700	47.000	47.200	
Total Liabilities	31.000	27.300	49.400	74.700	92.300	
Shares Outstanding	6.385	8.971	8.910	9.851	9.915	
Common Stockholder Equity	16.600	47.500	37.200	45.600	18.600	
Total Stockholder Equity	16.600	47.500	37.200	45.600	18.600	

Note: Figures in Millions of $ except: per share items, margins, yields, and ratios.

Source: IDD Information Services

STATE STREET

L. Roy Papp
L. Roy Papp & Associates

Company Profile

When I asked money manager Roy Papp for his favorite stock going into the new millennium, he quickly replied, "State Street, no question about it." When I reminded him this was the same company he picked in 1999, he was unmoved. "It's still my favorite. There isn't any stock I like better."

Although State Street was originally founded as a traditional bank in Boston back in 1792, it has grown into a much different company. Instead of making money from loans or other traditional banking activities, State Street provides a wide range of products and services for big institutional investors. "It offers safe-keeping and custodial services for a lot of mutual fund companies, corporations, pension funds, nonprofit organizations, and individuals with a high net worth," Papp observes. "State Street has more than $5 trillion in assets under its care."

The company began providing mutual fund services in 1924, shortly after these investments were created. State Street is the custodian for some 40 percent of all assets held by the nation's mutual fund portfolios. Unlike many of its competitors, State Street also offers accounting, daily pricing, and other administrative services to its various fund clients.

Although State Street already has a huge chunk of the available fund business in the United States, Papp believes the potential to capture more market share overseas is tremendous. "This is truly a global company," he says. "The growth rate of its non-U.S. custodianship business for the past five years has been about 35 percent annually, which means it doubles every two years." The current asset breakdown is 70 percent domestic and 30 percent overseas. State Street has offices in Austria, Australia, Canada, France, Germany, Japan, the People's Republic of China, and the United Kingdom. It also operates its own investment management division, with $525 billion in assets, including the SSgA family of mutual funds.

With more than 14,000 employees, the company prides itself on having the latest technology. "State Street spends tons of money updating its computer systems," Papp notes. He's also impressed with State Street's progressive management team. Papp says they are aggressive about stealing business away from competitors, even if that means underpricing them and settling for lower short-term profits.

State Street Chairman and CEO Marshall Carter is a former Marine Corps officer who was awarded the Navy Cross and Purple Heart during his two years of service in Vietnam. "Our commitment is clear," Carter says. "We continue to build our business for future growth by developing a broader product array for our customers." Among these products is Global Link, an integrated electronic market information, trade execution, and reporting platform, which includes unique currency markets research and other foreign exchange management tools. "In investment management, we are focused on continuing the expansion of both our global reach and diversified product lines," Carter adds. "Anticipating industry changes and investing to develop the resources to handle them before they occur is an important element of State Street's industry leadership. The market for services to institutional investors is large and growing. Analysts estimate the $6 trillion global mutual fund industry will grow 15 percent annually over the next five years, the $8 trillion pension fund industry 10 percent, the $9 trillion insurance industry 9 percent, and the $15 trillion asset management industry 10 percent."

Reason for Recommendation

In addition to those impressive numbers and that great potential, Papp says demographics are in State Street's favor. "You have a large increase in the baby boomers who are all saving a lot of money," he maintains. "They'll be putting their money into products that State Street is involved with. This is also a very well managed company. It has spent fortunes on computer software and is far ahead of the competition."

While the price of the stock has gone up since Papp originally recommended it in 1999, he points out that earnings are higher too. "Wall Street is finally pricing this company like a growth stock instead of like a bank," he rationalizes. "You're now looking at a stock that trades at roughly a market multiple."

There are two things that could derail State Street's impressive growth streak. One is the incredible amount of competition in the financial services industry. The second is that State Street will suffer if the red-hot mutual fund industry cools down, which some fear it could. "However, I'm betting that the international mutual fund market will grow, not slow down," Papp predicts. "This is clearly the best play on the global mutual fund industry and financial globalization that I know of."

Contact Information: State Street Corporation
225 Franklin Street
Boston, MA 02171
617-786-3000
www.statestreet.com

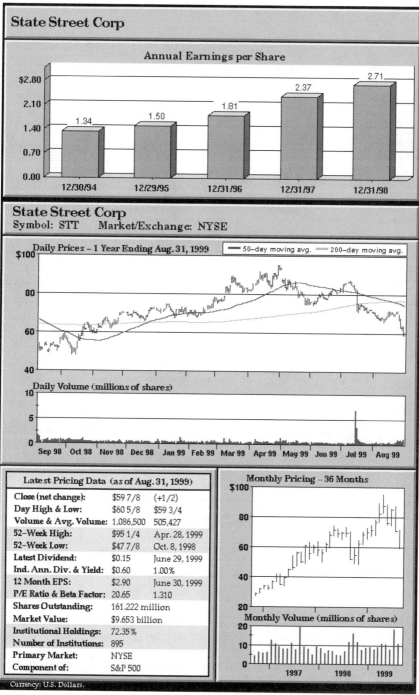

State Street Corp

Annual Earnings per Share

1.34	1.50	1.81	2.37	2.71
12/30/94	12/29/95	12/31/96	12/31/97	12/31/98

State Street Corp
Symbol: STT   Market/Exchange: NYSE

Daily Prices – 1 Year Ending Aug. 31, 1999   — 50-day moving avg.   — 200-day moving avg.

Daily Volume (millions of shares)

Sep 98   Oct 98   Nov 98   Dec 98   Jan 99   Feb 99   Mar 99   Apr 99   May 99   Jun 99   Jul 99   Aug 99

Latest Pricing Data (as of Aug. 31, 1999)		
Close (net change):	$59 7/8	(+1/2)
Day High & Low:	$60 5/8	$59 3/4
Volume & Avg. Volume:	1,086,500	505,427
52–Week High:	$95 1/4	Apr. 28, 1999
52–Week Low:	$47 7/8	Oct. 8, 1998
Latest Dividend:	$0.15	June 29, 1999
Ind. Ann. Div. & Yield:	$0.60	1.00%
12 Month EPS:	$2.90	June 30, 1999
P/E Ratio & Beta Factor:	20.65	1.310
Shares Outstanding:	161.222 million	
Market Value:	$9.653 billion	
Institutional Holdings:	72.35%	
Number of Institutions:	895	
Primary Market:	NYSE	
Component of:	S&P 500	

Monthly Pricing – 36 Months

Monthly Volume (millions of shares)

1997   1998   1999

Currency: U.S. Dollars.

Source: IDD Information Services

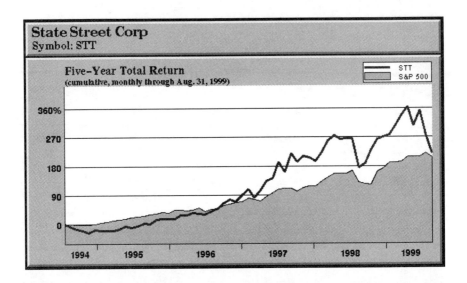

State Street Corp
Symbol: STT

Five-Year Total Return
(cumulative, monthly through Aug. 31, 1999)

STT
S&P 500

360%
270
180
90
0

1994 1995 1996 1997 1998 1999

SELECTED INCOME STATEMENT AND BALANCE SHEET ITEMS

INCOME STATEMENT	12/30/94	12/29/95	12/31/96	12/31/97	12/31/98	1 Year
Sales/Revenues	1,885.7	2,455.7	2,745.0	3,428.0	4,234.0	4,532.0
Cost of Goods Sold	N.A.	N.A.	N.A.	N.A.	N.A.	N.A.
Pre-tax Margin (%)	17.00	14.90	16.30	16.50	15.50	15.58
Operating Income	857.70	1,273.7	1,339.0	1,678.0	2,149.0	2,295.0
Net Income before Extras	207.40	247.10	293.00	380.00	436.00	466.00
Reported Net Income	207.40	247.10	293.00	380.00	436.00	466.00
Depreciation & Amortization	N.A.	N.A.	N.A.	N.A.	N.A.	N.A.
EPS from Net Income (Primary)	1.340	1.500	1.810	2.370	2.710	2.900
EPS from Net Income (Fully Diluted)	1.320	1.470	1.780	2.320	2.660	2.850
Dividend per Common Share	0.300	0.340	0.380	0.440	0.520	0.560
Dividend Yield (%)	2.10	1.51	1.18	0.76	0.74	0.66
Payout Ratio	0.22	0.23	0.21	0.19	0.19	0.19

BALANCE SHEET						
ASSETS						
Cash & Cash Equivalents	N.A.	N.A.	N.A.	N.A.	N.A.	
Inventories	N.A.	N.A.	N.A.	N.A.	N.A.	
Total Current Assets	N.A.	N.A.	N.A.	N.A.	N.A.	
Total Assets	21,730	25,785	31,524	37,975	47,082	
LIABILITIES & EQUITY						
Short Term Debt	649.10	5,564.2	649.00	609.00	431.00	
Long Term Debt	127.50	301.80	562.00	818.00	922.00	
Total Liabilities	20,498	24,198	29,749	35,980	44,771	
Shares Outstanding	153.758	164.776	162.308	160.836	160.665	
Common Stockholder Equity	1,231.3	1,587.5	1,775.0	1,995.0	2,311.0	
Total Stockholder Equity	1,231.3	1,587.5	1,775.0	1,995.0	2,311.0	

Note: Figures in Millions of $ except: per share items, margins, yields, and ratios.

Source: IDD Information Services

TELLABS

Alan Bond
Albriond Capital Management

Company Profile

As people communicate more both electronically and by phone, the need for systems to carry these data and voice signals is ever increasing. Tellabs is at the forefront of providing the equipment for getting these signals from one location to another. "The company designs, manufactures, and sells network access systems for voice, data, and video transportation," says Alan Bond of Albriond Capital Management. "These systems include fiber-optic equipment, or digital cross-connect systems." Tellab's products are used by telephone companies, long-distance carriers, cellular providers, cable operators, utilities, government agencies, and other business end users.

Over the years, Tellabs has gone from manufacturing analog-based products for the telecommunications industry to becoming a worldwide supplier of high-end digital systems. "Tellabs helps to manage and organize digital networks and network systems," Bond observes. "The company's biggest product is called Titan, which is a series of digital cross-connect systems that help to route telephone calls. Tellabs also manufactures multiplexers, which act as an interface between voice, data, and video devices."

The company's product breakdown is as follows. Digital cross-connect systems account for 57 percent of sales. This area includes the company's Titan 5500 series of software-intensive digital cross-connect systems and network management platforms. These systems, the company's flagship products, are used by telecommunication service providers in North America to build an infrastructure for wideband and broadband transmission. Network access products make up 11 percent of sales. Under this banner are digital signal processing (DSP) and local access products, including echo cancellers and T-coders; special service products (SSP) such as voice frequency devices; local access products; and the CABLE-SPAN system. Finally, managed digital networks account for 25 percent of sales and include the Martis DXX multiplexer, T1 multiplexers, and network management systems, which allow for fast speed transmission.

Reason for Recommendation

As the Internet continues to grow and users demand faster speeds, the race by service providers to build infrastructures that allow more bandwidth is intensifying. Bond predicts Tellabs will be a major beneficiary of this. "The way to think about the bandwidth concept is to picture a pipe that is being stuffed with a lot of information," he says. "You need equipment to quickly route all this information or the pipe will get plugged. That's what happened to America Online a few years ago. So many people signed on at once that the company didn't have enough bandwidth to handle it all. As a result, a lot of users got knocked off. The growth of the Internet has been a boom for Tellabs outside of the growth it would have experienced from just providing systems for normal voice transmission."

President and CEO Michael J. Birck is frank about the challenges faced by his company. He admits that times are changing and Tellabs will have to adapt to stay ahead of the competition. "Networks of the future will surely look and behave differently than those that populate all but the most recently constructed networks today," Birck predicts. That's why the company is aggressively working to develop products that account for this transition from voice to data transmission. Among other things, the company is developing ATM (cell-based) switching and transport systems and optical networking equipment. It is also expanding through acquisitions. Despite a failed attempt in 1998 to acquire CIENA Corporation and its portfolio of dense wavelength-division-multiplexer products, Tellabs did manage to buy out Coherent Communications Systems Corporation in 1998 for approximately $670 million in stock. Coherent is a major player in the global echo cancellation market.

Although Tellabs does have several competitors, including Lucent Technologies, it is Bond's stock of choice in this sector of the market. "This company has a history and a lot of knowledge," he says. "Tellabs builds the equipment that routes information once it leaves your office. This company has managed to grow at about 45 percent annually over the past five years, and that's without all of the Internet contracts I expect it to get in the future." The major risk, according to Bond, is that the big telephone companies could scale back their system build-outs and upgrades. The company would also be hurt if the cable companies made major inroads into providing local telephone access via cable.

Still, Tellabs has set an ambitious goal for itself—to triple revenues to $6 billion by 2003. Bond feels that's an attainable goal and says the stock deserves to sell at a slight premium to its growth rate. "I expect it to get up to at least $85 a share by the end of 2000," he says.

Contact Information: Tellabs, Inc.
4951 Indiana Avenue
Lisle, IL 60532
630-378-8800
www.tellabs.com

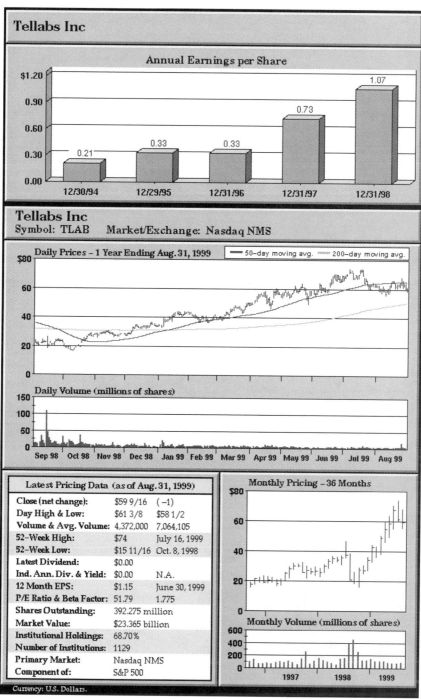

Source: IDD Information Services

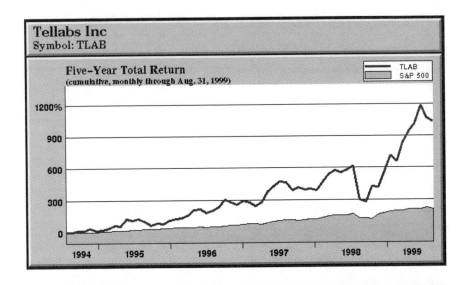

Tellabs Inc
Symbol: TLAB

Five-Year Total Return
(cumulative, monthly through Aug. 31, 1999)

TLAB
S&P 500

1200%
900
600
300
0

1994   1995   1996   1997   1998   1999

SELECTED INCOME STATEMENT AND BALANCE SHEET ITEMS

INCOME STATEMENT	12/30/94	12/29/95	12/31/96	12/31/97	12/31/98	1 Year
Sales/Revenues	494.20	635.20	869.00	1,203.5	1,660.1	1,954.9
Cost of Goods Sold	204.60	247.70	320.80	404.60	528.50	649.90
Pre-tax Margin (%)	19.80	25.60	20.20	33.20	35.50	33.25
Operating Income	102.10	159.20	243.60	363.50	536.90	641.70
Net Income before Extras	72.400	115.60	118.00	263.70	398.30	442.60
Reported Net Income	72.400	115.60	118.00	263.70	398.30	442.60
Depreciation & Amortization	19.500	23.700	32.600	46.900	56.100	79.100
EPS from Net Income (Primary)	0.210	0.330	0.330	0.730	1.070	1.150
EPS from Net Income (Fully Diluted)	0.200	0.320	0.320	0.710	1.040	1.120
Dividend per Common Share	0.000	0.000	0.000	0.000	0.000	0.000
Dividend Yield (%)	N.A.	N.A.	N.A.	N.A.	N.A.	N.A.
Payout Ratio	N.A.	N.A.	N.A.	N.A.	N.A.	N.A.
BALANCE SHEET						
ASSETS						
Cash & Cash Equivalents	51.500	92.500	90.400	109.00	234.70	
Inventories	51.900	67.700	78.500	89.600	122.40	
Total Current Assets	220.60	366.40	475.50	862.90	1,252.7	
Total Assets	390.10	552.10	743.80	1,183.4	1,627.6	
LIABILITIES & EQUITY						
Short Term Debt	0.000	0.000	0.000	0.000	0.000	
Long Term Debt	9.400	2.900	2.900	2.900	2.900	
Total Liabilities	97.200	119.00	152.60	250.30	251.10	
Shares Outstanding	349.152	355.192	359.306	363.254	388.902	
Common Stockholder Equity	292.80	433.20	591.30	933.10	1,376.6	
Total Stockholder Equity	292.80	433.20	591.30	933.10	1,376.6	

Note: Figures in Millions of $ except: per share items, margins, yields, and ratios.

Source: IDD Information Services

UNIPHASE

Joseph Battipaglia
Gruntal & Co.

Company Profile

"I think one of the big trends investors should be participating in is the convergence of telephony, data transmission, and computing," says Joseph Battipaglia, chairman of investment policy for Gruntal & Co. "Not only is it a high-growth area for the United States, as the confluence of these areas progresses, but it's also a huge opportunity overseas. As this infrastructure is built, it will require a huge capital investment, and those who can see this coming and participate will enjoy great investment returns."

Without question, Battipaglia believes the Internet is going to have a dramatic impact on everyone's life for years to come. But he isn't interested in e-commerce businesses or "pure" Internet plays. "You want to look at companies that are going to serve the direction of technology by way of database management, backboning technologies, switching, and so on," he insists. "The volume of consumption and traffic is going to rise dramatically. So you should stick with what I call the 'nuts and bolts' of the Internet, like Uniphase."

Uniphase is a leading supplier of active fiber-optic components. The company designs, develops, manufactures, and markets a wide array of telecommunications products, including semiconductor lasers, high-speed external modulators, transmitters, and optical modules used for fiber-optic networks in the telecommunications and cable television industries.

Without question, the communications industry is in a period of rapid change. Where you once had separate companies providing local and long-distance phone, cable TV, and Internet access, increasingly, these areas are converging and being serviced by the same providers. The one challenge faced by all companies in this area is the need to increase bandwidth, which is the speed by which data flow through one communication system to another. The more bandwidth, the faster and more information you can send through at one time. Estimates are that by the end of the year 2000, data traffic will be five times larger than voice traffic. Data traffic, of course, requires significantly faster speeds of transmission for optimum use.

In order to increase bandwidth, you must have a solid fiber-optic and wavelength division multiplexing (WDM) system in place. Fiber-optic systems use light to transmit a lot of information through tiny glass fibers that are smaller than a strand of human hair. WDM enables multiple wavelengths, or colors of light, to be transmitted through a single fiber. This lets communications firms significantly expand capacity without installing additional costly fibers.

Uniphase is involved in both of these technologies and strives to offer a "one-stop shopping" solution to its customers. "Uniphase should be a clear beneficiary

99

of the broader acceptance of WDM, increased submarine fiber-optic activity, higher WDM channel counts, the move of WDM into metropolitan markets, and cable television system upgrades," Battipaglia predicts. "New product introductions and capacity additions further enhance its outlook."

The company has evolved into a global operation with manufacturing facilities on three continents. Sales grew 64 percent in fiscal 1998, and Battipaglia expects it to keep up with that pace going forward. Uniphase is growing rapidly, in large part through key strategic acquisitions. "The company has a history of making complementary technology acquisitions at attractive prices," Battipaglia notes. In 1998 the company bought Philips Optoelectronics, a leading supplier of semiconductor lasers for the telecommunications and cable television (CATV) industries. "This addition was a major step towards achieving our goal of providing a complete high-performance optical component solution to our telecommunications and CATV customers," Uniphase Chairman and CEO Kevin N. Kalkhoven said. In 1999, Uniphase merged with competitor JDS Fitel to form JDS Uniphase, making the combined entity one of the largest and most advanced optical component and module manufacturers in the world.

Reason for Recommendation

Battipaglia feels that Uniphase has only begun to exploit its potential. According to him, "Four trends continue to expand the market for fiber-optic components: capacity additions to meet bandwidth demand; a deeper penetration of fiber into the network; the migration to all-optical networks; and the 'multiplier' effect of WDM. The multiplier effect is particularly attractive for components manufacturers. Every WDM channel addition requires more components, often multiple components of each type, per channel, and channels are being added rapidly as WDM gets faster."

Battipaglia is further impressed with Uniphase management. Still, he points out that the company's stock has exploded in recent years and admits it's no bargain at current prices. Nevertheless, Battipaglia believes there's plenty of upside from here. "This market is characterized by difficult entry barriers, robust demand, rapid technology changes, and manufacturing efficiencies that parallel those found in more traditional semiconductor manufacturing," he adds. Note that as this book went to press, Uniphase was in the process of changing its name to JDS Uniphase to reflect the integration of the merger. On completion, shares of the new company will trade on the Nasdaq under the symbol JDSU.

Contact Information: Uniphase Corporation
163 Baypoint Parkway
San Jose, CA 95134
408-434-1800
www.uniphase.com

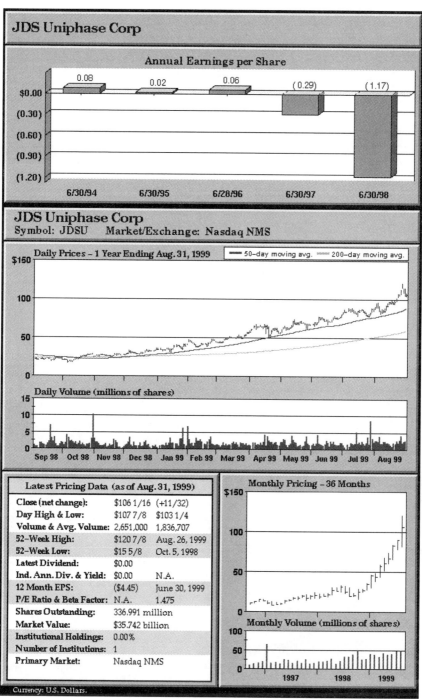

Source: IDD Information Services

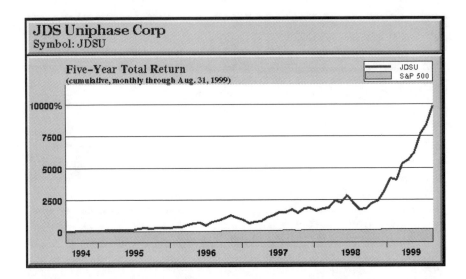

JDS Uniphase Corp
Symbol: JDSU

Five-Year Total Return
(cumulative, monthly through Aug. 31, 1999)

JDSU
S&P 500

SELECTED INCOME STATEMENT AND BALANCE SHEET ITEMS

INCOME STATEMENT	6/30/94	6/30/95	6/28/96	6/30/97	6/30/98	1 Year
Sales/Revenues	32.900	42.300	69.100	107.00	175.80	279.60
Cost of Goods Sold	19.100	22.900	34.200	52.700	82.000	N.A.
Pre-tax Margin (%)	10.30	2.60	9.80	(12.60)	(39.60)	N.A.
Operating Income	2.900	6.000	12.900	(16.800)	(73.000)	N.A.
Net Income before Extras	2.200	0.700	2.800	(18.900)	(81.100)	(167.40)
Reported Net Income	2.200	0.700	2.800	(18.900)	(81.100)	(167.40)
Depreciation & Amortization	0.900	1.200	2.100	4.700	10.100	N.A.
EPS from Net Income (Primary)	0.080	0.020	0.060	(0.290)	(1.170)	(4.450)
EPS from Net Income (Fully Diluted)	0.070	0.020	0.050	(0.290)	(1.170)	(4.470)
Dividend per Common Share	0.000	0.000	0.000	0.000	0.000	0.000
Dividend Yield (%)	N.A.	N.A.	N.A.	N.A.	N.A.	N.A.
Payout Ratio	N.A.	N.A.	N.A.	N.A.	N.A.	N.A.

BALANCE SHEET

ASSETS

Cash & Cash Equivalents	3.000	2.900	52.500	29.200	39.800	
Inventories	3.400	5.500	10.600	18.700	20.800	
Total Current Assets	23.300	24.200	127.00	133.70	165.00	
Total Assets	26.200	31.900	173.80	177.60	269.30	

LIABILITIES & EQUITY

Short Term Debt	0.100	0.000	0.500	6.100	0.000	
Long Term Debt	0.000	0.000	6.100	0.000	0.000	
Total Liabilities	4.900	7.000	20.600	27.900	51.400	
Shares Outstanding	35.248	38.064	64.392	67.688	76.380	
Common Stockholder Equity	21.300	24.800	153.20	149.80	217.90	
Total Stockholder Equity	21.300	24.800	153.20	149.80	217.90	

Note: Figures in Millions of $ except: per share items, margins, yields, and ratios.

Source: IDD Information Services

USG CORPORATION

Seth Glickenhaus
Glickenhaus & Co.

Company Profile

The name "Sheetrock" has become a generic term for describing an essential material used to manufacture homes. But Sheetrock is actually a trademarked brand of United States Gypsum Corporation, or USG for short. USG is one of the nation's leading manufacturers and distributors of building materials, including Sheetrock. It produces a wide range of products for use in both new construction and remodeling. "USG makes about one-third of all Sheetrock sold in this country," notes Seth Glickenhaus of Glickenhaus & Co.

USG's operations are divided into two core businesses. The first is North American Gypsum, which manufactures and markets gypsum wallboard and related products in the United States, Canada, and Mexico. In addition to Sheetrock, this area produces Durock cement board, Hydrocal gypsum cement, and Diamond building plaster. The second business is Worldwide Ceilings, which makes Acoustone ceiling tile, several brands of ceiling grid, and other interior systems products, including the Ultrawall relocatable wall system.

The company's most recent product introduction is a unique gypsum wood fiber panel for use in new construction. "The patented technology to produce this product builds on our expertise in continuous process manufacturing of gypsum wallboard and paper," says William C. Foote, USG's chairman and chief executive officer. "The resulting panels are strong and impact resistant." USG built a facility to produce the gypsum wood fiber product at its Gypsum, Ohio, plant, which came on line in 1999. This new family of products will be marketed under the company's newest brand name—Fiberock.

USG has manufacturing and distribution offices across the country. "It must have a strong presence in key locations since it doesn't make products that can be easily transported," Glickenhaus says. "The product is very brittle."

Without question, the company's fortunes rise and fall with the housing market. With a strong demand for housing, combined with low mortgage rates, demand is clearly on the rise both in the United States and abroad. The company notes that sales have been especially strong in eastern Europe, which is experiencing solid construction growth, as well as in the Middle East, Latin America, and Asia.

Reason for Recommendation

As far as Glickenhaus is concerned, this growth in demand should continue well into the future. "The reason I'm so bullish on the company is that virtually for the first time in history, the demand for Sheetrock is so great that it has caught up with USG's full production level," he explains. "There are builders who are at a bottleneck because they can't get enough Sheetrock in certain parts of the country."

It hasn't always been easygoing for USG. "Several years ago, the company came out of reorganization to prevent a takeover and racked up debt of about $2.5 billion," Glickenhaus says. "Since emerging from reorganization, it has reduced gross debt down to around $500 million."

In addition to its improving financials, Glickenhaus notes that USG has plenty of free cash flow and plans to buy back 5 million shares of stock. "It is steadily gaining market share and it's a low-cost producer that is putting in new machines, which will both reduce costs and increase capacity."

You should, however, be aware of a few negatives. First, the company faces potential legal liability in a huge class action lawsuit filed by people who were exposed to asbestos. Glickenhaus says the company is building up a reserve just in case, which will have a short-term impact on earnings. The other risk is that USG will suffer if the economy slows down along with construction. "However, my guess is that interest rates will fall if the economy cools, so I think the number of houses being built will remain pretty stable," Glickenhaus predicts. "This business isn't quite as cyclical as some might think. With the constant influx of immigrants to this country, there are a lot of people looking for homes. Plus, USG has three sources of business: 40 percent comes from new construction (a big factor in the growth of Sheetrock), 30 percent from remodeling (which goes up when the economy slows down), and the rest from commercial and industrial building."

Besides, Glickenhaus adds, the stock is inexpensive. "Despite the great growth USG is experiencing, the company's shares trade at a price-earnings multiple of around 7," he says. "The company has grown at around 28 percent annually over the last five years and it is continually expanding into other business lines." Glickenhaus estimates the company will earn around $8 a share in 2000 and expects the stock to get up to around $100.

Contact Information: USG Corporation
P.O. Box 6721
Chicago, IL 60680-6721
312-606-4125
www.usg.com

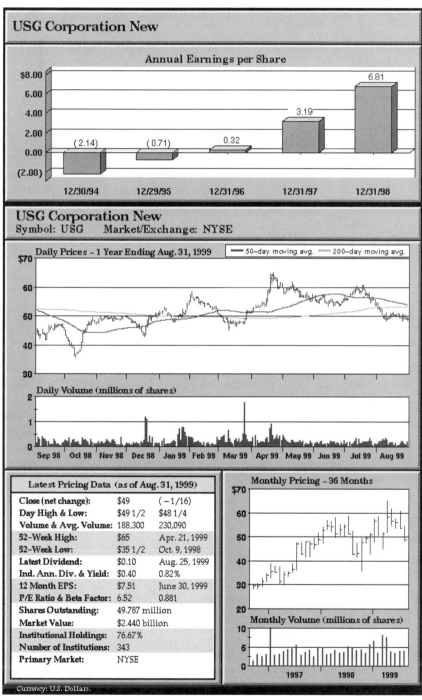

USG Corporation New

Annual Earnings per Share

	12/30/94	12/29/95	12/31/96	12/31/97	12/31/98
	(2.14)	(0.71)	0.32	3.19	6.81

USG Corporation New
Symbol: USG   Market/Exchange: NYSE

Daily Prices – 1 Year Ending Aug. 31, 1999   ▬ 50-day moving avg.   ▬ 200-day moving avg.

Daily Volume (millions of shares)

Sep 98 Oct 98 Nov 98 Dec 98 Jan 99 Feb 99 Mar 99 Apr 99 May 99 Jun 99 Jul 99 Aug 99

Latest Pricing Data (as of Aug. 31, 1999)		
Close (net change):	$49	(–1/16)
Day High & Low:	$49 1/2	$48 1/4
Volume & Avg. Volume:	188,300	230,090
52–Week High:	$65	Apr. 21, 1999
52–Week Low:	$35 1/2	Oct. 9, 1998
Latest Dividend:	$0.10	Aug. 25, 1999
Ind. Ann. Div. & Yield:	$0.40	0.82%
12 Month EPS:	$7.51	June 30, 1999
P/E Ratio & Beta Factor:	6.52	0.881
Shares Outstanding:	49.787 million	
Market Value:	$2.440 billion	
Institutional Holdings:	76.67%	
Number of Institutions:	343	
Primary Market:	NYSE	

Monthly Pricing – 36 Months

Monthly Volume (millions of shares)

1997 1998 1999

Currency: U.S. Dollars.

Source: IDD Information Services

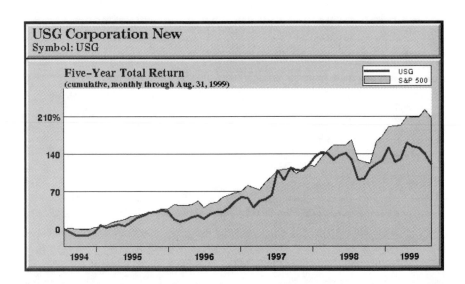

USG Corporation New
Symbol: USG

Five-Year Total Return
(cumulative, monthly through Aug. 31, 1999)

Legend: USG, S&P 500

(Chart y-axis: 210%, 140, 70, 0; x-axis: 1994, 1995, 1996, 1997, 1998, 1999)

SELECTED INCOME STATEMENT AND BALANCE SHEET ITEMS

INCOME STATEMENT	12/30/94	12/29/95	12/31/96	12/31/97	12/31/98	1 Year
Sales/Revenues	2,290.0	2,444.0	2,590.0	2,874.0	3,130.0	3,338.0
Cost of Goods Sold	1,689.0	1,605.0	1,711.0	2,017.0	2,165.0	N.A.
Pre–tax Margin (%)	(1.70)	2.70	5.10	11.10	17.10	N.A.
Operating Income	273.00	359.00	377.00	379.00	585.00	N.A.
Net Income before Extras	(92.000)	(32.000)	15.000	148.00	332.00	373.00
Reported Net Income	(92.000)	(32.000)	15.000	148.00	332.00	373.00
Depreciation & Amortization	84.000	236.00	234.00	197.00	81.000	N.A.
EPS from Net Income (Primary)	(2.140)	(0.710)	0.320	3.190	6.810	7.510
EPS from Net Income (Fully Diluted)	(2.140)	(0.710)	0.310	3.030	6.610	7.410
Dividend per Common Share	0.000	0.000	0.000	0.000	0.110	0.300
Dividend Yield (%)	N.A.	N.A.	N.A.	N.A.	0.22	0.54
Payout Ratio	N.A.	N.A.	N.A.	N.A.	0.02	0.04
BALANCE SHEET						
ASSETS						
Cash & Cash Equivalents	197.00	70.000	44.000	72.000	152.00	
Inventories	173.00	175.00	185.00	208.00	234.00	
Total Current Assets	644.00	491.00	503.00	640.00	797.00	
Total Assets	2,124.0	1,890.0	1,818.0	1,926.0	2,357.0	
LIABILITIES & EQUITY						
Short Term Debt	45.000	42.000	42.000	10.000	35.000	
Long Term Debt	1,077.0	865.00	706.00	610.00	561.00	
Total Liabilities	2,132.0	1,927.0	1,841.0	1,779.0	1,839.0	
Shares Outstanding	45.083	45.262	45.694	46.781	49.525	
Common Stockholder Equity	(8.000)	(37.000)	(23.000)	147.00	518.00	
Total Stockholder Equity	(8.000)	(37.000)	(23.000)	147.00	518.00	

Note: Figures in Millions of $ except: per share items, margins, yields, and ratios.

Source: IDD Information Services

VISX

Louis Navellier
Navellier & Associates

Company Profile

It's hard to imagine someone who wears glasses not preferring to throw their spectacles away in favor of having naturally perfect vision. Until recently, this was just a pipe dream. The only cure for correcting both nearsightedness and farsightedness was glasses and, more recently, contact lenses, or contacts. Contacts themselves were a revolution when they first appeared. But now several successful medical procedures can correct almost any type of vision problem, restoring sight in most cases to 20/20 or better.

Before we continue, it's important to discuss what causes poor vision in the first place. The human eye functions much like a camera. The cornea and lens focus light, the iris regulates the amount of light passing through the eye, and the retina is like a film that records the image. Images enter the eye through the cornea. When all is working well, the cornea bends the incoming image and causes it to focus on the retina. The retina then translates the image and relays it to the optic nerve, which sends it to the brain. If the cornea is not curved properly, it can't correctly focus on the light passing through it.

All of the newly approved medical procedures are designed to reshape the cornea. They have been met with enthusiasm and success. The first procedure to come on the scene in the 1980s was radial keratonomy (RK), which is effective for curing moderate cases of nearsightedness. With RK, the surgeon uses a knife to reshape the cornea's curvature by making precise microincisions to flatten the surface, allowing light to focus more precisely on the retina. Although this procedure is effective, recovery can be painful and it does involve incisions on the eye.

More recently, doctors have begun using two laser procedures with excellent results. One is photorefractive keratectomy, or PRK, in which submicron layers of tissue are removed from the surface of the cornea through the use of a laser. The laser reshapes the eye, resulting in improved vision. Another more recent variation of this procedure is Laser In-Situ Keratomileusis, or LASIK for short. In this procedure, a thin layer of the cornea is first folded back before the laser treatment begins. This, in turn, avoids damage to the surface of the cornea.

To perform either of these laser procedures, doctors need specialized equipment like that manufactured by Visx. Visx develops laser vision correction systems to treat nearsightedness, astigmatism, and farsightedness. The FDA-approved Visx Excimer Laser System, which sells for up to $500,000 each, removes submicron layers of tissue from the surface of the cornea to reshape the eye. The company estimates there are 157 million candidates for this procedure in the United States alone, not to mention the number in need of this surgery in other countries.

The laser treatment has only been approved for use in the United States since 1996, although it is also popular overseas, which is where many of the initial clinical trials were conducted.

The Visx System is a fully integrated medical device incorporating an excimer laser and computer-driven workstation. In order to perform a procedure, the doctor must purchase a VisionKey Card for each patient, which gives the doctor access to software upgrades and contains important patient data. As a result, in addition to selling the complete system, Visx gets a royalty of about $250 on each procedure performed through the sale of these cards.

"These systems are sold to both individual doctors and clinics," notes Louis Navellier of Navellier & Associates. "It's a great business and sales are booming. Sales are up over 120 percent in the past year. Earnings have grown 333 percent during that same time. Earnings revisions are growing faster, and the company has very fat operating margins combined with record profits." As Navellier puts it, the company and its stock are operating on all cylinders right now.

Reason for Recommendation

Navellier thinks more and more people will opt to have the Visx procedure, now that it has an established track record. "The company does have competition," Navellier admits. "But Visx has the best equipment, in my opinion, and it is very good at what it does. The stock also has incredible sponsorship in Wall Street, with very predictable earnings."

What should you watch out for? To begin with, several other eye correction procedures are currently awaiting FDA approval, many of which claim to be less invasive and safer than the laser procedures. There is also some question about the long-term effects of the Visx procedure as it has only been widely performed for the past few years. And the company faces a patent challenge by the original developer of the surgery. The other concern, which Navellier raises, is that this is a pretty expensive stock. Traders have been bidding it higher and higher right along with the company's continued good news. But Navellier believes the stock can still double in 2000, assuming these positive developments continue.

Contact Information: Visx, Inc.
3400 Central Expressway
Santa Clara, CA 95051-0703
408-733-0703
www.Visx.com

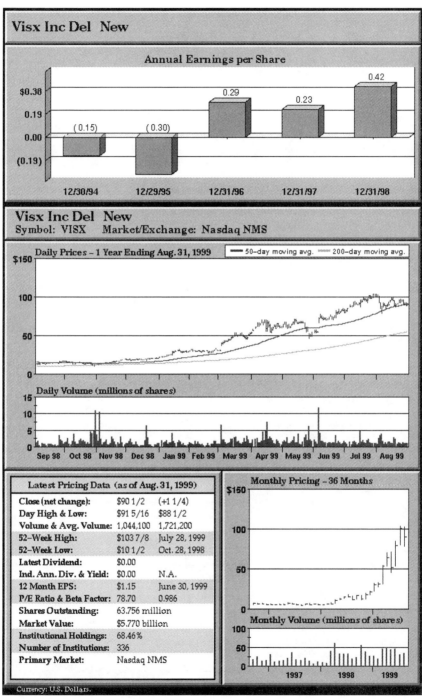

Visx Inc Del New

Annual Earnings per Share

	12/30/94	12/29/95	12/31/96	12/31/97	12/31/98
	(0.15)	(0.30)	0.29	0.23	0.42

Visx Inc Del New
Symbol: VISX   Market/Exchange: Nasdaq NMS

Daily Prices – 1 Year Ending Aug. 31, 1999   — 50-day moving avg. — 200-day moving avg.

Daily Volume (millions of shares)

Sep 98 Oct 98 Nov 98 Dec 98 Jan 99 Feb 99 Mar 99 Apr 99 May 99 Jun 99 Jul 99 Aug 99

Latest Pricing Data (as of Aug. 31, 1999)		
Close (net change):	$90 1/2	(+1 1/4)
Day High & Low:	$91 5/16	$88 1/2
Volume & Avg. Volume:	1,044,100	1,721,200
52–Week High:	$103 7/8	July 28, 1999
52–Week Low:	$10 1/2	Oct. 28, 1998
Latest Dividend:	$0.00	
Ind. Ann. Div. & Yield:	$0.00	N.A.
12 Month EPS:	$1.15	June 30, 1999
P/E Ratio & Beta Factor:	78.70	0.986
Shares Outstanding:	63.756 million	
Market Value:	$5.770 billion	
Institutional Holdings:	68.46%	
Number of Institutions:	336	
Primary Market:	Nasdaq NMS	

Monthly Pricing – 36 Months

Monthly Volume (millions of shares)

1997   1998   1999

Currency: U.S. Dollars.

Source: IDD Information Services

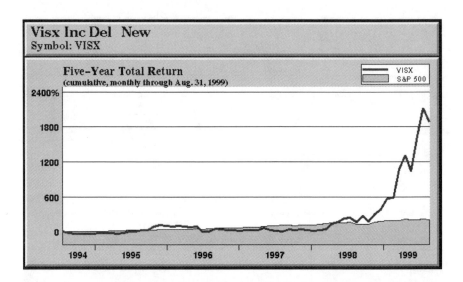

Visx Inc Del New
Symbol: VISX

Five-Year Total Return
(cumulative, monthly through Aug. 31, 1999)

Legend: VISX, S&P 500

SELECTED INCOME STATEMENT AND BALANCE SHEET ITEMS						
INCOME STATEMENT	12/30/94	12/29/95	12/31/96	12/31/97	12/31/98	1 Year
Sales/Revenues	17.900	16.700	69.700	68.600	133.80	194.20
Cost of Goods Sold	9.700	9.100	27.700	18.700	29.000	38.400
Pre–tax Margin (%)	(35.20)	(88.60)	26.70	23.30	22.30	53.40
Operating Income	(7.400)	(10.700)	14.400	15.400	59.300	98.700
Net Income before Extras	(6.300)	(14.800)	17.300	14.100	25.600	73.100
Reported Net Income	(6.300)	(14.800)	17.300	14.100	25.600	73.100
Depreciation & Amortization	0.600	0.600	1.200	1.900	2.100	2.500
EPS from Net Income (Primary)	(0.150)	(0.300)	0.290	0.230	0.420	1.150
EPS from Net Income (Fully Diluted)	(0.150)	(0.300)	0.270	0.230	0.390	1.100
Dividend per Common Share	0.000	0.000	0.000	0.000	0.000	0.000
Dividend Yield (%)	N.A.	N.A.	N.A.	N.A.	N.A.	N.A.
Payout Ratio	N.A.	N.A.	N.A.	N.A.	N.A.	N.A.
BALANCE SHEET						
ASSETS						
Cash & Cash Equivalents	11.200	32.300	24.900	30.000	29.900	
Inventories	3.800	6.700	5.800	4.700	6.800	
Total Current Assets	18.100	88.900	113.30	123.90	166.60	
Total Assets	20.600	91.100	119.70	130.40	176.60	
LIABILITIES & EQUITY						
Short Term Debt	0.000	0.000	0.000	0.000	0.000	
Long Term Debt	0.000	0.000	0.000	0.000	0.000	
Total Liabilities	6.700	11.200	20.400	20.100	37.600	
Shares Outstanding	44.100	60.696	61.620	61.448	61.598	
Common Stockholder Equity	14.000	79.900	99.300	110.30	139.00	
Total Stockholder Equity	14.000	79.900	99.300	110.30	139.00	

Note: Figures in Millions of $ except: per share items, margins, yields, and ratios.

Source: IDD Information Services

part

THE TOP MUTUAL FUNDS FOR 2000

A FEW WORDS ABOUT
MUTUAL FUNDS

Although mutual funds have been around for more than seven decades, they experienced a plethora of popularity in the 1990s. There are now some 10,000 funds on the market, which is roughly twice the number of issues on the New York and American Stock Exchanges combined.

You can literally find funds of every flavor, from conservative money market instruments to more aggressive funds investing in small-capitalization stocks (small-caps). It's easy to put money to work in a specific sector (like health care or technology), or diversify among a wide range of industries. It's even possible to take advantage of growth in exotic international markets, from Argentina to Zimbabwe, through funds.

The explosion of this industry is nothing short of phenomenal. Total fund assets stood at $500 million in 1940, skyrocketed to $500 billion in 1985, and exceed $5.5 trillion today. Assets continue to flow in at a rapid pace. Furthermore, you can buy funds practically everywhere, from the local bank to your nearby discount broker. There's even a multilevel marketing company offering folks a chance to peddle these investment pools door-to-door.

The Appeal of Mutual Funds

What led to this sudden popularity? To begin with, people are more concerned than ever about savings. Baby boomers realize that without a carefully crafted investment plan they could fall short when it comes time to retire.

In addition, many businesses, both large and small, use mutual funds to manage employee benefit and profit-sharing plans—a major growth area for the fund families that will continue to flourish for years to come.

Perhaps the number-one reason for the public's insatiable appetite for funds rests with the overwhelming amount of publicity they have received in recent years. More than a dozen personal finance magazines are currently available, all of which devote a lot of space to mutual fund investing. Moreover, virtually every major newspaper carries a regular column on funds, and financial commentators on radio and television continue to sing their praises.

Aside from all this free editorial space, the mutual fund companies themselves have spent millions educating and enticing the public to send in their hard-earned cash. The message is obviously getting through. Although it has slowed down a bit in recent months, new money is still coming into funds at a rapid rate.

Using Funds

There's no question that mutual funds make a great deal of sense regardless of how much you have to invest. Many of the experts featured in this book invest in funds themselves. Funds are most useful for equities. After all, the first rule of successful investing is *diversification.* You certainly don't want to put all your eggs in one basket when dealing with stocks.

When you buy a stock mutual fund, you automatically achieve instant diversification. Smaller funds, in terms of asset size, spread their money over dozens of companies, while larger ones may take positions in hundreds. Either way, your overall exposure is significantly reduced, though not entirely eliminated.

Funds make the process of investing a breeze. You simply send in a check and, for a small fee, hire a professional manager to make all investment decisions for you. What could be easier? It's even possible as well as advisable to accumulate wealth in funds over time through dollar cost averaging, a method in which you invest on a regular basis regardless of market conditions, enabling you to buy more shares when prices are down and less when they're up.

Just remember that not every fund is created equal. Roughly 75 percent of all stock funds actually underperform the unmanaged S&P 500 over time—rising to over 90 percent in the past few years. These underperformers are funds supposedly spearheaded by top-notch investment professionals. With so many choices (12,000 at last count), picking a fund is about as complicated as sorting through individual stocks. Therefore, the key to success rests with proper selection, which is the focus of Part 2.

The Downside of Funds

There are disadvantages to owning funds. To begin with, you have little control over exactly how your money is invested. Sure, you can buy a fund full of stocks, but you're not allowed to choose the companies. The fund manager is free to purchase anything he or she wants within the guidelines of the prospectus, without regard to your preferences.

In addition, fund companies can be extremely impersonal. Many are huge organizations that hire scantily trained representatives to answer shareholder questions. That's no problem if you just want to know your account balance or the fund's total return for a given year. However, should you have specific questions about what investments the fund is making or which stocks it recently purchased, you'll probably be out of luck. And you can forget about talking directly with the fund manager. That kind of access is almost unheard of.

Another problem is that good funds tend to grow quite large, which can hamper returns. A fund with $1 billion or more in assets is usually forced to diversify over dozens, if not hundreds, of companies. That makes it difficult to outperform the market because each stock probably only makes up a small percentage of the total assets. Therefore, when one or two issues double or triple in value, they have little impact on overall results. It's a case of being overdiversified.

Furthermore, funds are required to pay out any realized capital gains to shareholders each year, meaning you could have a tax liability even if you sit tight with your shares. Some of these gains will likely be short-term and taxed at higher ordinary income rates. Conversely, when you buy stocks, you don't experience a gain until you liquidate your holdings. If that's more than 12 months after making your initial purchase, your tax rate is capped at 20 percent under current law.

Finally, funds can take some of the fun out of investing. Many people find the process of hunting down stocks and then watching them rise (they hope) to be quite exciting. It's thrilling to match wits with the market in pursuit of profits. Because fund managers do everything for you, that pleasure is gone.

More on Asset Allocation

Still, mutual funds have a place in most portfolios, particularly for those more eager to spend time on the golf course or at the beach than reading through stock reports and monitoring price movements. If that describes you, simply choose from the following recommendations and relax.

I've divided the funds into four categories: aggressive growth, growth, growth and income, and international. Aggressive growth funds typically invest in the stocks of smaller companies, making them susceptible to dramatic short-term price swings but also potentially more rewarding. Growth funds these days generally hold a combination of small, midsize, and large companies, though the selections in this book tend to stick with the bigger names that are global powerhouses. Growth and income funds generally buy dividend-paying stocks to create a portfolio that provides you a respectable yield while reducing your overall risk. International funds, as you might guess, invest primarily (and sometimes exclusively) in foreign-based securities of all sizes. Although foreign funds are inherently risky because of such factors as currency fluctuations and political turmoil, they can actually help to reduce your portfolio's overall volatility as overseas markets don't necessarily move in tandem with U.S. markets.

Which types of funds should you buy? As a general rule, younger investors and those not requiring immediate income would be wise to focus on the more aggressive selections, while older and more conservative readers may want to pay close attention to the growth and income offerings.

I decided not to include pure bond funds for a couple of reasons. First of all, you can often do better by purchasing bonds, like Treasuries, directly from the government or through a discount broker. Furthermore, when you look at the evidence, one thing is clear: Over time, stocks provide the highest returns. Since 1926, the S&P 500 has compounded at an average annual rate of 11.2 percent compared with 5.3 percent for long-term government bonds and 3.8 percent for money market funds. That means it's impossible for your capital to grow significantly without putting a large portion of it into equities.

Unfortunately, the stock market doesn't always go up, and losses in any given period can be dramatic. Luckily, so can the rewards, as we've seen in recent years. That's why it makes sense for younger investors to be more heavily and aggressively invested in equities than older investors, although almost everyone should have a respectable exposure to stocks.

A rule of thumb states that a person should subtract his or her age from 100 and put that percentage in equities and the rest in bonds. So under this theory, if you're 40, you would have 60 percent of your assets in the stock market. Nevertheless, the late Philip Carret, the renowned investment legend who in 1928 launched what is now called the Pioneer Fund, called that philosophy nonsense. As he told me in a previous edition of *Wall Street's Picks,* "What difference does age make? That has nothing to do with it. Why, just because I'm [over 100], should I sell all my stocks and sit on bonds? I still have 75 to 80 percent of my money in stocks." (Carret died at the age of 101 in May 1998. At the time of his passing, most of his portfolio was invested in equities.)

Even if you need a monthly check to live on, stock funds remain a good choice. You can always redeem a set number of shares each month to produce the required amount of income (it's called a systematic withdrawal plan) while your principal continues to grow.

Though there are no magic formulas, here are some general stock and bond asset allocation guidelines for each age group that might even be considered somewhat conservative. In fact, several of my panelists argue that you should avoid bonds entirely.

Age	Suggested Weighting
Under 40	80% to 100% stocks, 0% to 20% bonds
40–50	75% stocks, 25% bonds
50–60	65% stocks, 35% bonds
60–70	60% stocks, 40% bonds
70+	50% stocks, 50% bonds

Selecting Your Funds

The next question: How many funds do you need? The answers vary widely; if you have less than $10,000 to invest, however, one or two funds are probably enough. When you get up to $50,000, it makes sense to buy around five. If your investment capital exceeds $100,000, it's possible to own eight or ten different funds. However, each fund should have a slightly different focus or investment objective. Otherwise, you could end up owning a bunch of funds holding the exact same companies.

A well-rounded collection of stock funds might include one with each of the following objectives: large company growth, large company value, small-cap growth, small-cap value, and diversified international. The market tends to favor various groups at different times. By investing in numerous areas, your chances of always making money increase greatly. My experts will offer more advice on this subject in Part 3.

Load versus No-Load

Fortunately, all of the funds listed in this book are offered on a no-load basis, meaning you won't pay any sales fees to get in or out, so every cent of your investment goes to work for you. You might ask, "How do the fund companies make any money then?" The answer is by charging an annual management fee, which is reflected in the fund's expense ratio. This fee is usually under 1 percent for bond funds, 2 percent for those invested in equities. You are never actually billed for this fee. Instead, it is taken directly out of the fund's daily net asset value (NAV), which is listed in the business section of most major newspapers.

It's important to note that both load and no-load funds carry management fees. The only difference is that load funds cost you up to 8 percent more. The load is simply a commission that comes off the top and goes directly into the pocket of the person who sells it to you, usually a broker or commission-based financial planner. The fund companies generally don't get a penny. Therefore, if you do your homework and read books like this one, there's no reason to ever pay a load to buy a fund. In fact, several studies have shown that, as a group, no-loads actually perform better than their load counterparts, which means they not only save you money but are also more profitable in the long run.

Buying Your Funds

After you figure out how many and which types of funds you want, it's time to decide where you should buy them. One option is to simply call the fund company directly to request a prospectus and application. You then merely fill in the blanks, send in a check for the required opening investment, and you're in business. Each confirmation slip comes with a coupon, enabling you to easily mail off additional contributions as often as you like, which is helpful for dollar cost averaging.

The latest and perhaps most convenient way to purchase funds is through the many national discount brokers, especially the big three—Charles Schwab, Fidelity Investments, and Waterhouse Securities. All offer no-transaction-fee programs, enabling you to buy hundreds of no-load funds from many different families without ever paying a commission. The brokers make their money through a service charge paid by the mutual fund companies. It doesn't cost you a penny more than if you were to buy the funds directly.

These no-transaction-fee programs are definitely worth investigating. They have two major advantages. The first is that all of your funds are consolidated on one easy-to-read monthly statement, which is very convenient. What's more, you can purchase shares and make trades on a specific day through your broker with a simple phone call. This saves you the hassle of writing out and mailing in a check, and it enables you to direct exactly when you want the trade to take place. With the U.S. Postal Service, it could take up to three weeks for your check to arrive.

A fund that can be purchased through any or all of the programs described above will be listed in italics at the end of each profile in the following pages. For more information on opening an account, just call the discount broker of your choice. All are accessible through the following toll-free numbers and Internet addresses:

Charles Schwab & Co.	800-845-1714	www.schwab.com
Fidelity Investments	800-544-9697	www.fidelity.com
Jack White & Company	800-233-3411	www.jackwhiteco.com
Muriel Siebert	800-872-0711	www.msiebert.com
Waterhouse Securities	800-934-4410	www.waterhouse.com

I have also included the Internet address for each featured fund that has one. By the way, if you are a serious fund investor, I suggest you check out my other annual investment guide, the *New York Institute of Finance Guide to Mutual Funds 2000* (Prentice Hall). This books goes into greater depth on how to construct a winning fund program, contains several model portfolios, and includes performance data on more than 8,000 funds from the respected rating service Value Line. You should be able to find the book at your local bookstore.

About the Recommendations

What follows are some specific picks for the year 2000 from the world's leading mutual fund authorities. There are three aggressive growth, three growth, three growth and income, and two international selections. Each description lists the fund's primary objective and investment focus (to help you construct a diversified portfolio) along with its past performance record, expense ratio, top holdings, management profile, and contact information. As you read, remember that *past performance is no guarantee of future results.* There are a lot of dogs in the mutual fund world, so stick with these gems and savor the rewards.

BRAZOS MICRO CAP

Louis Stanasolovich
Legend Financial Advisors

Fund Profile

Brazos Micro Cap has been able to accomplish what few other small company funds have over the past couple of years: it has actually made money for its shareholders. The relatively young fund, which was born at the beginning of 1998, focuses on the smallest 10 percent of all stocks, as measured by the Wilshire 5000 index. In other words, it owns the smallest and fastest-growing companies in America. Such companies often have market capitalizations below $200 million and are often ignored by analysts from the major brokerage firms.

The fund is managed by a team led by John McStay. The managers use a bottom-up research process, selecting companies based on their potential for strong revenue growth, earnings, cash flow, management strength, and product potential. They also filter their ideas through a series of valuation models, looking for such things as PE ratios and price per share growth rates. A member of the team visits almost all of the companies in the portfolio as an added layer of investigation. The overriding goal is to keep risk as low as possible.

Although the fund doesn't have much of a track record, the management team running the portfolio does. "The institutional manager that advises this fund, John McStay Investment Counsel, runs about $2 billion in small company stocks and has been around for many years," notes Louis Stanasolovich of Legend Financial Advisors. "They're not doing anything different with this fund than they do with the rest of their accounts, and they have an outstanding long-term track record." From 1987 through 1998, the management firm's institutional small-cap equity accounts returned an average of 21 percent a year after expenses compared with 11.9 percent for the Russell 2000 index, which is the benchmark that funds of this nature are judged by.

Stanasolovich likes the team's valuation discipline. "They don't want to buy a stock selling for a PE that's more than one times the growth rate," he says. "In microcap stocks right now, you can actually find companies with that kind of valuation." Manager McStay points out that small stocks have been in a bear market that few have recognized. He views this as a major opportunity. "Our . . . portfolio owns the highest-quality, fastest-growing companies in America," McStay maintains. "These companies are at relative valuation levels not seen since 1973. Today, smaller stocks are cheaper than [they were] following the serious market declines of the third quarter of 1990 and the fourth quarter of 1987."

The fund is relatively diversified, with a portfolio of around 50 stocks. It has also been tax efficient, although it's impossible to tell whether that will continue as the fund's track record is so short.

Reason for Recommendation

Stanasolovich agrees with McStay that there are great values to be had in the small-cap market—his favorite play to capture those potential gains. "I'm usually not thrilled about funds run by a team," he admits. "But in this case they have eight managers who are all owners running the fund. They are also the analysts. The other thing I like is that they're planning to close the fund when it reaches $200 million in assets. What's more, all the managers invest in the fund. And they have a lot of experience, an average of 21 years each, yet they are all in their 40s and 50s. To me that's important. I don't like managers who are too young or too old because I want to make sure they'll be around for many years to come."

As for negatives, Stanasolovich would like to see the fund's expense ratio come down, but he emphasizes it's in line with others in this category. The fund also has a steep minimum initial investment requirement of $10,000, although you can start an IRA for as little as $500.

How much of your money should be in a fund like this? Stanasolovich's view is different from most. He believes investors could put up to 40 percent of their U.S. equity allotment in this asset class. However, many advisers suggest a more subdued weighting of 10 to 20 percent. (You can find more advice on this subject by reading through the manager profiles in Part 3.)

Minimum Initial Investment: $10,000 ($1,000 for IRAs)

Contact Information: Brazos Micro Cap
615 East Michigan Street
Milwaukee, WI 53202-5207
800-426-9157
www.brazosfund.com

Because of the fund's small size and
limited operating history, performance
information is unavailable.

Source: IDD Information Services

Top 10 Holdings	Key Statistics	
Bright Horizons Fam. Sol.	Sales Load (max)	0.00%
Cinar Cl B	Redemption Charge (max)	0.00%
Education Mgmt.	Expense Ratio	1.60%
Orthodontic Centers	Management Fee	1.20%
Concentra Managed Care	12b-1 Marketing Fees	0.00%
Blue Rhino	PE Ratio	35.02
Serologicals Hldg.	Dividend Yield	0.00%
Boron Lepore & Assoc.	Turnover Ratio	N/A
Paymentech	Beta Factor	N/A
Pervasive Software	Total Assets	$97 mil.

PROFUNDS ULTRA BULL

Paul Merriman
Paul A. Merriman & Associates

Fund Profile

If you're a megabull seeking to wring the highest returns out of the stock market, Paul Merriman has a fund for you. However, this market-timing expert has two warnings. He cautions the fund is appropriate only for market timers or those willing to forget about it for a good 20 years, because it is going to bounce like a wild tennis ball. And he warns that if we get into a bear market, this fund will fall faster than a stone thrown from the top of the Empire State Building.

With those caveats in mind, Merriman recommends the ProFunds Ultra Bull Fund. "You can think of this as a souped-up index fund," Merriman says. "The fund is designed to give investors a performance that is twice as high as Standard & Poor's 500 index." In other words, if the S&P 500 is up 10 percent, ProFunds Ultra Bull should theoretically be up 20 percent. Conversely, if the S&P falls 10 percent, this fund should plummet 20 percent.

The nondiversified fund (meaning it can keep a high percentage of assets in just a few securities) is generally not invested in individual stocks. Instead, it holds such exotic instruments as stock index futures contracts and options. "It contains a basket of T-bills, derivatives, options, and futures, with some occasional stocks thrown in," Merriman observes. While those investments alone might sound scary to some, especially after the Long-Term Capital Management debacle in 1998, Merriman emphasizes that these instruments are being used much differently in this fund. "There is a big difference between using derivatives for leverage and using them for speculation," he says. "The people who ran Long-Term Capital Management were speculators. The managers of the ProFunds Ultra Bull Fund use derivatives to generate performance that should double the market."

In the fund's short life, its managers have been moderately successful in achieving that goal, though by no means perfect. In 1998, the fund's first full year in existence, ProFunds Ultra Bull returned 42.95 percent compared with 28.58 percent for the S&P 500.

The fund is the brainchild of Michael L. Sapir, who is known for developing innovative and unusual financial products. He was involved in creating the first prime rate fund, a fund investing exclusively in developing market securities, and the first general account annuity. The fund itself is managed by both Louis Mayberg and Dr. William Seale. Mayberg is an experienced investment banker, and

Dr. Seale has more than 25 years of experience in financial research, commodities, derivatives, hedging, and futures.

Ultra Bull is just one turbocharged fund the ProFunds family offers. The family also has a cousin to the the Bull fund, aptly named the Ultra Bear. As you might have guessed, Ultra Bear is designed to double the return of the S&P 500—only in the *opposite* direction. Such a fund can be extremely dangerous in a roaring bull market. In addition, the family offers bull and bear funds designed to mimic the technology-heavy Nasdaq 100 index.

The fund family warns that its investments are best used as part of a market-timing strategy or to hedge an existing portfolio. "This is one of the only fund families that welcome timers," Merriman notes. "I'm the first to admit that a normal market-timing strategy won't outperform a buy-and-hold approach in a bull market. It will only reduce risk. However, a fund like this gives you the potential to outperform because you are theoretically earning double the return of the market when you are fully invested. This is the only way I know that a timer can beat the market when the S&P is going straight up." It may also be an appropriate compliment to a plain-vanilla S&P 500 fund in times when you are especially positive about the outlook for stocks.

Reason for Recommendation

In addition to being perfect for market timers, Merriman points out that this fund is also a great addition to the college fund of a small child or a young person's retirement account. That's because the market has a strong upward bias. So if investors have many years to ride out the fluctuations, he expects this fund will reward them handsomely.

"It is also perfect for an IRA," he insists. "You normally can't leverage money in a retirement account. You're not allowed to buy anything on margin. However, you can purchase a fund like Ultra Bull."

You'll pay more for this fund than for a standard index fund. The expense ratio for Ultra Bull is 1.33 percent a year compared with around .20 percent for the Vanguard S&P 500 Index Fund. Of course, the potential gains are much higher, assuming the market is going in the right direction. The fund also has a high minimum investment requirement of $15,000. Merriman says that over time he expects this fund to return an average of 18 percent annually, which is well above the 11 percent historical return of the S&P 500, but with a heightened amount of volatility.

Minimum Investment Requirement: $15,000

Contact Information: ProFunds Ultra Bull
7900 Wisconsin Avenue, Suite 300
Bethesda, MD 20814
888-776-3637
www.profunds.com

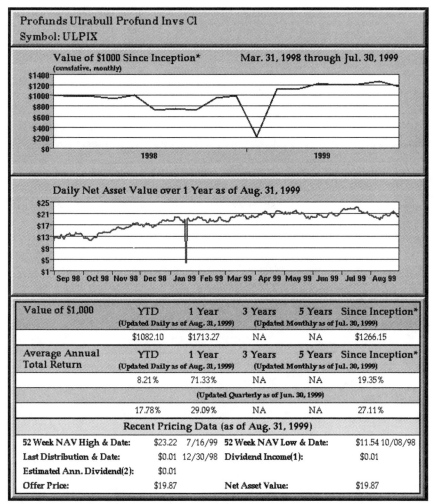

Profunds Ulrabull Profund Invs Cl
Symbol: ULPIX

Value of $1000 Since Inception* (cumulative, monthly)   Mar. 31, 1998 through Jul. 30, 1999

Daily Net Asset Value over 1 Year as of Aug. 31, 1999

Value of $1,000	YTD (Updated Daily as of Aug. 31, 1999)	1 Year	3 Years (Updated Monthly as of Jul. 30, 1999)	5 Years	Since Inception*
	$1082.10	$1713.27	NA	NA	$1266.15

Average Annual Total Return	YTD (Updated Daily as of Aug. 31, 1999)	1 Year	3 Years (Updated Monthly as of Jul. 30, 1999)	5 Years	Since Inception*
	8.21%	71.33%	NA	NA	19.35%
	(Updated Quarterly as of Jun. 30, 1999)				
	17.78%	29.09%	NA	NA	27.11%

Recent Pricing Data (as of Aug. 31, 1999)

52 Week NAV High & Date:	$23.22 7/16/99	52 Week NAV Low & Date:	$11.54 10/08/98
Last Distribution & Date:	$0.01 12/30/98	Dividend Income(1):	$0.01
Estimated Ann. Dividend(2):	$0.01		
Offer Price:	$19.87	Net Asset Value:	$19.87

Source: IDD Information Services

Top 10 Holdings	Key Statistics	
S&P 500 Index (put)	Sales Load (max)	0.00%
US Treasury Note	Redemption Charge (max)	0.00%
S&P 500 Option (call)	Expense Ratio	1.33%
S&P 500 Option (call)	Management Fee	0.75%
S&P 500 Option (call)	12b-1 Marketing Fees	0.00%
S&P 500 Option (put)	PE Ratio	N/A
S&P 500 Option (put)	Dividend Yield	0.08%
S&P 500 Option (put)	Turnover Ratio	N/A
	Beta Factor	N/A
	Total Assets	$92 mil.

ROYCE SPECIAL EQUITY

Don Phillips
Morningstar

Fund Profile

What small-cap fund is the head honcho of noted fund-rating service Morningstar buying for 2000? It's a fund that he admits is a little extreme but has a lot of the things he likes. "I look for funds that let you tap into the talents of a great manager," says Morningstar President and CEO Don Phillips. "Royce Special Equity is run by Charlie Dreifus, who is a great manager." Royce Special Equity was launched in April 1998, but Dreifus has a long history of investing in small-cap stocks. "He ran the Quest for Value fund in the late 1970s and early 1980s," Phillips notes. "He also ran Lazard Special Equity in the late 1980s and into the early 1990s."

Royce Special Equity invests in small-cap and micro-cap companies with market capitalizations below $500 million. Dreifus is a disciplined value investor who traces his roots to the teachings of Benjamin Graham and Abraham Briloff. He attempts to find inexpensive stocks with high returns on assets and low leverage. Specifically, he looks for companies with some or all of the following characteristics: unrecognized assets, ability to operate effectively in adverse environments, recently changed management, substantial or growing cash flow, a large ownership stake by management, and conservative financial reporting policies.

"Dreifus has an intriguing style," Phillips insists. "He's looking for very small and very cheap companies. Right now his holdings have average PE ratios of around 11. That's not 11 times sales, as is the case with some of these Internet start-ups. It's 11 times earnings. In the past, he's had periods of just spectacular performance." As Dreifus puts it, "A fundamental principle in our investment approach is to buy what we believe are good businesses at inexpensive prices."

But you don't get great returns without taking risks. Dreifus believes in concentration, even in this inherently volatile area of the market. At last check, 40 percent of his fund's assets were in the top ten holdings. The industry sectors with greatest weightings included consumer and industrial products along with industrial services. As you would expect with a value fund, technology, financial services, and health care had relatively slim representation. "This approach is much different from his boss Chuck Royce (a noted micro-cap investor and chairman of the Royce Funds), who has historically owned several hundred stocks in his fund portfolios," Phillips notes.

Reason for Recommendation

"I like this fund because I like the approach Dreifus takes and I like that he's looking at companies few others are following," Phillips says. "He's also got the courage to stick with his convictions." The previous funds Dreifus has managed had low turnover, which Phillips predicts will carry over to this fund. That means he frequently trades his positions, which should translate into greater tax efficiency. "He buys for the long haul and has a real eye for value." Dreifus himself says he's committed to long-term investing, not short-term trading or speculating.

In addition to liking this specific fund, Phillips also is fond of the small-cap sector in general. "I believe in finding a great manager with an appropriate vehicle to showcase his or her best work," Phillips shares. "I think Dreifus is a great manager and this fund is his vehicle. Then I want to overlay that with an area that's greatly out of favor. Small-caps definitely fit the bill."

Dreifus predicts that the names in his portfolio will soon start to bear fruit. "It is possible that small-cap and micro-cap stocks could see renewed interest because of ongoing valuation discrepancies, mergers, LBOs (limited buyouts), or other factors," he says. "In our opinion, valuation and performance generally correlate over full market cycles."

Phillips admits that he's a bit of a contrarian by nature, so he's naturally attracted to funds like this in the first place. "You want to buy funds like this, not when they're topping the charts, but when no one wants to own them," he insists. "It's also refreshing to have a seasoned manager who buys underfollowed, underappreciated stocks with a long-term view, especially in this era of day traders and people more focused on the noise of security movements than the value of a company."

Among the negatives you should be aware of: The fund has a hefty minimum initial investment requirement of $50,000. Fortunately, you can get in for less through some of the discount brokers and for just $2,000 if you're opening up an IRA. The fund also has a 1 percent redemption penalty if you sell your shares within one year.

Minimum Initial Investment: $50,000 ($2,000 for IRAs)
(Available without a transaction fee through most of the major discount brokers.)

Contact Information: Royce Special Equity Fund
1414 Avenue of the Americas
New York, NY 10019
800-221-4268
www.roycefunds.com

Because of the fund's small size and
limited operating history, performance
information is unavailable.

Source: IDD Information Services

Top 10 Holdings	Key Statistics	
Garan Inc.	Sales Load (max)	0.00%
AMPCO-Pittsburgh	Redemption Charge (max)	0.00%
Lawson Products	Expense Ratio	N/A
Chromcraft Revington	Management Fee	N/A
National Presto Inds.	12b-1 Marketing Fees	N/A
Value Line	PE Ratio	11.5
Superior Uniform Group	Dividend Yield	2.2%
Met-Pro Corp.	Turnover Ratio	N/A
Aceto Group	Beta Factor	N/A
Farmer Bros. Co.	Total Assets	$3 mil.

DODGE & COX STOCK

Michael Hirsch
Advest

Fund Profile

The Dodge & Cox Stock Fund celebrates its 35th anniversary this year. This value-oriented fund is run by a team of managers with an average of 21 years experience working for the fund's advisory firm, which has been providing professional investment management to individuals trusts, corporations, and institutions since 1930. The managers look for stocks with favorable growth outlooks plus increasing earnings and dividends. They also place emphasis on each candidate's financial strength and economic background.

"The managers have a very disciplined approach," says Michael Hirsch, a portfolio manager with Advest who specializes in mutual funds. "I normally have a rule against buying funds run by teams. I prefer funds managed by individuals. However, I think these guys have their hands on the right pulse of the market."

Hirsch has been a fan of the Dodge & Cox style for a long time. "I remember being in their office years ago," he recalls. "They were showing me a chart of what happens to supposed growth stocks when they get battered down for one reason or another, become value stocks, and then boom and become growth stocks again. They believe that Wall Street's attraction to growth versus value is as cyclical as individual stocks are. They're looking for battered down growth stocks that will become growth stocks again. And they've done a great job at it."

Long term, there's no question about that. But as for most value managers, the past several years have not been so kind. Fund Chairman Harry R. Hagey noted that 1998 was the fund's "most disappointing one-year period of relative performance [to the S&P 500] in Dodge & Cox's history." The problem? Wall Street was more interested in faster-growing technology, pharmaceutical, and retail companies, which the fund doesn't own. "Our portfolio was not invested in many of these high-performing stocks because, in our judgment, they had been highly valued at the beginning of the year, and we believed that there were more attractive investments elsewhere," Hagey explains. "Clearly, there was a large penalty for not owning these companies."

Nevertheless, Hagey points out that the fund's value-oriented approach also significantly lagged the market during two prior periods: in the early 1990s, when the United States went into recession, and in the 1970's in the midst of "Nifty Fifty" mania. "Both were times when a narrow group of highly valued securities dominated the return for the index as a whole," he says. "In both cases, these dif-

131

ficult periods were followed by a number of years of good relative performance for the fund. While there can be no assurances, we are hopeful that post-1998 will prove to be similar, and thus we are committed to maintaining our value-oriented approach to investing." That's what Hirsch means by discipline—sticking to your knitting even when the going gets tough.

Hirsch recalls the managers talking with him about their purchase of IBM several years ago. "The stock had gone from around $140 to $40," he shares. "There was even talk about IBM's going out of business because the world had passed it by. I was visiting Dodge & Cox and asked Harry [Hagey] why they bought a company that looked to be so deep in trouble. He explained it to me from A to Z. Of course, now they have a stock that almost quadrupled in price since they bought it. But they knew line-by-line why they bought it in the first place."

The portfolio remains broadly diversified with around 75 names. Less than 30 percent of all assets are in the top ten of the largest holdings.

Reason for Recommendation

In addition to being fond of Dodge & Cox's disciplined style, Hirsch is cautious about the overall market. He therefore feels a fund like this, which takes a more conservative stance, could do well in the year ahead. As Hagey puts it, "Our in-depth research, investment discipline, and long-term focus give us the staying power to hold investments in times of uncertainty." Of course, if the recent fancy for racy growth stocks continues, this fund won't keep up.

Another potential downside is the fund's size. Assets have grown significantly in recent years, from just $173 million in 1990 to more than $4 billion today. "Dodge & Cox went unnoticed for a long time because it doesn't do any proactive marketing," Hirsch says. "What happened is that it was discovered by a couple of Fortune 500 401(k) plans and the money started rolling in." However, Hirsch insists size isn't a problem for the fund. "If you look at the names in the portfolio, you'll see the managers are buying some very large companies," he says.

Other positives about the fund include a small turnover rate, meaning the managers clearly like to buy and hold their best ideas, and a very low expense ratio.

Minimum Initial Investment: $2,500 ($1,000 for IRAs)

Contact Information: Dodge & Cox Stock Fund
P.O. Box 9051
Boston, MA 02205-9051
800-621-3979
www.dodgeandcox.com

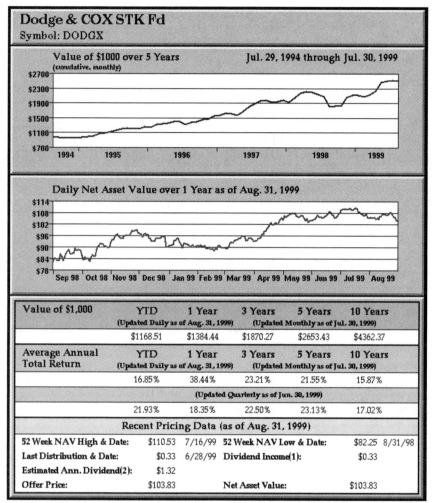

Dodge & COX STK Fd
Symbol: DODGX

Value of $1000 over 5 Years (cumulative, monthly)   **Jul. 29, 1994 through Jul. 30, 1999**

$2700
$2300
$1900
$1500
$1100
$700

1994   1995   1996   1997   1998   1999

Daily Net Asset Value over 1 Year as of Aug. 31, 1999

$114
$108
$102
$96
$90
$84
$78

Sep 98 Oct 98 Nov 98 Dec 98 Jan 99 Feb 99 Mar 99 Apr 99 May 99 Jun 99 Jul 99 Aug 99

Value of $1,000	YTD	1 Year	3 Years	5 Years	10 Years
	(Updated Daily as of Aug. 31, 1999)		(Updated Monthly as of Jul. 30, 1999)		
	$1168.51	$1384.44	$1870.27	$2653.43	$4362.37
Average Annual Total Return	YTD	1 Year	3 Years	5 Years	10 Years
	(Updated Daily as of Aug. 31, 1999)		(Updated Monthly as of Jul. 30, 1999)		
	16.85%	38.44%	23.21%	21.55%	15.87%
	(Updated Quarterly as of Jun. 30, 1999)				
	21.93%	18.35%	22.50%	23.13%	17.02%

Recent Pricing Data (as of Aug. 31, 1999)

52 Week NAV High & Date:	$110.53	7/16/99	**52 Week NAV Low & Date:**	$82.25 8/31/98
Last Distribution & Date:	$0.33	6/28/99	**Dividend Income(1):**	$0.33
Estimated Ann. Dividend(2):	$1.32			
Offer Price:	$103.83		**Net Asset Value:**	$103.83

Source: IDD Information Services

Top 10 Holdings	Key Statistics	
General Motors	Sales Load (max)	0.00%
FDX	Redemption Charge (max)	0.00%
Union Pacific	Expense Ratio	0.57%
Pharmacia & Upjohn	Management Fee	0.50%
Kmart	12b-1 Marketing Fees	0.00%
Motorola	PE Ratio	30.57
Alcoa	Dividend Yield	1.32%
Citigroup	Turnover Ratio	19.00%
Dow Chemical	Beta Factor	0.84
News ADR Pfd.	Total Assets	$4.7 bil.

WHITE OAK GROWTH

Bob Markman
Markman Capital Management

Fund Profile

White Oak Growth manager James Oelschlager believes there will be three primary drivers of growth in our economy going forward—technology, health care, and financial services. As a result, he's loaded his fund with stocks from companies in these sectors. Yet he doesn't own that many names. In fact, at last count he had fewer than 25 stocks in the portfolio. And he won't flinch at putting 5 percent or 6 percent in a single idea. "It's a very concentrated fund focused on large U.S. companies," says Bob Markman of Markman Capital Management.

It's exactly the kind of fund Markman is telling his clients to buy these days. As you'll learn from Markman's profile in Part Three of this book, he's convinced the best place to be in the stock market for the foreseeable future is in big U.S. multinational companies. He specifically is enamored of the same three sectors as Oelschlager.

"I like that Oelschlager runs this fund using a top-down approach," Markman says. "He looks at which areas and industries he expects to win down the road. He's concluded, as I have, that the top three will be tech, financial services, and health. I don't know how anybody can dispute that. He's one of the few guys who's got the guts to say, 'Why should I go with number four or five? I want to be in one, two, and three."

Oelschlager keeps about half of his portfolio in technology stocks, with the rest divided between health care and financial services. Because of this heavy concentration, the portfolio is obviously more volatile than many others in the category of growth funds. If you define risk as volatility, this is a risky fund," Markman points out. "But I think it's very unrisky in terms of losing money from it over any reasonable holding period. I don't think Andy Grove [chairman of Intel] goes to bed at night thinking his portfolio is risky because he holds a lot of Intel stock. If you believe in what you own, and you own good companies, your risk is reduced. Besides, if you're concerned about month-to-month volatility, you probably shouldn't be in the stock market in the first place."

White Oak Growth remained in relative obscurity until the media took notice of Oelschlager's performance several years ago. Since then, assets have skyrocketed from around $25 million to more than $1.4 billion. But Markman insists size isn't a problem. "That's one of the great things about investing in large-cap U.S. stocks. You eliminate the size question," he says. "If you're investing in names like Microsoft and General Electric [not necessarily names owned by White Oak], you can be a $20 billion fund and it makes no difference. You won't move the market. You're in stuff that's superliquid. So you have a much greater likelihood of persistency of performance. A lot of small-cap funds do start to go backwards as assets increase. But it's much less likely to happen with a fund like this. White Oak is a great fund for investors to gain exposure to an asset class where they can eliminate one of the major risks of being in mutual funds."

White Oak Growth has a single-digit annual turnover rate, which means Oelschlager rarely trades his holdings. This leads to increased tax efficiency. "There was no distribution whatsoever in 1998," Markman says. "It's one of the most tax-efficient funds out there. Oelschlager is very disciplined. The fund is certainly more tax efficient than an S&P 500 fund and has made investors more money." Oelschlager says he looks for stocks that will do well for several years, not just the next few quarters. He likes to let his winners run but won't hesitate to sell his losers. Another positive is the fund's annual expense ratio, which is less than 1 percent. That's well below the industry average among actively managed growth funds.

A lawyer by trade, Oelschlager started in the investment business in 1969 running Firestone's pension fund. He went out on his own in 1985, although Firestone is still his largest client. He has suffered from multiple sclerosis since the age of 31 and is confined to a wheelchair. Markman says that has no impact on his ability to pick great stocks. "You won't see him jumping out of a building in *Money* magazine, like some fund managers do," he quips. "But other than that, his mind is as sharp as ever." Incidentally, Oelschlager also has a comanager, Doug MacKay, who helps him run the portfolio and is a research analyst.

Reason for Recommendation

"Among everything else, this fund is in the areas that are likely to do best going forward," Markman maintains. "There will be lots of bumps along the way, but when the dust settles the winners in the global economy are going to be technology, financial services, and drug stocks. Owning a portfolio structured around these areas almost inevitably has to be a winner."

Minimum Initial Investment: $2,000
(Available without a transaction fee through most of the major discount brokers.)

Contact Information: White Oak Growth Fund
P.O. Box 419441
Kansas City, MO 64141-6441
888-462-5386
www.oakassociates.com

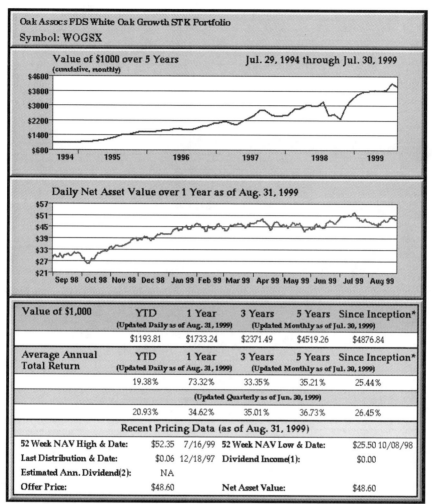

Oak Assocs FDS White Oak Growth STK Portfolio
Symbol: WOGSX

Value of $1000 over 5 Years (cumulative, monthly)   Jul. 29, 1994 through Jul. 30, 1999

Daily Net Asset Value over 1 Year as of Aug. 31, 1999

Value of $1,000	YTD	1 Year	3 Years	5 Years	Since Inception*
	(Updated Daily as of Aug. 31, 1999)		(Updated Monthly as of Jul. 30, 1999)		
	$1193.81	$1733.24	$2371.49	$4519.26	$4876.84

Average Annual Total Return	YTD	1 Year	3 Years	5 Years	Since Inception*
	(Updated Daily as of Aug. 31, 1999)		(Updated Monthly as of Jul. 30, 1999)		
	19.38%	73.32%	33.35%	35.21%	25.44%
	(Updated Quarterly as of Jun. 30, 1999)				
	20.93%	34.62%	35.01%	36.73%	26.45%

Recent Pricing Data (as of Aug. 31, 1999)			
52 Week NAV High & Date:	$52.35 7/16/99	52 Week NAV Low & Date:	$25.50 10/08/98
Last Distribution & Date:	$0.06 12/18/97	Dividend Income(1):	$0.00
Estimated Ann. Dividend(2):	NA		
Offer Price:	$48.60	Net Asset Value:	$48.60

Source: IDD Information Services

Top 10 Holdings	Key Statistics	
Tellabs	Sales Load (max)	0.00%
Applied Materials	Redemption Charge (max)	0.00%
Lucent Tech.	Expense Ratio	1.00%
MBNA	Management Fee	0.74%
Cisco Systems	12b-1 Marketing Fees	0.00%
Linear Tech.	PE Ratio	40.51
Intel	Dividend Yield	0.00%
Citigroup	Turnover Ratio	6.16%
Eli Lilly	Beta Factor	1.51
Morgan Stanley/Dean Witter	Total Assets	$1.8 bil.

WILSHIRE LARGE COMPANY GROWTH

Harold Evensky
Evensky, Brown & Katz

Fund Profile

As Harold Evensky puts it, the Wilshire Large Company Growth Fund is "kind of out of left field." In other words, it's not really an index fund, but it's not exactly actively managed either. The fund is run by the folks who created the Wilshire 5000 index, which is a widely recognized benchmark consisting of all publicly traded stocks in the United States. (The name is something of a misnomer as the index actually contains more than 7,000 stocks.)

"What Wilshire does is take the 2,500 largest companies from the index in terms of market capitalization," Evensky explains. "They then take the 750 largest ones out and split that smaller universe into a couple of components—growth and value. Their Large Company Growth Portfolio gets those companies showing such attributes as strong sales growth, solid earnings growth, and a high price-to-earnings multiple." The rest go to Wilshire's sister Large Company Value Fund.

While not a pure index fund, manager Thomas Stevens does have a limited number of names to choose from. However, he is given latitude in selecting which companies to actually include in his portfolio. Although the fund typically owns some 200 names, Stevens often concentrates on those he considers the best. "In the most recent report, Microsoft was the largest holding at almost 8 percent. The second was General Electric at 7.5 percent," Evensky observes. "So he makes some pretty major commitments to the more obvious growth stocks." If Stevens's opinion on the economy or specific industry factors changes, he'll usually switch from one stock to another instead of raising cash.

Stevens says he looks for strong fundamentals, using a proprietary process that pays close attention to such measures as five-year earnings growth, return on equity, and sales growth ratios. "We believe this is indicative of . . . high-quality companies and demonstrates an established record of sustained growth and corresponding earnings," Stevens says. "The Large Company Growth Portfolio seeks out these high-quality companies exclusively rather than trying to identify next year's turnaround success story in hopes of hitting a home run."

Wilshire Large Company Growth Fund has consistently outperformed the S&P 500 over the past few years. Of course, it has been invested in just the right stocks and focuses on that segment of the market most in favor at this time. Nev-

139

ertheless, Evensky says it stands apart from its peers in its category. "You're talking about a fund that is normally 100 percent invested at all times, that has almost no style drift, and that has a very clear vision of where the money should be and where it will stay," he says. "It expertly captures the large-cap growth part of the market, which means you'll do very well when that part of the market is going up. This is a fund that has basically had a five-star Morningstar rating forever and beaten the pants off everything else," Evensky says. "It's reasonably tax efficient and cost efficient too."

Style drift is something Evensky pays close attention to. When you buy a fund, say a large-cap growth fund, you expect the manager to buy big companies. However, most actively managed funds give their managers a lot of flexibility in choosing names for the portfolio. It's conceivable that a fund labeled "large-cap" will own some small-cap or mid-cap names—referred to as style drift, which means the manager buys names outside the fund's primary mandate. Another form of style drift occurs when the manager claims to be a value investor but owns a lot of high-priced growth stocks. Evensky avoids style drift managers because they can throw his asset allocation models out of whack.

Reason for Recommendation

Unlike his colleague Bob Markman, Evensky doesn't believe investors should put all of their money in big U.S. stocks. He favors a more diversified approach, which includes a sprinkling of small and international companies. Truth be told, he feels value stocks will do better than growth over time. But he certainly thinks you should own a generous portion of large U.S. growth stocks in your portfolio. He views this Wilshire fund as his favorite way for gaining access to that segment of the market. "I like the manager and the fact that I will be fully invested exactly where I want my money to be," he says. "I know that by owning this fund, I'll have significant positions in the hot stocks of the day. And on both a pure and relative basis, this fund has done demonstrably better than both the market and those managers looking to add value to this area. Few have performed any better. For people that want to get major plays in growth, this fund is a great way to do it."

Minimum Initial Investment: $2,500
(Available without a transaction fee through most of the major discount brokers.)

Contact Information: Wilshire Large Company Growth Fund
P.O. Box 60488
King of Prussia, PA 19406-0488
888-200-6796
www.wilfunds.com

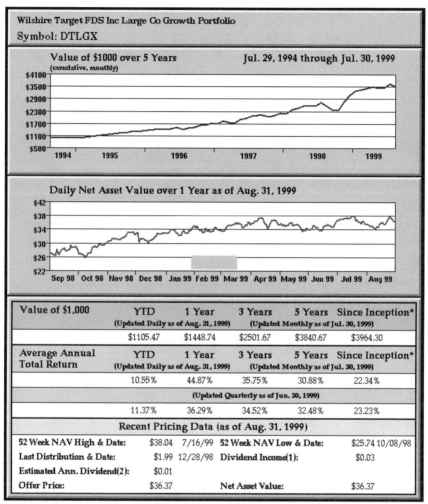

Source: IDD Information Services

Top 10 Holdings	Key Statistics	
Microsoft	Sales Load (max)	0.00%
General Electric	Redemption Charge (max)	0.00%
Wal-Mart	Expense Ratio	0.73%
Cisco Systems	Management Fee	0.25%
Intel	12b-1 Marketing Fees	0.25%
Merck	PE Ratio	34.70
Coca-Cola	Dividend Yield	0.05%
American Intl. Group	Turnover Ratio	57.00%
Pfizer	Beta Factor	0.98
Bristol-Myers Squibb	Total Assets	$412 mil.

AMERISTOCK

Thurman Smith
Equity Fund Research

Fund Profile

Thurman Smith loves to find small, undiscovered funds with big potential for his *Equity Fund Outlook* newsletter. In his mind, Ameristock is just such a fund. "This is not an obvious fund that people would pick up," he says. "But it is a great fund and it's relatively safe." Smith says Ameristock is especially appropriate for this book. You see, he believes in trading around his fund positions with some degree of frequency. A fund he recommends today could wind up on his sell list tomorrow. And given that this book only comes out once a year, he wanted to find a fund that readers could hold for many years to come. "This really is a fund you could comfortably own for a long time," he says.

Ameristock is run from fund manager Nicholas Gerber's bedroom in Moraga, California. (That's fine with Smith who works out of his home too.) Before founding the fund in 1995, Gerber was an index fund portfolio manager with Bank of America and ran a futures index fund before that.

Ameristock seeks consistent long-term returns by investing in large, well-known, established American companies—household names that you would all be familiar with. Gerber combines both an active and passive approach. On the active side, he looks for stocks with low price-earnings ratios and high dividend yields because he's a value-oriented investor. "He really doesn't want to pay too much for what he buys," Smith says. "Before buying a stock, he wants to get a sense of what the company is doing and its prospects for growth. He does consider growth but uses value techniques to determine whether to buy."

On the passive side, Gerber's a buy-and-hold investor who rarely trades. He says this reduces brokerage commissions and keeps taxable gains to a minimum.

Unlike funds from big families, Ameristock is clearly a bare-bones operation. Shareholder reports are photocopied instead of being printed on fancy paper. Gerber even answers his own phone when investors call with questions about the fund. Such cost savings are passed directly on to shareholders in the form of a relatively low expense ratio and terrific returns. "Ameristock has tracked nicely above both the S&P 500 and Wilshire 5000 from day one with low volatility," Smith points out. "My research shows this fund is about 65 percent as risky as the Wilshire 5000, which is my preferred benchmark. It has the best risk-reward ratio of any fund in its category."

Despite Gerber's value orientation, he generally remains fully invested in a portfolio of 40-plus names. "It's about the perfect size—not too big or too small," Smith insists. "A lot of funds in this area have 100-plus names, which tends to dissipate the performance of the strongest-gaining stocks." The fund has no yield to speak of, even though Smith puts it into the growth and income category. "That's actually good for taxable investors as they aren't going to get any substantial year-end income distributions," he maintains.

Reason for Recommendation

Smith views Ameristock as a core holding that could fit comfortably into every investor's portfolio. Given Smith's admittedly semipassive approach, you might wonder why you should buy Ameristock instead of an index fund. Smith has a quick answer for that. "Because it performs better," he insists. "The fund has been a very consistent performer."

The downside, as Smith puts it, is that the fund suffers from the "What happens if the manager gets run over by a bus?" syndrome. "Any time you have a one-man shop like this, your risk is that if something happens to your manager, there's nobody to serve as a backup," he observes.

Because Gerber is only 37, losing him is not likely to be a problem any time soon. In fact, Gerber recently told shareholders he didn't plan to retire for 30 years and hoped he'd still be at the helm of Ameristock at that time. "In a market in which valuations are crazy, it's nice to know you can still find a fund like this that is only about three-quarters as expensive as the market in terms of price-earnings ratio, price-to-cash flow, and price-to-book ratio," Smith says. "That makes this a compelling choice for those just now coming into the market, which is very expensive." And for those already invested, it may be a good portfolio addition or replacement for a lagging large U.S. fund you may already own. "This is a fund you buy and only look at once in a while," Smith concludes. "It's not exciting, but it will let you sleep well at night."

Minimum Initial Investment: $1,000

Contact Information: Ameristock
1301 East Ninth Street, 36th Floor
Cleveland, OH 44114
800-394-5064
www.ameristock.com

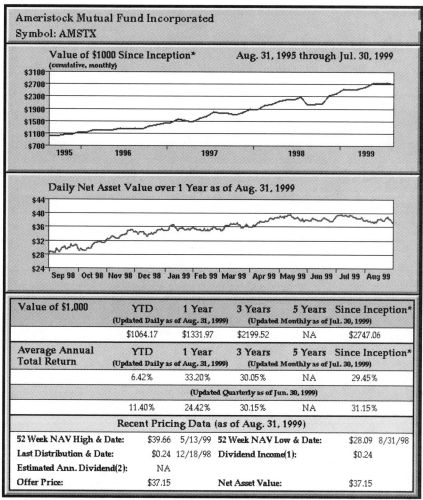

Ameristock Mutual Fund Incorporated
Symbol: AMSTX

Value of $1000 Since Inception* (cumulative, monthly)   Aug. 31, 1995 through Jul. 30, 1999

Daily Net Asset Value over 1 Year as of Aug. 31, 1999

Value of $1,000	YTD	1 Year	3 Years	5 Years	Since Inception*
	(Updated Daily as of Aug. 31, 1999)		(Updated Monthly as of Jul. 30, 1999)		
	$1064.17	$1331.97	$2199.52	NA	$2747.06

Average Annual Total Return	YTD	1 Year	3 Years	5 Years	Since Inception*
	(Updated Daily as of Aug. 31, 1999)		(Updated Monthly as of Jul. 30, 1999)		
	6.42%	33.20%	30.05%	NA	29.45%
	(Updated Quarterly as of Jun. 30, 1999)				
	11.40%	24.42%	30.15%	NA	31.15%

Recent Pricing Data (as of Aug. 31, 1999)			
52 Week NAV High & Date:	$39.66 5/13/99	52 Week NAV Low & Date:	$28.09 8/31/98
Last Distribution & Date:	$0.24 12/18/98	Dividend Income(1):	$0.24
Estimated Ann. Dividend(2):	NA		
Offer Price:	$37.15	Net Asset Value:	$37.15

Source: IDD Information Services

Top 10 Holdings	Key Statistics	
Sara Lee	Sales Load (max)	0.00%
Ameritech	Redemption Charge (max)	0.00%
Ford Motor	Expense Ratio	0.90%
Fannie Mae	Management Fee	1.00%
Philip Morris	12b-1 Marketing Fees	0.00%
IBM	PE Ratio	27.17
Caterpillar	Dividend Yield	0.64%
Dow Chemical	Turnover Ratio	11.85%
General Motors	Beta Factor	0.84
Chevron	Total Assets	$114 mil.

JANUS GROWTH AND INCOME

Janet Brown
DAL Investment Company

Fund Profile

Janus Growth and Income is definitely not the most conservative fund you'll find in this category. "It is predominately a large-cap growth portfolio with a strong bias toward growth," notes Janet Brown of DAL Investment Company. "It's basically a fund that buys growth at a price, but it maintains a significant technology weighting. That's one reason I'm optimistic about its prospects for 2000. I really think technology will continue to drive the market."

This fund was run for almost a decade by Janus star manager Tom Marsico, who left the firm at the end of 1997 to found his own fund company. (His new clone of this fund, Marsico Growth & Income, was one of the featured funds in *Wall Street's Picks for 1999* and remains highly recommended.) The fund's current manager, David Corkins, joined Janus as a research analyst in 1995 and took over the fund when Marsico left. Before joining Janus, Corkins had no formal retail money management experience, having served as the chief financial officer of Chase U.S. Consumer Services, which is Chase Manhattan's mortgage business.

"I really don't think the manager at Janus is all that important," Brown maintains. "I feel [Chief Investment Officer] Jim Craig, who manages the flagship Janus fund, pretty much runs the equity side of the business there. I doubt the managers have a lot of latitude over which stocks they own in their portfolio, which isn't necessarily a bad thing."

By charter, 75 percent of the fund's assets are invested in stocks chosen strictly for their growth prospects. The remaining money is put into income-producing securities. "The income producers tend to be dividend-paying stocks and the occasional convertible preferreds," Brown points out. Larger multinational companies with dominant competitive positions are currently most favored by Corkins. "Great companies," he notes, "have three things in common: strong management, a good business, and stable earnings. I'm also looking for a catalyst, an intangible, something that will spark growth others might miss."

"Corkins tends to be a long-term holder and wants management teams he's comfortable with," Brown says. "Since filling Marsico's shoes last August, he has cut down on volatility, increased the number of issues in the portfolio, and toned down the sector bets. He views a good company as one that earns high returns of capital, is protected from competition, and has management that appreciates shareholder value."

One thing common to almost all funds in the Janus group is the stocks held in the family's various portfolios. You won't find major differences in the top holdings of this fund compared with Janus's most aggressive offering. That's because managers at Janus are known for sharing their ideas and research with each other. Even the firm's worldwide fund has a large stake in many of the same stocks found in this portfolio. "We call it the watercooler effect," Brown says. "The managers at Janus obviously share ideas because all of their funds own the exact same holdings." The Janus funds further tend to be extremely concentrated, with the best ideas making up a significant portion of its top ten holdings.

The overall Janus strategy calls for taking a bottom-up approach to stock selection, which means identifying individual companies with strong earnings growth potential that may not be recognized by the market. Brown also notes that Janus has been more lax in terms of valuing stocks of late. "It has gotten away from more of the traditional measures, such as price-earnings ratios, and is now focusing more on items like cash flow," she says. "I think that's good because many of the old accounting standards just don't apply to these newer technology-driven companies. Intangibles are not on the balance sheet, so a lot of these companies don't look as good when you examine older valuation standards such as price-to-book. CIO Jim Craig believes earnings per share can be misleading and that return on capital provides a better measure of profitability. I'm convinced that this focus is the key to Janus's success."

Reason for Recommendation

In addition to liking the fund's large technology stake, Brown notes that Janus Growth and Income has strong weightings in several other sectors she likes, including pharmaceuticals, cable television, and multimedia. While this may not be the best growth and income fund for extremely conservative investors, it's a shining star in the category. "I think it's fair to say this fund will be less volatile than the S&P 500," Brown offers. "But it has extremely good upside potential. Not only that, but it has outperformed the S&P 500 in recent years, which is pretty remarkable given the kind of environment we have been in. It's also much less volatile than many of the other Janus funds. So if people are tempted to buy a fund from that family because of the great performance the past few years, yet they want to temper their risk, this is a fine choice."

Minimum Initial Investment: $2,500 ($500 for IRAs)
(Available without a transaction fee through most of the major discount brokers.)

Contact Information: Janus Growth and Income
P.O. Box 173375
Denver, CO 8217-3375
800-525-3713
www.janus.com

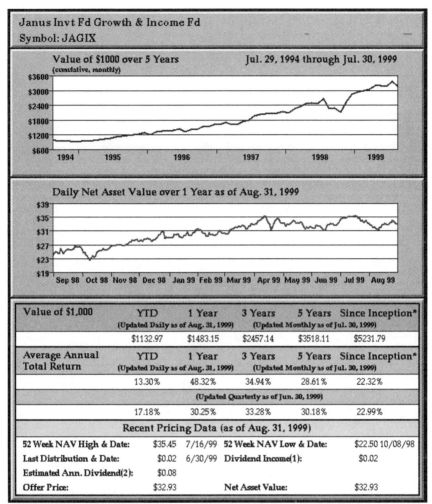

Janus Invt Fd Growth & Income Fd
Symbol: JAGIX

Value of $1000 over 5 Years (cumulative, monthly) — Jul. 29, 1994 through Jul. 30, 1999

Daily Net Asset Value over 1 Year as of Aug. 31, 1999

Value of $1,000	YTD (Updated Daily as of Aug. 31, 1999)	1 Year	3 Years	5 Years	Since Inception*
			(Updated Monthly as of Jul. 30, 1999)		
	$1132.97	$1483.15	$2457.14	$3518.11	$5231.79

Average Annual Total Return	YTD (Updated Daily as of Aug. 31, 1999)	1 Year	3 Years	5 Years	Since Inception*
			(Updated Monthly as of Jul. 30, 1999)		
	13.30%	48.32%	34.94%	28.61%	22.32%
	(Updated Quarterly as of Jun. 30, 1999)				
	17.18%	30.25%	33.28%	30.18%	22.99%

Recent Pricing Data (as of Aug. 31, 1999)

52 Week NAV High & Date:	$35.45	7/16/99	52 Week NAV Low & Date:	$22.50 10/08/98
Last Distribution & Date:	$0.02	6/30/99	Dividend Income(1):	$0.02
Estimated Ann. Dividend(2):	$0.08			
Offer Price:	$32.93		Net Asset Value:	$32.93

Source: IDD Information Services

Top 10 Holdings	Key Statistics	
Cisco Systems	Sales Load (max)	0.00%
Time Warner	Redemption Charge (max)	0.00%
Microsoft	Expense Ratio	0.96%
Comcast	Management Fee	0.75%
Nokia	12b-1 Marketing Fees	0.00%
AT&T Liberty Media	PE Ratio	45.39
General Electric	Dividend Yield	0.31%
America Online	Turnover Ratio	95.00%
MCI WorldCom	Beta Factor	1.05
Sun Microsystems	Total Assets	$4.9 bil.

VANGUARD TOTAL STOCK MARKET

Sheldon Jacobs
The No-Load Fund Investor

Fund Profile

When most people think of index funds, the S&P 500 immediately comes to mind. Without question, that's the most popular index around these days. But Sheldon Jacobs, editor and publisher of *The No-Load Fund Investor,* feels there's a much better index for people to invest in. It's the Wilshire 5000, a benchmark that represents the entire U.S. stock market. "Most of the money follows performance, which is why so many people are flocking to the S&P 500," Jacobs explains. "These investors don't understand indexing. They are just following what I consider to be a mania."

As a quick review, index funds simply try to match the performance of a specific benchmark. Unlike actively managed funds, they don't attempt to beat the market. In fact, by definition an index fund will always underperform its benchmark by the amount of its expense ratio.

While some 80 percent of the Wilshire 5000 is almost identical to the S&P 5000, the remaining 20 percent contains hundreds of small-cap and mid-cap names. "At some point, the leadership in this market is going to change, and the small-caps will begin outperforming the large-caps," Jacobs predicts. "At that point, funds that track the Wilshire 5000 are going to romp all over the S&P 500."

Jacobs's preferred fund for tracking the Wilshire 5000 is the Vanguard Total Stock Market Portfolio, although he emphasizes he likes all funds that follow this benchmark. He singles out Vanguard because it's the most inexpensive of the bunch, charging annual expenses of just 0.20 percent. Despite its name, the Wilshire 5000 seeks to track a much larger universe of more than 7,400 stocks, which means it is by far the most diversified equity fund you can buy.

Even though Jacobs has been a proponent of index funds for years, he's best known for picking actively managed funds. Nevertheless, he says that over the past year or so, he's made a major effort to include the Vanguard Total Stock Market Portfolio in his model portfolios. "I normally recommend people index no more than one-half of their entire portfolio," he points out. "It makes a good core. The rest you can flesh out with other kinds of funds. For example, if you're a conservative investor, "I think you'll find the index fund to be too volatile as it does have above-average risk. In that case, you could put half of your money in the index fund and the rest in something like utility, real estate, or equity income funds." On the flip side, Jacobs says if you're an extremely aggressive investor, you'll probably want to put the other half of your portfolio into small-cap or technology funds. "There are always funds that beat the index," he admits. "I've been recommending certain large-cap focus funds that are doing two or three times better than the index. But this is a great core holding."

Reason for Recommendation

Beyond that, this is one fund you can buy and hold forever. You don't have to worry about the manager suddenly leaving because the portfolio management process is entirely automated. As an added bonus, the Vanguard Total Stock Market Portfolio, like most index funds, is extremely tax efficient, meaning it doesn't pay out much in the way of taxable distributions at the end of the year.

Another reason Jacobs likes the Wilshire 5000 better than the S&P 500 is that he believes small-cap and mid-cap stocks will soon take a leadership position in this market. When that happens, the Wilshire 5000 will profit because it has part of its portfolio in this area of the market. "If the smaller companies do start to take off, and you own the S&P 500, you'll have to sell part of it to buy these other stocks," Jacobs notes. "That will cause you to lose a big part of your tax efficiency."

Incidentally, Vanguard's high-profile senior chairman, John Bogle, who brought indexing to the masses, calls this his favorite index fund. He says he too prefers the Wilshire 5000 even though Vanguard's S&P 500 is the second largest fund in the nation.

Jacobs describes the Wilshire 5000, and specifically the Vanguard Total Stock Market Portfolio, as the ultimate no-brainer. "As long as the market's going up, or at least some part of it, this fund is going to work," he contends. And while Vanguard's fund is available at no cost directly through the fund company, if you trade through one of the discount brokerage supermarkets, Jacobs suggests you look at the Wilshire 5000 fund from Wilshire Target Funds. It has a slightly higher expense ratio but is available without a transaction fee through most of the supermarkets. As an added bonus, it's run by the same firm that created the index. For more information on the Wilshire fund, call 888-200-6796.

Contact Information: Vanguard Total Stock Market Portfolio
P.O. Box 2600
Valley Forge, PA 19482
800-662-7447
www.vanguard.com

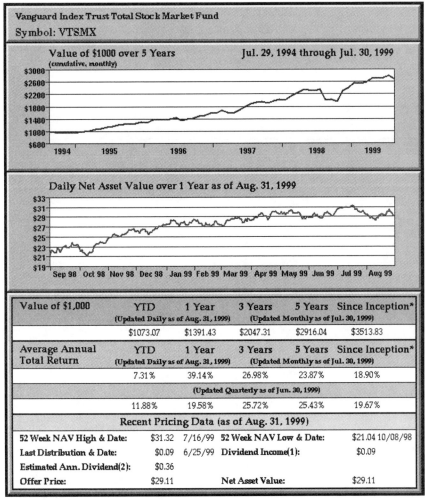

Source: IDD Information Services

Top 10 Holdings	Key Statistics	
Microsoft	Sales Load (max)	0.00%
General Electric	Redemption Charge (max)	0.00%
Wal-Mart	Expense Ratio	0.20%
Intel	Management Fee	At Cost
Merck	12b-1 Marketing Fees	0.00%
Pfizer	PE Ratio	33.73
Cisco Systems	Dividend Yield	1.21%
Exxon	Turnover Ratio	3.00%
AT&T	Beta Factor	1.00
IBM	Total Assets	$13 bil.

ARTISAN INTERNATIONAL

Stephen Savage
The No-Load Fund Analyst

Fund Profile

When it comes to investing in international stocks, Artisan International manager Mark Yockey "really gets it," according to Steve Savage. Savage is editor and publisher of *The No-Load Fund Analyst* and is impressed with more than just Yockey's great long-term track record. "He understands the key issues that affect foreign companies," Savage says. "There are certain people in the world who have an incredible ability to assess company management and understand what the major issues are. Yockey is one of those people."

Yockey is a self-described bottom-up investor who uses a number of different techniques to find winning stocks. He begins by assessing the world landscape to figure out which countries he wants to put money in. "There are political and regional economic issues that will drive the fundamentals of the underlying companies, and he is aware of that," Savage observes. The research process focuses on industries or investment themes that offer accelerating growth prospects. From here, Yockey seeks companies that can capitalize on that growth. He favors countries with improving or rapidly expanding economies and avoids stock markets that he considers to be overvalued.

In terms of individual companies, Yockey concentrates on well-managed businesses with above-average balance sheets, increasing earnings, and dominant or increasing market shares in strong industries. Stocks are sold when they become overvalued, the company shows deteriorating fundamentals, or he's able to find a more attractive investment for the money.

Yockey and his analysts travel frequently to visit companies and talk with managers. He's been spending much of his time of late in Europe, which is where a majority of the fund is invested. "While newspaper headlines continue to highlight the macroeconomic slowdown in Europe, [I] believe investors are underestimating companies' ability to grow their margins, much like what occurred in the United States during the 1980s," Yockey says. "We make it our business to look beyond the headlines in order to focus on promising concepts and trends that point to sustainable long-term growth potential in our investments." Yockey has a very small position in Asia, which he believes is still rife with economic and political risk. "We may build existing positions there opportunistically, but we do not expect to make large allocations to that region in the near term," he says. The fund maintains only a token weighting in the emerging markets.

Before joining Artisan in 1995, Yockey posted a stellar performance during his six-year tenure as manager of the United International Growth fund. In 1998, Artisan International beat 98 percent of its peers, prompting fund rating service Morningstar to crown Yockey international manager of the year. As a result, assets have quickly been flowing into the fund. So far, Savage doesn't view that as much of a problem. Not yet, at least. "One of the fortunate things is that international funds have fallen into general disfavor right now, so good funds that get attention in this sector aren't overrun with assets as you would expect with domestic funds," Savage explains. "Because the whole group hasn't done that well relative to the United States, even the most popular international funds aren't attracting a lot of money."

Reason for Recommendation

Savage doesn't believe in betting big on any particular asset class, whether international or otherwise. "But I've always felt, and will always feel, that it makes sense for an investor to have an international component in their portfolio," he maintains. "For one thing, a lot of great companies are overseas, and it doesn't make sense to rule them out. For another thing, foreign markets tend not to correlate with the United States. This lack of correlation can be used to bring down the overall risk of a portfolio without compromising the long-term potential. It's really a great deal."

Therefore, Savage believes every investor should own at least one international fund. "How much you should put in it depends on your individual circumstance, but I think a sensible range is from 10 to 30 percent," he adds. And a sensible international fund to own, says Savage, is Artisan International. "Wherever we invest, we intend to maintain our focus," Yockey insists. "[We intend] to find high-quality companies that can profit from emerging trends in stable economies and to purchase their stocks at attractive valuations." Adds Savage, "This fund is run by a small group that has developed a great investment culture."

Minimum Initial Investment: $1,000
(Available without a transaction fee through most of the major discount brokers.)

Contact Information: Artisan International Fund
P.O. Box 8412
Boston, MA 02266-8412
800-344-1770

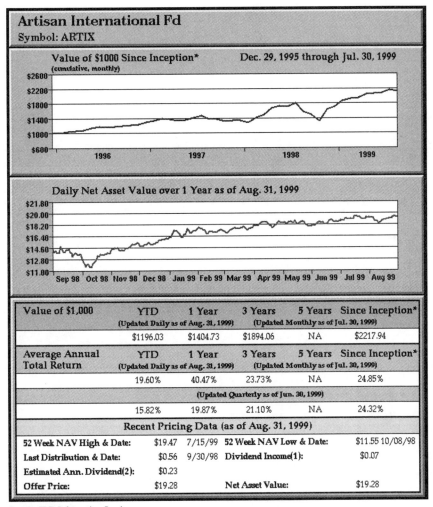

Artisan International Fd
Symbol: ARTIX

Value of $1000 Since Inception* (cumulative, monthly) **Dec. 29, 1995 through Jul. 30, 1999**

Daily Net Asset Value over 1 Year as of Aug. 31, 1999

Value of $1,000	YTD	1 Year	3 Years	5 Years	Since Inception*
	(Updated Daily as of Aug. 31, 1999)		(Updated Monthly as of Jul. 30, 1999)		
	$1196.03	$1404.73	$1894.06	NA	$2217.94

Average Annual Total Return	YTD	1 Year	3 Years	5 Years	Since Inception*
	(Updated Daily as of Aug. 31, 1999)		(Updated Monthly as of Jul. 30, 1999)		
	19.60%	40.47%	23.73%	NA	24.85%
	(Updated Quarterly as of Jun. 30, 1999)				
	15.82%	19.87%	21.10%	NA	24.32%

Recent Pricing Data (as of Aug. 31, 1999)

52 Week NAV High & Date:	$19.47	7/15/99	52 Week NAV Low & Date:	$11.55 10/08/98
Last Distribution & Date:	$0.56	9/30/98	Dividend Income(1):	$0.07
Estimated Ann. Dividend(2):	$0.23			
Offer Price:	$19.28		Net Asset Value:	$19.28

Source: IDD Information Services

Top 10 Holdings	Key Statistics	
Metronet Comms.	Sales Load (max)	0.00%
Colt Telecom Grp.	Redemption Charge (max)	0.00%
Securicor	Expense Ratio	1.45%
UBS	Management Fee	1.00%
Global Telesystems Grp.	12b-1 Marketing Fees	0.00%
Racal Electronics	PE Ratio	29.60
TeleWest Comms.	Dividend Yield	0.18%
Nortel Networks	Turnover Ratio	109.42%
Banca Popolare di Brescia	Beta Factor	0.78
United Intl. Hldgs.	Total Assets	$1.1 bil.

VANGUARD INTERNATIONAL VALUE
Robert Bingham
Bingham, Osborn & Scarborough

Fund Profile

Even though Bob Bingham's not a market timer by nature, he feels international value stocks are ripe for the picking in 2000. After all, they represent the best of the two most out-of-favor worlds—international and value. "Just as growth has been favored in the United States for the last several years, it has been favored in most of the international markets as well," Bingham observes. The best fund for gaining exposure to this asset class, according to Bingham, is Vanguard International Value, one of the few pure international value plays. Most other funds in this category follow a more blended approach.

Although Vanguard is best known for its indexing prowess, International Value is actually an actively managed fund. The current manager, Wilson Phillips of the advisory firm Phillips & Drew, took over in 1996. "Phillips is a fairly disciplined guy who follows a strict value approach," Bingham says. "One thing I like is that he's kept at least 20 percent of the portfolio in Japan since taking over. That move hasn't made investors a lot of money until recently, but I like international managers with that kind of discipline. You don't know which regions are going to do well over any given period, so you want to be well represented across the spectrum. Japan, despite its problems, still represents a major portion of the world's total stock market capitalization."

Phillips believes that research is crucial when it comes to investing in international stocks. He and his analysts visit around 1,450 companies a year for on-site inspections. Phillips looks for companies that are statistically cheap. By that he means they have an above-average yield and relatively low price as measured by earnings, book value, and cash flow. He also prefers companies that are out of favor and with motivated management teams.

Phillips decides whether—and how much—to invest in each country by first examining each market's relative value. Securities are sold when a more attractive investment comes along. "We believe that the best investment returns are achieved by buying companies that have underperformed and whose valuations are depressed and by selling those that have risen to high valuations, even if their immediate prospects for higher profits look assured," Phillips says. Turnover has averaged around 49 percent annually over the past five years, although Phillips notes the fund is generally managed without regard to tax ramifications.

In addition to buying stocks, Phillips can enter into foreign currency contracts. This helps protect holdings against unfavorable short-term changes in exchange rates. The fund can also invest in a limited number of futures and options contracts.

During the most recent period, Vanguard International Value had 65 percent of its portfolio invested in Europe, 30 percent in the Pacific, and 5 percent in the emerging markets. "The fund's position in Japan, which at about 22 percent of net assets is slightly larger than Japan's 21 percent position in the EAFE [international stock market] Index, naturally raises lot of questions," Phillips admits. "That nation's poor economic outlook is well documented and does not provide much comfort but is probably already reflected in depressed stock prices. We recognize the severity of Japan's economic problems but believe our position is justified by the low valuations and, more important, by growing signs that change is happening."

Because Phillips feels the valuations of many large-capitalization stocks are unjustified, he has been focusing on midsized and smaller companies, which he considers to be more attractively priced.

Reason for Recommendation

Bingham emphasizes that what he likes most about Vanguard International Value is that it provides you pure representation in an area of the market he expects to do well in 2000—international value. "This fund stands out because of its extremely low expense ratio," he adds. The fund's advisory firm, Phillips & Drew, also has a financial incentive to maintain good relative performance. Under the agreement with Vanguard, the company operates under an incentive/penalty fee structure. In years when the fund's performance bests that of its benchmark index, the management fee is increased. Conversely, in years when the fund underperforms the benchmark, the fee is decreased.

Bingham believes investors could put up to one-half of the international stock portion of their portfolio into a values-based fund like this. "This is an investment most people wouldn't pick right now because it certainly hasn't done well compared to many U.S. funds," Bingham admits. "But I feel the kinds of stocks it buys are positioned to do very well over the next several years."

Minimum Initial Investment: $3,000 ($1,000 for IRAs)

Contact Information: Vanguard International Value
P.O. Box 2600
Valley Forge, PA 19482-2600
800-662-7447
www.vanguard.com

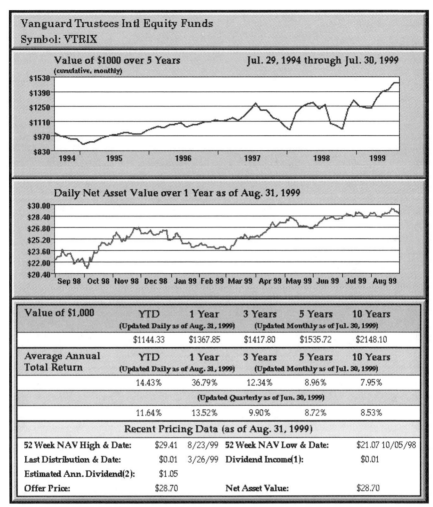

Vanguard Trustees Intl Equity Funds
Symbol: VTRIX

Source: IDD Information Services

Top 10 Holdings	Key Statistics	
Electrolux Cl B	Sales Load (max)	0.00%
Elf Aquitaine	Redemption Charge (max)	0.00%
Akzo Nobel	Expense Ratio	0.52%
Shell Transp. & Trad.	Management Fee	0.48%
Matsushita Elec.	12b-1 Marketing Fees	0.00%
Nestle	PE Ratio	30.26
Novartis	Dividend Yield	3.62%
Allied Domecq	Turnover Ratio	0.52%
Bayer	Beta Factor	0.65
BG	Total Assets	$924 mil.

part

UP CLOSE WITH THE EXPERTS

GETTING TO KNOW WALL STREET'S FINEST

As always, this is my favorite part of the book. Now that you've read about the many stocks and mutual funds my distinguished panelists are buying in the year 2000, it's time to learn a little bit more about what makes them so great. What follows are biographies of each expert, presented in alphabetical order. You'll find a picture (so you can see they're not only savvy but also good-looking), followed by a brief overview of what they do and how they got where they are. Every profile ends with thoughts on the biggest mistakes investors make and strategies for success in the stock market. Also included is the panelist's occupation, birth date, educational background, market outlook, and the best and worst investments they've ever made.

Each luminary has a different way of choosing stocks and/or a unique field of expertise, so you will get a truly diversified list of disciplines and techniques to help you become a better buyer and seller of both stocks and mutual funds.

I'm often asked what characteristics the world's greatest investors share. After doing some careful analysis, I came up with five traits they all seem to have in common. First, they have adopted very specific strategies that they consistently follow regardless of what's happening with the overall market. Clearly, there isn't just one technique that works all the time. Nevertheless, if you develop a system you understand and heed without fail, over time you will make a lot of money. Second, the pros are highly suspicious of hot tips and anything recommended by a stockbroker. Many go so far as to say people should avoid taking the advice of a broker altogether because most are mere salespeople who don't know much about the market to begin with. Third, the masters don't pay attention to what they see and hear on the news. Instead, they ignore the day-to-day direction of the Dow and focus on uncovering new ideas while closely following the holdings in their own portfolio. Fourth, the wealthiest investors avoid market timing. They are always fully invested, although the specific stocks and funds they hold might change depending on their outlook for such things as interest rates and the economy. Fifth, and this should come as no surprise, the gurus all agree that diversification is the secret to achieving long-term investment success.

It's interesting to note that only a handful of these experts actually majored in business or planned to invest other people's money for a living. I guess that goes to show you don't need a Harvard MBA to become a first-class portfolio manager. It's also striking how open and easygoing most of these living investment legends are. Even though they work in a fast-paced, often frenetic industry, these folks have a great deal of confidence and faith in their decisions. They aren't constant traders yet are willing to accept both success and failure, and aren't afraid to move on when they're wrong. Without question, they understand the true essence of what makes the stock market work.

In addition to giving you a lot of insight into who these people are, the profiles will teach you how to pick stocks and mutual funds, when to sell, and what to expect from your investments in the future. You are sure to uncover valuable advice you can profit from for decades to come.

One last observation is that most of my panelists remain optimistic going into the new millennium but wouldn't be surprised to see some sort of correction during the year. More important, they warn that stock market returns are likely to be more in line with their historic norms of between 8 and 10 percent in the new century. In other words, it's time to lower your expectations. If my panelists are on the money again, as they have been in the past, careful stock and fund selection will be of vital importance.

Now let's hear from them about how to properly pick your investments now and into the future.

JOSEPH BATTIPAGLIA

Gruntal & Co.

Joe Battipaglia remains one of the most bullish investment strategists on Wall Street. He's telling Gruntal & Co.'s aggressive clients to keep 100 percent of their assets in equities this year. But that's nothing new for Battipaglia. He's been positive on the market since getting into the investment business back in 1982. "There are really three reasons I feel so good about stocks," he explains. "In descending order, you have diminishing inflation, the fact that economic activity has been on an upswing, and a consumer confidence level that keeps improving. These conditions merit investors having a substantial exposure to equities."

He believes short-term rates will remain in the area of 5 percent, with inflation running between 2 and 2.5 percent for the foreseeable future. That, in his mind, is a formula for continued gains in the market. "There are only two things, in my view," he explains, "that will derail the bull market: the onset of a big recession in the United States or a new round of spiraling inflation. Without those, you have a continued strong market with a tendency for equity prices to go higher."

Battipaglia was introduced to the stock tables in *The Wall Street Journal* by his father at a young age. But after getting an MBA from the Wharton School, he went into the corporate world as a financial analyst with Exxon. "My initial position was to work on five-year business plans," he says. "I learned what it meant to be in a pyramidal organization, where you were expected to advance only in your particular discipline." Battipaglia wanted to explore other opportunities. He was investing his own portfolio in stocks on the side and decided that might be fun to do full-time. "I liked the entrepreneurial and risk-taking aspects of the investment industry plus, structurally, investment firms are pretty much on a horizontal plane," he adds.

So Battipaglia got on the phone and started calling some of his classmates and contacts from Wharton. Within a few days, he had offers to become everything from an odd-lot bond trader to an institutional salesman. "In 1981, I took a position with a small broker-dealer out of Philadelphia called Elkins & Co.," he says. "I was a man of many hats. I did some analysis, helped out in the underwriting of investment banking, and worked on the rollout of an IRA product. As the bear market we were in at the time started to wither and die, Elkins decided to sell out to Bache, which viewed everyone at the firm as either a salesman or overhead. It was clear to me I had to tell them I was a salesman in order to keep my position. So I spent one year as a broker, thinking that would give me enough time to figure out what my other choices were."

In his search for new opportunities, he came across Gruntal & Co., which had just 300 brokers in the New York area and was looking to establish a presence in

Philadelphia. "The firm wanted to build up its research department, which consisted essentially of two people," Battipaglia notes. "I joined as the third person and started following anything that was interesting. My first recommendations included AT&T, Centocor, and Vanity Fair Corporation." In 1986, Gruntal asked him to come to New York, and four years later he was named director of research and given a larger staff of analysts. "I became head of our in-house money management business in 1993," he adds. "Then, in early 1997 I was named chief investment strategist and am now a partner as well."

There are two main focuses of Battipaglia's job. First, he gives an overall recommendation as to how much exposure clients should have to equities. As you know, for those willing to accept the volatility, he thinks that percentage should be quite high. And he doesn't expect this bullish environment to end anytime soon. What about the argument that stocks are overvalued, given the market's meteoric rise? Battipaglia doesn't buy it. "I think you've got to take a top-down approach to looking at markets and flip it over," he insists. "Whenever you come from a high inflationary period to a low inflationary period, assets can rise 15-fold to 20-fold during the next cycle. We still have a long way to go."

As part of his job, Battipaglia recommends specific companies that clients of the firm should consider investing in. His favorite themes currently include pharmaceuticals, technology, transportation, financial services, and telecommunications. "When evaluating individual stocks, I'm looking for what I would call an anomaly in the market," he shares. "That is, the market's valuation of the stock is not on point with the company's true fundamental condition. This could be caused by investors not realizing how strong the company's franchise is, an event that causes it to temporarily stumble, or a positive unexpected new product or development."

Occupation: Chairman of Investment Policy, Gruntal & Co. LLC
New York, New York

Birth Date: October 28, 1955

Education: BA, Boston College, 1976
MBA, Wharton School, University of Pennsylvania, 1978

Biggest Mistake Investors Make: "Not selling stocks based on a discipline. You need to know when you're going to sell before you go in."

Best Investment: Buying pharmaceutical stocks in the 1970s and holding on

Worst Investment: Cambridge Biotech (Purchased in the late 1970s for around $6 and eventually went down to zero.)

Advice: "Have a clear sense of the broad fundamentals and stay focused on the creation of company value."

Market Outlook: Bullish

ROBERT BINGHAM

Bingham, Osborn & Scarborough

Bob Bingham has unquestionably had an adventurous life. "It took me until I was 33 to find what I loved and the kind of work that was my passion," he says. "I have always believed that if you're not sure about what you want to do forever, you choose something that presently engages you. That's what I have always done." Managing money through mutual funds is what has engaged Bingham for the past 16 years. But before getting into this profession, he had a chance to travel and work around the world. After graduating from Amherst College in 1970, he drove a 12-year-old Volkswagen from Europe to Nepal. He later spent time in Japan. Along the way, he worked as a ski instructor, English teacher, disc jockey, chemical salesman, and landscaper.

Bingham finally settled down in 1981, when, at the age of 31, he found himself unemployed and contemplating what to do next. His wife suggested he'd be good at helping people with their investments, even though he had no formal training in this field. A short time later, he spotted an ad in *The Wall Street Journal* from a financial planning firm seeking commission-based account executives with "no experience necessary." He applied and got the job. Four years later, he and his Amherst classmate, Ed Osborn, formed Bingham, Osborn & Scarborough, a San Francisco–based investment firm that manages more than $450 million, mostly through mutual funds.

Bingham is both a financial planner and investment manager. He says his profession combines several of the activities he likes most. "I love teaching, and this gives me an opportunity to teach both clients and junior partners-to-be," he says. "I also enjoy variety, and this business changes its composition daily."

Bingham uses mutual funds instead of individual stocks and bonds because he's convinced they enable him to construct more sophisticated portfolios. "Mutual funds have become the medium of exchange in the securities markets," he maintains. "It used to be it was individual issues. But modern portfolio theory changed the ball game. It's been quite convincingly demonstrated that asset allocation is what makes the difference in long-term investment performance."

He cites one study that shows 94 percent of performance in a portfolio comes from asset allocation compared with 4 percent for stock selection and 2 percent for market timing. "If you believe that, you want to diversify among markets, not individual securities," he concludes. "To do that, unless you have millions of dollars, you must be able to purchase and sell portfolios of securities that represent those markets. Mutual funds enable you to do that."

Bingham first decides which asset classes he wants represented. He then goes out to find funds for this representation. "We throw all of the available funds in our database up on a computer screen and probably the single biggest factors we look at are expense ratios, turnover, and consistency of management," he shares. "We don't like star funds, because once the star leaves, you have a major change of management. We'd rather see stability in the overall management company, not just the individual pulling the trigger."

Right now, his portfolio strategy for an aggressive investor calls for a mix of 70 percent stocks and 30 percent bonds. Of the stock portion, 27 percent is in large U.S. companies, 16 percent in small U.S. companies, 19 percent overseas, 5 percent in technology, and 3 percent in real estate investment trusts. Of the bond portion, 20 percent is in short-grade to intermediate-grade U.S. bonds, 5 percent in high-yield bonds, and 5 percent in foreign bonds. "We'd have bonds in a portfolio even for a younger investor," he points out. "We feel it is our job to keep clients invested. If you go through a huge downturn and don't have the cushion provided by bonds, people will get out at the bottom. Bonds allow them to stay with the program in tough times."

Fund turnover in his typical portfolio is low, ranging from 10 to 20 percent a year. Bingham will sell a fund if it's no longer doing what it was "hired" to do. "That doesn't happen very much because we're not trying to find the number-one fund in the business," he notes. In fact, Bingham has increasingly been moving towards using index funds across the board.

When you walk into Bingham's San Francisco office or talk to him on the phone, you're bound to hear the sounds of classical music playing in the background. "I'm a pretty energetic person and I like the calming effect of the music," he says. "It probably keeps me a little more even-keeled." Away from the office, Bingham is an avid squash player and loves to visit the ski slopes. "Athletics is a major outlet for me," he adds.

Occupation: Partner, Bingham, Osborn & Scarborough
San Francisco, California

Birth Date: October 7, 1948

Education: BA, Amherst College, 1970

Biggest Mistake Investors Make: "Following the herd and hot money. The worst thing you can do is read the headlines, see what's hot, and invest in it."

Best Investment: Vanguard S&P 500 Index Fund (He's owned it for the past ten years, and it has outperformed most of his other funds.)

Worst Investment: Investing in a real estate limited partnership in the 1980s (It lost 80 percent of its value in six years.)

Advice: "Develop a philosophy for how you'll make your money grow and make sure it's long term–oriented.

Market Outlook: Cautious (More positive on small-caps and international.)

ALAN BOND

Albriond Capital Management

Alan Bond recently bought stock in what will likely be his best investment ever. He purchased all of the remaining shares of his investment firm from his former business partners. He now owns his company, with $720 million in assets, outright. How does it feel to be completely in control? "It's a little more hectic, but the day-to-day management of the business really hasn't changed," he insists. Bond also changed the name of his firm to Albriond, which is a combination of his full name: Alan Brian Bond.

It was a vacation to Disney World at the age of ten that first set the stage for Bond's successful career on Wall Street. After returning home to Queens, New York, his parents gave him the chance to decide which stocks his $3,000 college fund would be invested in. "We had just been to Disney World, the place was packed, so I said, 'Let's buy some Disney,'" he remembers. "I also thought we should buy some Delta Airlines because it was the preferred provider of transportation to Disneyland." He rounded out his portfolio with shares of GM. "Those three stocks helped to pay for Dartmouth College and the Harvard Business School," he says.

After Harvard, Bond joined Goldman Sachs and pursued his goal of being involved with the stock market full time. "I was what's called a research salesman on the institutional desk," he explains. "I would advise portfolio managers on what they ought to buy or sell. But ultimately I wanted to be the trigger puller and make those investment decisions myself, as opposed to telling others, 'This is what I really think you ought to do.'" That opportunity came almost three years later with W. R. Lazard & Co., which brought Bond on board to develop its equity management division. By 1991, however, he longed for something different. "The firm was changing course and had many different divisions," he recalls. "I told the founder I loved what I was doing so much that I wanted to pursue it without the distractions of other divisions and so forth. I wanted to start my own firm."

Bond went out on his own at the age of 30 with the help of some business partners. He admits that starting his own firm today would be much more difficult. "There are so many firms and mutual funds that it makes it hard for someone new to stand out," he observes. While Bond has never invested professionally during a bear market, he expects that eventually he will. "I think there is something to the 'New Era' thinking, in that productivity enhancements in the last six years have really driven what I call USA, Inc., to be more efficient," he surmises. "But this can't go on forever."

Still, Bond feels the opportunities for individual investors have never been greater. "I've got to believe you have more people following the stock market now than ever in history," he maintains. "That's probably due to a lot of factors, including people being more worried about their retirement benefits than did past generations. Plus, with the market making double-digit gains year after year, they're looking at passbook interest rates and opting for another alternative that's more compelling, and that's the stock market." Interestingly enough, Bond has nothing against the proliferation of day traders, claiming the volatility they generate creates opportunity for professionals like him.

Bond seeks three different objectives in managing his portfolios: aggressive growth, large-cap growth, and mid-cap growth. "I start my screening for stocks based on a set of quantitative criteria," he shares. "If I can find companies trading at a discount to their growth rate, I zero in on those first. I look for earnings growth of better than 15 percent over a three-year to five-year period. I typically want a beta of less than 1.5. The return on equity should be better than 15 percent. I also prefer a price-to-cash flow ratio of less than 10." With his ideas in hand, Bond crafts his portfolios. "I think of these stocks as lumps of clay and then begin to decide what to do with them," he offers. "I rank them based on relative valuation, earnings strength, and profitability. For example, I like companies that are growing at 20 percent yet selling for ten times earnings."

After the numbers have been crunched and filtered, Bond performs fundamental analysis, what he calls the "meat" of the process. "I'll go out and talk with top company executives and see how happy and enthusiastic the workers are," he says. His sell discipline is equally rigid. "Typically, once I've achieved a 25 to 30 percent return on a holding, I'll take some profits," he says. "I also generally get out of a stock whenever it declines 15 percent from my cost. Another test I now perform is I take the stock's 52-week high and my cost, add both numbers together, and divide by two. This is my threshold of pain for my winners. If the price falls below that magic number, I'll sell."

Occupation: President, Albriond Capital Management LLC
New York, New York

Birth Date: August 8, 1961

Education: BA, Dartmouth College, 1983
MBA, Harvard Business School, 1987

Biggest Mistake Investors Make: "Sticking with winners for too long and not knowing when to get out."

Best Investment: America Online (The stock is up about 800 percent since he bought it in May 1998.)

Worst Investment: CML (Purchased it for $15 in 1991, rode it to $30, sold it for $11, and watched it go down to $3 in less than two years.)

Advice: "Always be on the lookout for the next great investment."

Market Outlook: Bullish

ART BONNEL

Bonnel Growth Fund

Art Bonnel believes the Dow will hit 100,000 by 2025, although he contends he's being a bit conservative. "That reflects an average annual return of 9.25 percent, although historically it's been a bit higher," he says. "There will be corrections of 10 to 20 percent along the way, but there'll be buying opportunities." Bonnel is bullish on the long-term prospects for the market because as people live longer, he believes they'll conclude they must invest in equities to achieve the highest possible return on their money.

For the past 12 years, investing has been a family affair for Bonnel. He runs the $120 million Bonnel Growth Fund out of his home in Reno, Nevada, with the help of wife Wanda. She uses her accounting background to scour through dozens of earnings reports and 10-Qs each day in search of companies growing fast enough to be considered by her picky husband. Art Bonnel then scrutinizes each candidate by subjecting it to a four-part test.

To begin with, earnings must be up from the previous year. "I don't care how much, I just want to see them up," he explains. If they're down, he passes or sells the issue if it's already in his portfolio. Next, the current ratio (current assets divided by current liabilities) should be 2 to 1. "If a company is having problems, for whatever reason, it shows up in the current ratio," he notes. Step three examines the amount of long-term debt on the balance sheet (he doesn't want to see it increasing), and the debt-to-equity ratio must be no more than 30 percent. Finally, Bonnel looks at insider holdings. He likes top management to own at least 15 percent of the company, reasoning, "I want them to be motivated to increase the value of their personal wealth."

If a company checks out in all four categories, Bonnel glances at a Standard & Poor's tear sheet for a brief description of the business and views a few charts. "I want to see a stock basing out or in a minor uptrend," he explains. "I don't want to catch a falling piano." A stock is unloaded if earnings go down or he sees meaningful selling by insiders.

Once Bonnel finds a promising idea, he likes to buy it at a reasonable price. "When I look at a company, I generally don't like to pay more than half the earnings growth rate," he insists. "In other words, if earnings are up 100 percent this year, I don't want a PE of more than 50. What I attempt to find are companies with PEs in the 20 range."

You'll notice he doesn't talk to company management or visit his potential investments. That's because, in his mind, the numbers don't lie, but people sometimes do. "Company officers can tell you anything they want and that things are great," he says. "I look at what the accountants tell us, not what company officers say they're doing. What's their debt level like? What are their current assets? You can tell me any story you want, but I want to see audited numbers."

In addition, he doesn't limit himself to any particular area of the market, meaning you'll find both large and small companies in his portfolio. "I'll buy anything that looks attractive," he says. "Sometimes I'll buy a company that hasn't been doing well for a couple of years but suddenly gets its act together, resulting in increased earnings."

While Bonnel claims his earnings-driven strategy works well in most markets, he warns it's not infallible, admitting he is wrong 35 to 40 percent of the time. Furthermore, when his companies report a disappointing quarter, they are often hammered by Wall Street. Still, he doesn't believe his discipline is unnecessarily risky. "In a bear market, good stocks go down, mediocre stocks go down, and poor stocks go down," he explains. "However, if you're in companies that are doing well, they will bounce back faster."

This strategy has helped Bonnel to produce an impressive record. Before being offered his own fund by United Services in 1994, he managed the MIM Stock Appreciation Fund for five years, generating an average annual gain of 18 percent. "I stick with this system through good times and bad," he insists. "There are slow periods when my style of investing goes out of favor, but then it tends to come back because I'm looking at companies that are growing."

Right now, he's especially interested in mid-cap stocks. "I'm finding some pretty good buys out there," he says. "The past few years have been difficult for this part of the market. Investors have been putting their money into companies with more predictable earnings."

Occupation: Portfolio Manager, Bonnel Growth Fund
Reno, Nevada

Birth Date: August 20, 1945

Education: BS, University of Nevada, 1968

Biggest Mistake Investors Make: "Watching stocks too closely and worrying about every tick."

Best Investment: Charles Schwab & Co. (Bought for $20 in August 1998 and sold for $150 in April 1999.)

Worst Investment: Comtronix (Paid $20 a share and discovered the company was cooking the books; got out at $1 before it went to zero.)

Advice: "You can make more money with patience than brilliance. The true genius of investing is recognizing the direction of a trend, not attempting to pick market tops or bottoms. Also, if you find you have made a mistake, you should cut your losses."

Market Outlook: Bullish

ELIZABETH BRAMWELL
Bramwell Capital Management

Although Elizabeth Bramwell is known for being a first-rate growth manager, when we last chatted she talked a lot about looking for attractively valued stocks. "There are some especially good opportunities in companies with market capitalizations under $5 billion, below which they start to lose a lot of institutional support," she observed.

Bramwell has been managing money for more than three decades. But growing up, she never had much of a financial vocabulary. Her father was a musician and never discussed the stock market. As a young girl, Bramwell dreamed of becoming a doctor and wound up majoring in chemistry at Bryn Mawr College. However, she found economics to be more exciting. So after graduation, she enrolled at the Columbia Business School, where she got an MBA in finance.

Among her Columbia classmates was famed money manager Mario Gabelli. Both began their professional career as analysts at the same time at different firms, although they occasionally crossed paths. In 1985 Gabelli asked Bramwell to join his money management firm as director of research. Two years later, in April 1987, she was tapped to launch the Gabelli Growth Fund. Bramwell wrote the fund's investment philosophy and made all of the buy and sell decisions. From the start, Bramwell often posted a better performance than her value-oriented boss, and the media took notice. Assets in Gabelli Growth quickly swelled to $700 million with some 60,000 shareholders. During her tenure, the fund posted an average annual return of 16.6 percent.

Following a highly publicized dispute, Bramwell parted ways with Gabelli in 1994 and started her own fund, Bramwell Growth, six months later. "I left [Gabelli] with the idea that if I were going to go out on my own, I too could start a business and succeed," she says.

Bramwell's investment discipline has evolved over the years. "When I started out, I worked on analyzing emerging public companies, so I like to own emerging, smaller names," she explains. "However, I also don't want to ignore some of the larger firms when they are big movers." In addition to running Bramwell Growth, which contains companies of all sizes, Bramwell Capital is subadviser to the Selected Special Shares Fund, which concentrates on small-cap and mid-cap stocks. The firm also subadvises a fund sponsored by Sun America.

Bramwell prides herself on being both a top-down and bottom-up analyst. "From a top-down standpoint, I think about things like inflation, interest rates, tax rates, currencies, and political events," she says. "I'm always thinking about the future, projecting earnings and the multiples on those earnings. I then relate those

175

multiples to the underlying growth rates." Her ideal objective is to buy companies at discounts to their future growth rates.

From a bottom-up, more sector-specific perspective, she looks for sector trends, such as accelerating use of technology. "Several things are happening that will be enormously positive for numerous technology companies," she maintains. "One is electronic commerce. Another is the explosion in new communications. I also think that the eventual subsiding of the Y2K jitters will be positive for a lot of businesses in the technology sector." In addition, Bramwell is fond of companies that are big users and/or providers of outsourcing, which she sees as an expanding emerging trend.

Once Bramwell has determined which areas of the market she's most interested in, she begins looking closely at specific companies. "I'm trying to figure out how they're going to grow going forward with new products and markets," she tells me. "Are the margins going to expand, and what's happening with tax rates? Do they need to raise more money, or will they buy back shares?" Attending conferences and company road shows that come through the Big Apple, where her office is located, provides useful insight. "Companies make 30-minute to 45-minute presentations in New York that are followed by a question-and-answer period," she notes. "Having other analysts and portfolio managers there [in the room] asking questions provides for a synergistic briefing."

Bramwell carefully monitors her holdings on a daily basis and looks for strong indications of change before deciding to move on. "I'll sell when I think the fundamentals are deteriorating or if the macroeconomic picture changes," she shares. "I'll also sell if I think I've found a better opportunity elsewhere. In that case, I'm willing to sell one stock to go into another."

Occupation: President and CIO, Bramwell Capital Management
New York, New York

Birth Date: December 1, 1940

Education: BA, Bryn Mawr College, 1962
MBA, Columbia University, 1967

Biggest Mistake Investors Make: "Being emotional."

Best Investment: Amazon.com. (Bought in May 1997 for a split-adjusted $2.94 a share.)

Worst Investment: U.S. Satellite

Advice: "Understand what you're buying. Act with knowledge, not compulsively."

Market Outlook: Bullish

JANET BROWN

DAL Investment Company

Janet Brown's approach to investing is the exact opposite of traditional asset allocation. "We believe a sure way to underperform is by allocating a percentage of your portfolio to an underperforming sector and stick with it through thick and thin," she says. "I think many of the asset allocators out there are coming around to our way of thinking." In other words, instead of owning a little bit of everything, including large, small, and international stocks at all times, she believes in going only with the winners in the current market cycle. As this book went to press, that was predominately large company U.S. growth stocks. "I believe your best chance for beating the market is by following the leaders."

Brown and her former boss, Burton Berry, devised a unique strategy for selecting funds in the late 1970s. They call it "upgrading." The results of their research are printed each month in *NoLoad Fund*X,* a newsletter published by Brown's firm. "The first thing we do is classify the funds in our database by risk," she explains. "We then look at current performance over the past 12-, 6-, 3-, and 1-month periods. Next, we take a simple performance average during those four periods, give funds in the top 15 some bonus points, and rank each one by its performance-based score." It's a purely quantitative process, which calls for purchasing funds based on returns alone. The background of a manager isn't really a consideration. The best five funds in each risk category are recommended for purchase. When a fund's performance drops, thus booting it out of the top five, Brown recommends switching into another winner. There are some exceptions, however. She tells investors not to put more than 25 percent in international or small-cap stocks, even when they are the best performers, because they are too risky.

The logic behind this system is pretty straightforward. Every fund manager has a certain investing style that works well in some environments and poorly in others. "For instance, large-cap growth stock pickers have been doing well over the last few years because that's where the market leadership has been," Brown says. "But there will be periods when small-cap managers do better. There are also certain sectors that come and go out of vogue. Investing is quite cyclical because of changing economic fundamentals. It's easy to identify areas of outperformance after the fact, but they're impossible to forecast."

Brown's discipline calls for staying fully invested at all times. If it works as designed, you'll always be in the right place at the right time. "The system should continually keep you in those funds that have gotten it right because they're in the best stocks or sectors. They might even be in cash if the market's going down," she adds. A high-performing fund usually maintains its momentum for an average of six months, though Brown says some have stayed in the spotlight for as long as two and one-half years.

Following the leaders means paying capital gains taxes each time you make a trade. In retirement accounts, that's not a concern. But in taxable portfolios, Brown admits it doesn't always make sense to switch around so much. "You really have to look at whether upgrading will result in enough increased performance to make the trade pay off," she admits. "To be truthful, in the last few years it often hasn't because you've been able to get good results in almost all domestic market environments."

Brown entered the fund business through a rather unconventional channel. After graduating from college with a degree in architecture and art, she went off to Brussels with a friend. She needed a job and wound up working for a large insurance brokerage firm as a fund administrator. "The company sold mutual funds, mostly to U.S. servicemen," she recalls. "In order to do my job, I had to get licensed. I began to study investments, and particularly funds. I quickly concluded that no-loads were the way to go." Unfortunately, her European employer only peddled load funds, which carried steep 8.5 percent sales charges. Brown moved back to San Francisco three years later and thought about becoming a stockbroker. "I knew I wanted to be in the investment business but found brokers did more sales work than investment management," she says. "I also felt there was a conflict of interest between the broker and the client as it was a commission-based relationship. Then a friend of mine introduced me to Burt Berry, who had started an investment firm using only no-load funds. He hired me as his assistant in 1978 when we had less than $10 million under management. The two of us developed this upgrading strategy." In 1997 Berry sold most of the firm to Brown and her partners.

Brown's upgrading system seems to be effective and has been given high marks by *The Hulbert Financial Digest.* "It's not complicated, but it really does work," she says.

Occupation: President, DAL Investment Company
San Francisco, California

Birth Date: November 10, 1950

Biggest Mistake Investors Make: "Having a short-term outlook and not riding through corrections."

Best Investment: Rydex OTC (It more than doubled in about a year.)

Worst Investment: Continuing to own value funds in 1998 (although they came back a bit in 1999).

Advice: "Take a long-term view and only stick with funds that are doing well in the current environment."

Market Outlook: Cautiously optimistic

SUSAN BYRNE

Westwood Management

 Growing up in Pasadena, California, Susan Byrne didn't even know what Wall Street was. She wound up there in a most unconventional way. At the age of 24, following her short-lived first marriage, Byrne headed for New York with her four-year-old son and a lot of ambition. "I thought New York would be a neat place to go and start my grown-up life," she recalls. "I had my choice of three secretarial jobs, and the one that paid the most was with E. F. Hutton." By always volunteering, overselling her abilities, and yearning to make more money, she eventually was able to talk her way into a job as a research editor at another brokerage firm. "It wasn't a very glamorous job," she admits. "I took all of the material from the analysts and edited it into proper English."

From there, she became a member of the firm's investment team, specializing in political economics, an area she studied in college. "I loved this job and felt I had really found something that I not only enjoyed but could also make a contribution to," she confides. "I was also encouraged by my clients. They would say, 'Based on the way you look at things, Susan, you should really consider managing money.'" One thing led to another, and in 1977 she was hired as an apprentice portfolio manager by Banker's Trust. Two and one-half years later, she was offered a chance to work as an assistant treasurer and in-house pension fund manager at GAF Corporation. "This job gave me the opportunity to clearly demonstrate an ability to manage money. In the bank you had committees and guidelines. Here I was on my own," she recalls. "I was with them for almost four years and, with their blessing, started my own firm, Westwood Management, on April 1, 1983." GAF was her first client.

Byrne maintains that this route might seem unusual, but it was a typical experience for women her age during that time. "There was a horrible bear market in the early 1970s, and the securities industry wasn't attracting a bunch of people," she explains. "My first five years in the business were from 1970 to 1975. These were terrible times, and there wasn't a lot of competition. Today the firms want to see a certain type of person from the best and brightest schools."

Byrne admits she started her own company because she knew that was the only way she'd ever become a big player in the business. "I was waiting for these firms to come knock down my door and make me a partner, which was clearly not happening," she explains. "So I decided to start my own company and demonstrate to myself and my peers that I had a talent for managing money." She began with $35 million and today has grown that to more than $2 billion in private accounts and mutual funds.

You don't gather that much money unless you know how to make it multiply, and Byrne has clearly proven she does. Her first rule of investing is to avoid losing your capital. "That may sound silly, but it's one of those things people sometimes forget," she says. "I begin with a top-down viewpoint by looking at what's happening with inflation. If the environment seems right for financial securities, I look at a combination of the expected 12- to 18-month economic cycle along with the outlook for corporate profits, interest rates, inflation, and the dollar."

She then chooses stocks by searching for a catalyst that can drive a company's share price higher. Once she's found that, she looks at what other analysts are saying about the stock and will only buy if she thinks they are underestimating its potential. "This sounds easier than it is, because we only own about 40 stocks out of a universe of 6,400. So you can see that we agree with other analysts 95 percent of the time," she notes. "We'll only invest in those companies that we are highly confident will come through with a positive earnings surprise."

Her perfect stock sells for a PE ratio that's well below its growth rate. "I use a lot of screening techniques and am especially looking for companies that have had a positive earnings surprise greater than the most recent earnings revision," she shares. "For instance, a company that's supposed to earn $2 a share in a calendar year would equate to a company that's supposed to earn 50¢ a quarter. If it just reported first-quarter earnings of 60¢, and the earnings revision for the year is less than $2.40 (60¢ multiplied by four quarters), I'd take a hard look at it." Every stock in her portfolio has a price target based on her estimated forward-looking growth rate. She'll either sell when it hits her target or revise that number higher if the fundamentals warrant it. Byrne says her primary goal is to buy value stocks that ultimately turn into high growers.

Occupation: President and CIO, Westwood Management
Dallas, Texas

Birth Date: August 5, 1948

Education: Attended but didn't graduate from the University of California at Berkeley

Biggest Mistake Investors Make: "Trying to time the market. If it's long-term money, just put it in the market and forget about it."

Best Investment: Dell Computer (She bought it for a split-adjusted $3.50 a share and sold out for $80 in 1997.)

Worst Investment: Buying options in an IRA some 26 years ago.

Advice: "Be a steady investor and have a set plan for when you will evaluate your portfolio. Put money in the market on a regular basis."

Market Outlook: Cautious, especially on large-cap growth stocks

JAMES COLLINS

Insight Capital Research & Management

Jim Collins is convinced that mid-cap stocks will enjoy the next big move in the U.S. market. "Why the mid-caps?" he asks. "Because once portfolio managers determine that the large-caps are overpriced, they will shift into the next most liquid group—the mid-caps." Even though Collins specializes in small-cap stocks, his firm, Insight Capital, invests money across the board. He even runs a value portfolio, although he's known for being a heavy momentum player. "My hottest product is a tax-advantaged growth portfolio that was up 72 percent in 1998," he says. "We take about half of the money in the portfolio and put it into ten large, established growth companies with a projected earnings growth of 15 percent annually for the next three to five years. We put the rest in 40 smaller companies with an earnings growth of at least 20 percent."

Collins began following the stock market in high school for an unorthodox reason. He wanted to own a manufacturing plant some day and knew he would have to come up with capital to do it. He figured learning about stocks would give him the knowledge he needed to raise cash. But things didn't turn out as he planned. "After graduating from college with an engineering degree, I went into the Navy," he reflects. "For about ten years, I tried everything conceivable out there to get an edge on the marketplace."

After his tour of duty was over, he joined General Electric as an engineer and spent his off-hours trading stocks. He managed to turn $1,500 into $487,000 in just four years. "I hadn't been at GE very long before I was making more money trading stocks than I was as an engineer," he confesses. "I was pretty much a speculator and trader in those days. I ran a concentrated portfolio of over-the-counter stocks. I typically held no more than six to eight names at a time, with most of the money invested in three issues." His portfolio eventually zoomed to $1.5 million before plummeting back down to $30,000 after a series of bad gambles. "I took that money, married a lovely girl from Asheville, North Carolina, and as soon as I graduated from the Harvard Business School, we took off for Europe and spent the whole $30,000 traveling for three months," he says. "I never looked at it as money. I just looked at it as a score. My thinking is still pretty much the same. I want to rack up as big a score as I can."

So far, that's exactly what he's done. His firm is ranked in the top tier of all money managers in the nation. His *OTC Insight* has been the number-one investment newsletter over the past ten years, according to the *Hulbert Financial Digest,* producing a total return of 1,494 percent, or 31.9 percent annually.

Collins's first professional job in the industry was working as a stock picker for a mutual fund company in 1967. He later became a stockbroker before starting his own firm in 1983. "I'm primarily a fundamentalist in what I do," he explains. "I have a three-step buying process: running quantitative screens, doing fundamental analysis, and then what I call performance analysis. Performance analysis for me is really taking a look at the relative strength of a stock."

He maintains a database of around 8,000 stocks, which he screens every morning. "First and foremost I like to find stocks with a track record of beating the market over a long period of time," he reveals. "The primary purpose of the screening is to see if a company has a track record of beating the market. Then I move on to fundamental analysis to verify that the industry looks good and that the company is a notch ahead of the rest of the players in its business. I then like to dig deeper to see that earnings are indeed growing rapidly, preferably by 20 percent a year or better, and that there is a solid cash flow."

Because he demands such strong growth, he most often gravitates toward smaller stocks that trade over the counter. The average company in his portfolio should grow its earnings by 33 percent in 2000. "The number-one reason I'll sell a stock is because it's not beating its benchmark index," he adds. In his non-tax-efficient accounts, this can lead to extremely high turnover.

As previously mentioned, Collins also runs a more value-oriented portfolio. But his definition of value is a little different from most. "We're really looking for growth companies that are out of favor for whatever reason," he says. "Sometimes a company will miss a quarter or get downgraded. We'll watch to see where it bottoms, but we don't try to go bottom fishing. We try to pick it up after it turns back up. So we're following the trends with some of the fallen angels."

When Collins wants to escape the hustle and bustle of the investment world, he and his wife travel. They recently took a trip to South America and occasionally go hiking in England.

Occupation: President, Insight Capital Research & Management
 Walnut Creek, California

Birth Date: August 26, 1934

Education: BEE, Georgia Tech, 1956
 MBA, Harvard Business School, 1963

Biggest Mistake Investors Make: "Panicking and hitting the sell button at the wrong time; being greedy and thinking there's easy money to be made."

Best Investment: Cisco Systems (First bought it in 1991 and still owns it.)

Worst Investment: Gantos (Purchased shares of this clothing company in the 1980s for between $9 and $12 per share; got out around $5.)

Advice: "Focus on the fundamentals of a company and keep your money in stocks on an up-trend."

Market Outlook: Bullish

ELIZABETH DATER

Warburg Pincus Asset Management

Elizabeth Dater is sticking with small-cap stocks even though nobody else seems to like them much these days. "The turnaround isn't going to happen overnight because they've been out of favor for a long time," she admits. "But we've seen periods like this before, and small-caps usually come back and do spectacularly well. Besides, I have never believed people should have 100 percent of their U.S. equity money in small-caps to begin with. I believe your allocation [to this asset class] should be between 10 and 25 percent, depending on your risk tolerance."

Dater is a growth investor who looks for tiny, well-managed companies with the potential to become the large blue chips of tomorrow. "If I'm successful, the businesses I follow will have very little recognition when I start investing in them but a lot by the time I'm ready to sell," she says. "I look for companies with proprietary products and services along with access to the capital they need to fund their growth. I like companies with low debt to equity and a high return on equity because these tend to be the most profitable businesses." Most important, Dater takes a close look at management, which she believes is essential for determining whether an upstart will succeed or fail. "Management must be able to articulate a clear vision and business plan that I can benchmark them to and watch as the plan progresses," she explains. "I also like management to have an incentive to hold an equity ownership position to make sure its interests are aligned with the shareholders."

Because many small-cap companies aren't making much money, it isn't always easy to determine how much they are worth. Dater's rule is to buy a company at a PE ratio below its growth rate. She also diversifies among 75 to 85 names to spread out her risk. "I rate each company in my portfolio as either a core holding or changing dynamic," she adds. "At least 75 percent are core holdings. These are companies with the strongest earnings momentum, unique business models, and best management. The other 25 percent, the changing dynamics, are put on close watch to make sure they grow as I expect. This would include the Internet stocks. If they don't work out, they get replaced."

It seems only fitting that Dater wound up as a panelist on the PBS program *Wall $treet Week with Louis Rukeyser* shortly after launching her career in the investment business. She's been a great communicator interested in the performing arts all of her life. As a young girl, she was a dancer and planned to teach drama. But after graduating from Boston University in 1966, she instead decided to tour the world as a flight attendant for Pan American World Airways.

Two years into this vocation, she got married, which in those days essentially meant forced retirement from the airline. Dater hopped on over to a temporary employment agency that specialized in helping former stewardesses find new careers.

"They sent me to Wall Street working for Lehman Brothers," she recalls. "The first year on the job I sat in Bobby Lehman's office answering phones. He was ill at this point, and I talked to his estate lawyer every day. His lawyer told me I should consider a career in this business. I spent a few days on the trading desk with a couple of high-pressure institutional salespeople and really got into it." Before long, she was working for the department full-time, picking up some accounting and economics courses at night.

As luck would have it, Dater began her adventure in investing right at the peak of a roaring bull market. "I then had the unique opportunity of spending the next 11 or 12 years waiting for the next one to come around," she quips. "It got pretty rough in the mid-1970s." Dater left Lehman Brothers in 1971 to become an assistant portfolio manger at Fiduciary Trust Company. "I worked my way up to the research department, where I became an analyst," she says. "I developed a fair amount of expertise in the area of media communications, which was a very under-followed industry at that point. There was this funny little business called cable just starting up to help improve the reception of TV signals. I was one of the first people to cover that industry."

By the time she left Fiduciary Trust to join Warburg Pincus in 1978, a year after becoming a panelist on *Wall $treet Week,* she was a vice president. "When I joined Warburg Pincus as a securities analyst, it was very small with only $300 million under management. As there were only a few of us here, I viewed it as a real entrepreneurial opportunity, which is why I made the switch." Warburg Pincus's roots are in venture capital, a market Dater was no stranger to. Many of the media companies she followed were little more than tiny upstarts when she began covering them. Today she heads up Warburg's small-cap and postventure capital effort and also runs a few mutual funds.

Occupation: Managing Director, Warburg Pincus Asset Management
New York, New York

Birth Date: May 13, 1945

Education: BFA, Boston University, 1966

Biggest Mistake Investors Make: "Not sticking to their own investment beliefs."

Best Investment: Affiliated Publications (First bought as an IPO in the early 1970s and ultimately made 30 to 40 times her original investment.)

Worst Investment: WPP Group (Purchased in 1988 for $12 and wound up selling out for around $3 a few months later.)

Advice: "Stick to your investment philosophy and don't sell good companies too early."

Market Outlook: Bullish

DAVID DREMAN

Dreman Value Management

When it comes to being unconventional, David Dreman doesn't mind being at the head of the class and even sails around in a yacht aptly named *The Contrarian.* It's an instinct Dreman says he likely inherited from his 89-year-old father. "He was always sort of a natural contrarian, so the instinct came very naturally," he says. Dreman grew up watching his dad work at his small investment and commodities firm in Winnipeg, Manitoba. There was never any question in Dreman's mind when he was growing up that he would one day be a professional stock picker.

After graduating with a business degree, he worked for his father for several years trading stocks on the Toronto exchange before coming to the United States in search of more excitement. "The American markets seemed to be much broader and volatile, which created more opportunity," he reflects. "I thought they were more interesting because the Canadian market was primarily composed of industrial and mining stocks. I came here for what I thought would be a one-year look at the U.S. markets and I've been here ever since."

Dreman started out as a research analyst and later senior editor with Value Line before becoming an investment officer with the brokerage firm J&W Seligman. He finally went out on his own in 1976 and has been practicing his low PE contrarian strategies ever since. "I define a contrarian as someone who buys out-of-favor stocks that are cheap relative to the market," he explains. "Major opportunities almost always come at times when markets are panicky. That's when major money can be made. We seem to have one crisis or another every two or three years." Dreman attempts to profit from the doom-and-gloom predictions that he figures are a bunch of nonsense. For example, he made a lot of money in 1990 when analysts began bad-mouthing the banks. Then, when the threat of health care reform emerged and the White House began trashing the pharmaceutical companies in 1993, Dreman scooped up shares at around eight times earnings.

Dreman's father always told him the consensus of the experts was usually wrong. That's why he believes his contrarian strategy works so well. "One of the most important things to money managers is finely tuned earnings estimates," he observes. "What I've found in my research is that the chance of an analyst being within a plus or minus 5 percent range of his or her estimate in 20 quarters is 1 in 100 billion. It shows you how this is a loser's game." Contrarians, on the other hand, don't try to forecast the future precisely. If anything, they take advantage of the fact that earnings surprises create temporary havoc with good stocks.

A low price-earnings ratio is important to Dreman because studies show inexpensive stocks perform best over time. That's why he begins his search for companies by running a computer screen that brings names selling at below-market PE ratios to his attention. "I also want an above-average dividend yield and good fundamentals," he adds. "I'm trying to buy companies that are likely to increase earnings at an above-average rate relative to the S&P 500 for the foreseeable future." Dreman says right now value stocks are as cheap relative to growth as they have been in a generation.

It's no surprise that this contrarian often finds his best ideas after reading about some impending disaster. "I love bad news from a good stock that isn't permanent," he reveals. "I like to exploit the market's overreaction. But I won't touch a company that has really serious problems. I'm looking for a crisis that I believe the Street and analysts have overreacted to and is not as serious as it looks at first glance." Once he buys a stock, Dreman sets a moving target based on valuation. "I'll sell a stock when it reaches a market multiple," he says. "I'll also get rid of it if the economic conditions change and I see bad times ahead or am wrong in my fundamental analysis. Finally, if a stock doesn't work out over a three- to four-year period, I'll sell."

In addition to managing the Kemper Dreman High Return Fund, Dreman oversees some $5.5 billion in private and institutional money. He has written several books on investing and is a regular columnist for *Forbes*. He spends much of the year working out of his home in Aspen, Colorado, although his official headquarters are in New Jersey. "The markets are like a 19th century battlefield," he says. "There's smoke and you're masked in an enormous amount of contradictory information. It requires good decision making, and there's a lot of tension. Most people seem to buckle in. I love it."

Occupation: Founder and Chairman, Dreman Value Management LLC
Jersey City, New Jersey

Birth Date: May 6, 1936

Education: Bachelor of Commerce, University of Manitoba, 1957

Biggest Mistake Investors Make: "Abandoning their discipline at precisely the wrong time."

Best Investment: Capital One Financial (Bought it for $1 in 1990, and it is now worth around $180.)

Worst Investment: King's Department Store (The stock went from $12 to $1 about 15 years ago.)

Advice: "Stick to your discipline. Also realize you don't have to take big risks to make money. You're better off buying a good diversified portfolio of safe, blue chip stocks than trying to hit the ball out of the park."

Market Outlook: Bearish on growth, but bullish on value stocks. "I think we're in the middle of a bubble," he says.

HAROLD EVENSKY

Evensky, Brown and Katz

Harold Evensky believes most mutual funds charge too much for mediocre performance and he's doing something about it. Evensky is one of 13 members of the Alpha Group, a consortium of financial advisers from around the country. The Alpha Group is using its muscle and proxy voting power to pressure fund companies to cut costs. "We'll reject managers solely on the basis of high fees," Evensky boasts. "The reason it hasn't been more of an issue [for everyone else] until now is because returns have been so high that no one has noticed how much they were paying."

Evensky is a true pioneer in the field of financial planning. After a short stint running his own construction company, he became a stockbroker some 20 years ago and found he wasn't very good at cold calling to round up clients. "I read about financial planning, which was something brand-new back then," he recalls. "I enrolled in a program to learn about it and started giving seminars on financial planning to develop my business." He soon decided to target more sophisticated and wealthy clients, though his employers weren't comfortable with how he did business. So in 1985 he rejoined his old partner from the construction business and went out on his own.

"Our firm was opened as a financial-planning practice," Evensky explains. "We set up our own broker-dealer in order to maintain total control and flexibility. We did big, multi-hundred-page comprehensive plans for a very substantial fee and then implemented them on a commission basis." When discount broker Charles Schwab introduced a program allowing independent planners to trade no-load mutual funds with minimal transaction costs, Evensky switched over and became a totally fee-based adviser, charging his clients a percentage of their assets under management instead of a load or commission. "We are not money managers," he says. "We hire money managers [usually through mutual funds]. Our focus is on the asset allocation, not the selection process."

Once Evensky and his staff prepare a plan, they begin the process of finding the right funds by looking for managers who invest in specific asset classes. He uses both index and managed funds, although he now weights index funds more heavily than before. "We use active managers in areas where we believe there's a possibility they'll outperform net of costs and fees, namely in small-cap growth and international," he says.

When it comes to active funds, Evensky doesn't like eclectic managers who are willing to buy anything. "We also don't look at specialty funds," he confides. "The managers at specialty funds tend to be the newest ones. It's where they're put to try their teeth. We generally don't want managers with huge concentrations in any one area, and we stay away from domestic managers with excessive foreign positions."

Next, he eliminates all candidates with high fees and consistently poor performance. "We avoid those in the bottom half of their asset class for the last five years or the bottom third for the last three years," he notes. "Our experience says if they've been that consistently close to the bottom, they'll probably stay there." He then checks to see if the fund has grown too large, if it's run by a manager with a trackable record, and whether it has a high degree of turnover (which he doesn't like). "In addition, we absolutely, irrevocably avoid what I call the *Money* magazine fund of the last ten minutes," he emphasizes. "We think that is a guaranteed solution for buying high and selling low."

As a final step, Evensky will often consult with members of his Alpha Group, who take turns interviewing potential managers. "We're looking for commitment, brains, and passion. We reject what we consider to be pomposity, simplicity, and marketing hype," he says.

The financial-planning profession has come a long way since Evensky joined it, especially over the last few years. "We've seen amazing growth in this industry," he observes. "The industry has gone through a huge amount of turbulence. But the end result is that the people who have stayed in it and those who are entering it today tend to have a very serious commitment to the concept and philosophy of planning as a process."

Occupation: Partner, Evensky, Brown & Katz
Coral Gables, Florida

Birth Date: September 9, 1942

Education: BA, Cornell University, 1965
MA, Cornell University, 1967

Biggest Mistake Investors Make: "Not knowing what they want to accomplish and not having an investment plan."

Best Investment: Marrying his partner Deena Katz.

Worst Investment: Managers Intermediate Mortgage Fund (Bought it four years ago and when interest rates spiked up, he lost 15 percent of his money.)

Advice: "Make a plan before you invest."

Market Outlook: Cautious

AL FRANK

The Prudent Speculator

Al Frank isn't afraid to admit he's a naturally cheap guy. "I'll still go to a discount gas station a mile away to save three or four cents a gallon," he concedes. "I like to get things on sale, and when I travel, I always look for the lowest fare." Frank traces his frugality back to his childhood. Both of his parents were uneducated tailors who never had a lot of cash.

As a youngster, Frank was bored with homework and wanted to do nothing more with his life than work at a print shop. "I had no intention of going to college," he admits. "I was a mediocre student. I graduated in the lowest quartile of my high school class." But because many of his classmates enrolled at Los Angeles City College, Frank decided to join them. "It was the best educational institution I ever attended," he contends. "I was still planning to be a printer and thought I'd take a business major for two years to learn how to run my print shop. But after one semester, I decided I didn't want to be a business major after all." Frank transferred to UCLA with dreams of becoming a cinematographer. He practically flunked out and enlisted in the Army instead. After his discharge, he hitchhiked to New York, working briefly for the *New York Times.* He then married his first wife and came back to California to earn a bachelor's degree at UC Berkeley. Next, he moved to Las Vegas, then back to New York, and over to Europe before returning to California to get two master's degrees at California State University, Los Angeles. At the same time, he worked on a PhD at UCLA.

Frank is unquestionably a man who loves adventure. But his search for what to do with his life ended one day after his mentor at UCLA introduced him to the stock market. He quickly developed a passion for it. "I was studying the stock market while working as an assistant professor," he recalls. "In 1977 one of my friends suggested that I write an investment newsletter, and another wanted me to manage money. I decided to register with the SEC and started *The Pinchpenny Speculator,* which is the original name of *The Prudent Speculator.*" It was just a hobby at first. Frank mailed out around 100 letters and managed some $65,000. That all changed in 1983, when *The Hulbert Financial Digest* crowned his publication the year's number-one performer. "All of a sudden I had 1,000 subscribers and then 6,000," he exclaims. "Before long, I was grossing $2 million a year." Everything was going great until the crash of 1987. Frank was fully margined, and his model portfolio lost more than 55 percent of its value that year. "I personally had a $2 million portfolio," he recalls with dread. "After the crash, it was worth $400,000. I made the money back in two years, but most of the subscribers I lost never returned."

Frank now works out of his home in Santa Fe, New Mexico, and maintains an office in Laguna Beach, California, where his partner, John Buckingham, does most of the actual stock research these days. He also has his own mutual fund. Frank follows about 850 companies at any given time and pays close attention to such fundamental factors as price-to-book value, price-to-cash flow, price-to-sales, and PE ratios along with debt and return on equity. "In the beginning, when I was doing this myself, I just used *Barron's*. Twenty years ago you could find stocks selling for six times earnings, 60 percent of book value, and yielding 6 percent," he remembers. "They were called 'The Triple Sixes.'"

His computerized database is much more sophisticated now but stocks that cheap are hard to find in today's market. Nevertheless, Frank's overriding goal remains the same: to uncover stocks that he expects to double within three to five years. "Once I spot a company that looks promising, I send for 10-Ks and 10-Qs," he adds. "I then estimate a value for each stock, and if the current selling price is below 50 percent of my target, it's a buy." Frank rarely visits a company or talks with management. "I've never found a chief executive who didn't see the problems at his corporation as anything but opportunity," he notes. Frank is a big believer in diversification and has learned a lot from studying the work of his mentor, Benjamin Graham. "His was one of the first books I ever read," Frank reveals. "Graham's idea that you should buy undervalued stocks because they provide a cushion of safety was very impressive to me." And even though these value techniques haven't really paid off in recent years, Frank is convinced value stocks will make a comeback. "People are buying hopes and dreams in this market," he insists. Frank readily admits that about 30 percent of the stocks he recommends are never profitable. "But the other 70 percent range from barely profitable to exceptionally profitable," he claims.

Occupation: Publisher, *The Prudent Speculator*
Laguna Beach, California

Birth Date: April 19, 1930

Education: BA, UC Berkeley, 1956
MA, California State University, Los Angeles, 1962–1965

Biggest Mistake Investors Make: "Being impatient, panicking out before the market realizes the value of a corporation, and not doing your homework."

Best Investment: SunAmerica (Bought for a split-adjusted 38¢ a share in 1980 and sold for $50 in 1997.)

Worst Investment: A couple of savings and loans that were forced out of business and went down to zero in the 1980s.

Advice: "Realize that if you have a good system, you'll be right about your investment decisions around 75 percent of the time. But if you're right just two out of four times, you'll make a great return."

Market Outlook: Bullish

SETH GLICKENHAUS

Glickenhaus & Co.

At the age of 85, Seth Glickenhaus has lost his faith in his fellowman. "I used to believe this country was more than ready for democracy," he says. "Now I realize people shouldn't be allowed to vote without passing a test on the major issues of the day. They're not electing the right people. The present system is an utter abomination." As further proof, he points out that the stock market usually goes up every time Congress adjourns. But Glickenhaus certainly isn't apathetic. He gets involved whenever possible, supports medical research, and helps the downtrodden. He feels many of our current problems have been caused by a general "dumbing down" of America. "The school systems in our big cities have deteriorated," he says. "The rest have been forced to simply prepare children for exams rather than how to think."

At an age when most people do very little, Glickenhaus prides himself on constantly keeping busy. He still works full-time at his New York investment firm, which is regarded as one of the country's top value shops. This colorful manager once had dreams of becoming a medical doctor. But after graduating from Harvard some 66 years ago, he was convinced by Herbert Salomon of Salomon Brothers to give up a chance to go to law school in favor of working as a broker. "I agreed to take a job with him for three months on the condition that if it didn't work out, I'd go back to school," Glickenhaus recalls. "It worked out, but I left in 1938 because I was generating about $25,000 a week in profits for the firm, though they were paying me just $48."

He managed to earn his law degree by going to night school and went on to work for a little brokerage shop that folded a few months after he joined it. "The owner was a dipsomaniac," Glickenhaus contends. He first thought it served him right for leaving what could have been a cushy future at Salomon. But then Glickenhaus and one of his colleagues had an idea. They convinced the defunct brokerage shop's principals to let them take over, after promising to return the $25,000 the principals had invested in the company. "They agreed, and in a few months we had paid them back and turned it into our own firm," he recalls. "We ran it through 1946, although I went off to war for a while, and my partner took over until I came back." That was when Glickenhaus started what, in effect, was the first hedge fund. "If someone had invested $10,000 with us, by the time we wound the fund up 13 years later, that person would have walked away with something on the order of $300,000."

Glickenhaus made out much better as he and his partner were entitled to 50 percent of the fund's profits. At that point, Glickenhaus was a multimillionaire and figured his performance so far would be a tough act to follow. Glickenhaus next decided to finally pursue his dream of becoming a medical doctor at the age of 46. "I did my premed work at Columbia and was admitted to the Einstein Medical School," he says. "The lure of Wall Street got to me again. I quit school and started my own firm, Glickenhaus & Co. All I did at first was trade for my own account. This went on for about ten years."

Then some rich friends asked him to manage their retirement accounts, and he agreed. Since that time in 1972, his firm has grown to overseeing some $6 billion. He's developed an impressive record that has placed him among the top 1 percent of all investment managers in the nation.

Glickenhaus calls himself a cautious investor who is more concerned about downside risk than the quality of earnings. "When I look for a stock, I want to find outstanding management," he reveals. "I'm also very price conscious. I love overlooked companies that have come down in value for one reason or another that I feel is invalid. I also like companies with a lot of cash flow that will be used to buy back the stock." Furthermore, he seeks out names that are either industry leaders or low-cost producers, and he wants to buy them for less than their intrinsic value or for what a reasonable person would pay for the entire business. "I look for stocks selling for very low price-earnings multiples," he adds. "I also examine a company's dividend policy and profit margins."

Glickenhaus deals almost exclusively with large-cap stocks. He has several strict sales rules. "Let's assume I buy a stock and I think its price is going to go up 80 percent in two years," he offers. "If its price does go up that much and it's not a bargain any more, I'll sell it. Another reason for selling is if a stock goes up too much too fast; I'll get rid of it to avoid losing my gain."

Occupation: Senior Partner, Glickenhaus & Co.
New York, New York

Birth Date: March 12, 1914

Education: BA, Harvard College, 1934
LLB, New York University Law School, 1938

Biggest Mistake Investors Make: "Managing their own funds without professional guidance."

Best Investment: Chrysler (Bought when Lee Iacocca first came on board.)

Worst Investment: An environmental company (he forgets the name) that went from $23 to zero in 1994.

Advice: "Carefully research your investments and pay attention to downside risk. Also, beware of current trends."

Market Outlook: Bearish

MICHAEL HIRSCH

Advest

Although Michael Hirsch recently went to work for a broker-dealer, he still thinks people are better off investing in mutual funds than in individual stocks. "The markets are getting more volatile and owning a portfolio of stocks simply does not provide the necessary diversification from my perspective," he says. "A portfolio of individual stocks is just too risky. And even though I work for a brokerage firm, I still say what I've said for 25 years: Who would you rather have picking stocks for you? A commissioned salesman or a portfolio manager who only earns money if the value of his or her portfolio goes up?"

Hirsch is gratified to see that much of the investing public seems to agree with him, judging from the amount of cash flooding into funds. He was investing in funds long before they were popular. "I started managing money in funds in 1975 and remember getting a 45-minute interview with the assistant pension officer at Chrysler to convince him to let me manage some of its money," he recalls. "I spent the first 30 minutes explaining what a mutual fund was. He had no idea."

Hirsch was also one of the first to show the world how to build an entire portfolio using nothing but carefully selected funds. "I saw what was happening with the market, even in the 1970s, in terms of volatility and whatnot, and realized funds were an efficient way to diversify," he says. His underlying thesis was that because institutional investors constantly change their preferences for sectors and styles, one must be ready to shift around at any time. In this environment, funds offer the most flexibility. When Hirsch started out, there were just 125 funds. Today, by some counts there are more than 12,000 funds in the United States alone. "There are too many in my opinion," he contends. "Funds are becoming like commodities, and that confuses the hell out of the public. It's become so bad that people truly need professional help. I think the same due diligence investors always had to perform on individual stocks is now required for mutual funds as well."

Before joining Advest in early 1999, Hirsch managed the FundManager family of mutual funds. These are mutual funds that invest in other funds based on a given objective. The idea behind these instruments is that investors can buy just one fund and let a manager put together a complete portfolio. "It's a trend that's really catching on. There is even a fund-of-funds association," he notes. "Mutual funds are the way to go because the markets are moving more rapidly, and the individual has no way to effectively compete with the institutions by going directly into stocks. What bothers me is the naiveté that's out there. The problem is that most people are new to funds and expect the market to keep going up. They have unrealistic expectations and will bail out at the first sign of trouble."

When choosing funds, Hirsch always prefers the tortoise to the hare. "Slow and steady wins the race," he maintains. "I get nervous when one of my funds winds up in the top 10 percent." He looks at what he calls his "three Ps" when evaluating funds: performance, people, and the process. "I want consistent performance over the long term, not spectacular performance over the near term," he explains. "If you only look at funds that have stayed in the top half of their peer group for the last three years, that will knock out 90 percent of all candidates."

Next he looks at the people. "I like funds run by individuals, not committees," he says. "I believe investing is an art, not a science. You can't paint the Mona Lisa by committee. I want strong-willed individuals with demonstrated investment management talents who are putting their reputations on the line each day." He also seeks fund managers who can describe their investment style and discipline in 25 words or less, and he demands that they do their own research instead of depending on analysts from other brokerage firms. "People who rely primarily on third-party research are doomed to mediocrity," he insists.

The final "P" is the process. "I have to satisfy myself that each manager is bringing a different area of expertise to the totality of my clients' portfolios," he says. "I don't look at labels. I look at the investment approach. That's how you build in the downside protection, because any particular investment will fail at some point." Hirsch maintains one of the main differences between managers who oversee private money and those with funds is that a fund manager's record is on public display each day. Private managers are accountable only to their clients, and even then it's not always clear-cut how well they are doing. "

Hirsch works out of both New York and Israel. His wife and two youngest children live in Tel Aviv, and Hirsch regularly commutes between both locations.

Occupation: Portfolio Manager, Lynvest Group at Advest
New York, New York

Birth Date: February 7, 1945

Education: BA, Brooklyn College, 1966

Biggest Mistake Investors Make: "Going for yesterday's hot fund. Novice investors look at who has the best record over the past few months and blindly rush in."

Best Investment: He won't say to avoid offending any of his past or present fund managers.

Worst Investment: He won't reveal this one for the same reason.

Advice: "Invest for the long term. Buy a good basket of funds and stick with them."

Market Outlook: Very cautious

SHELDON JACOBS

The No-Load Fund Investor

Sheldon Jacobs has made a career of forecasting. In an earlier life, he spent 25 years predicting which shows people would watch on television for both ABC and NBC. Now he predicts which mutual funds will perform best in the future. He also has a forecast for how long the seemingly nonstop growth of the mutual fund industry will continue. "Until the next bear market comes along," he says. "Then we'll probably get a fairly sizable amount of consolidation."

One reason Americans are in love with funds, Jacobs surmises, is because there's really no better financial alternative available right now. "Real estate returns were great through the 1970s and part of the 1980s, but that's not true anymore [in many parts of the country]," he explains. "In a real sense, the stock market's the only game in town."

Jacobs first discovered no-load funds in the early 1970s, while working in television. He was instantly hooked. He went on to write his first book, *Put Your Money in Your Pocket,* in 1974 and began publishing a quarterly no-load fund newsletter from his kitchen table five years later as a sort of hobby. When the bull market took off in 1982, Jacobs walked into his boss's office at NBC, just four years shy of his scheduled retirement, and quit his job. His new mission in life was to teach others how to successfully invest in funds. His *No-Load Fund Investor* newsletter now has around 18,000 subscribers. He also publishes two annual mutual fund guides and manages some $400 million in discretionary accounts along with partner Bob Brinker, host of the popular ABC radio weekend program *Moneytalk.*

Jacobs is clearly a big believer in funds. "I own only one individual stock, and I'm a professional in this field," he maintains. He notes that funds have two distinct advantages: diversification and professional management. There is, however, one exception to his all-fund rule. "You should buy equities through a mutual fund unless you know more about a stock than Wall Street does," he offers. That doesn't mean getting a hot tip from a broker or the Internet. Instead, he's referring to the inside information one gains through working for a particular company or industry. As he puts it, "Everybody owns IBM, so there's no edge for the individual investor. There's only one negative to buying mutual funds instead of individual stocks. You can't control the tax situation. You're at the mercy of when the portfolio manager decides to take his capital gains. Other than that, I don't think there's any reason to buy individual stocks." He also argues that almost everyone should have a significant equity component in his or her portfolio. "If you're wealthy and don't need the money, you should keep a minimum of 60 to 70 percent in stocks, no matter what your age," he insists.

Jacobs admits that funds are less advantageous as a vehicle for purchasing Treasuries, although he believes junk bonds should always be bought through funds because of the diversification they provide.

What's the best way for investors to select individual funds? "You start with past performance, then you adjust it for other factors, such as where you think the market's going, which stock groups will be hot, the size of the fund, things like that," he says. "You've got to get beyond the numbers." But Jacobs admits it was a lot easier for him to pinpoint which television shows would be popular in his former career than picking which funds will act best in the future. "If I just had to do a guesstimate, I could have probably made a run-of-the-mill prediction on television audiences with an error rate of maybe 2 or 3 percent," he says. "On mutual funds, if I get within 25 percent, I'm doing great."

Jacobs concedes he failed to predict how enormously popular funds would become when he entered the business full-time in 1979. "I bought an existing newsletter when I started *The No-Load Fund Investor*," he recalls. "The man who sold it to me said that the mutual fund newsletter would never be as big as his other publication, which focused on stocks, because more people buy stocks than funds. He was wrong. I think funds are the only sane way to go. If you do it on your own now, you're competing against all of these professionals. It makes more sense just to hire them. Plus, they'll do a better job. Over and above their picking prowess, they'll diversify properly, and they'll be there every day."

Although he expects to see a bear market or two along the way, Jacobs predicts the market's future direction from here will remain up. As for his own career, he's only willing to look out for the next three years or so. "I've been telling everybody that I'll consider retirement in the year 2001," he says. "But I honestly don't have any firm plans either way right now."

Occupation: Publisher and Editor, *The No-Load Fund Investor*
Irvington-on-Hudson, New York

Birth Date: January 29, 1931

Education: BA, University of Nebraska, 1952
MBA, New York University, 1955

Biggest Mistake Investors Make: "Not taking enough risk."

Best Investment: Mutual Shares (Recommended in the first issue of his newsletter in 1979 and held on until manager Michael Price left in 1998.)

Worst Investment: "I can't remember any major disasters."

Advice: "Diversify."

Market Outlook: Bullish

LARRY JEDDELOH

The Institutional Strategist

Although Larry Jeddeloh might not be a household name, his buy and sell recommendations determine how some $70 billion dollars are invested. Jeddeloh provides research to more than 100 institutions around the world, including Deutsche Bank, Mitsubushi Banking, and William Blair & Co. He advises portfolio managers on everything from how to allocate money among various countries and currencies to which individual stocks look most promising. Even though he focuses on companies of all sizes, he's especially fond of smaller stocks, which provide more opportunity because they're covered by fewer analysts.

Jeddeloh began investing in the stock market as a college student during the 1973–74 bear market. "I remember the Dow was down to around 575," he says. "I used to load trucks at night to pay my way through school and started talking to this guy at work. He told me he bought Braniff at half of book value. I thought that might be interesting, so I went out and bought Braniff too. The thing doubled in about a month when the market rallied. I thought this was the greatest thing I'd ever seen. I was hooked."

He took a job as a broker for four years following graduation before deciding to get an MBA. He also began teaching two college courses on investing. "The more I got into the theoretical side of the market, the more I grew interested in it," he reflects. "After getting my MBA, I was given the opportunity to become an analyst for a Minneapolis institutional research firm called the Leuthold Group." Jeddeloh stayed there for seven years before responding to an ad in the *Financial Times* to become chief strategist for the Union Bank of Switzerland in Zurich. "I had developed an interest in international investing, and you couldn't learn it here in Minneapolis because no one was doing it," he says. After a two-year stint overseas, he came back and ran the investment advisory division of a Minnesota bank before founding The Institutional Strategist in 1995. "Primarily what we do is institutional research," he notes. "It's both global in nature and United States–oriented. We don't sell our work to the public." One-third of Jeddeloh's business comes from big banks in Europe, a market on which he's very bullish. He spends at least four months of the year traveling around the world and also manages money for some individuals and pension plans.

Jeddeloh and his team of researchers prepare reports showing not only where they think the economy and various stocks markets are going but also which stocks appear to be the most attractive. "I like companies that are relatively underfollowed and out of favor," he points out. His theory is that if you buy companies that are ignored by other analysts, their share prices will move dramatically higher once they're discovered. He's usually willing to wait about six months for this to happen.

Most of Jeddeloh's recommendations usually sport low PE ratios and sell below book value. "I like to buy earnings growth at a discount," he explains. "I also want to see a theme or story surrounding the stock. That's because stocks can be cheap and stay cheap for a very long time. There has to be some catalyst to get them to move. I look for stocks that have all of these characteristics but also some imminent change that will make the valuation increase."

Before a stock gets his nod, he likes to talk with company executives, customers, suppliers, and competitors. In addition, he wants to get a good price but one not too good to be true. "I don't buy stocks that are down 50 to 60 percent just because they're down," he cautions. "A lot of those things will keep right on falling. So I use a quick technical check to make sure the stocks are stabilizing on the chart." His institutional customers tend to follow his recommendations very closely, and he admittedly often moves the market.

Jeddeloh recommends selling either when earnings disappoint or there is a fundamental change in the company. "I don't sell just because the price has gone up," he emphasizes. "Sometimes I'll hold a stock for four or five years, maybe even longer."

Jeddeloh contends that small investors now have the best opportunity in years to profit from buying individual stocks. "The institutions manage so much money that they're limited as to what they can buy," he insists. "The little guy can purchase smaller, underresearched companies that are ignored by the institutions. In addition, they can be nimble and take advantage of price discrepancies. For instance, they get opportunities to buy large-cap stocks at bargain prices from time to time when the big guys bail out, thus artificially depressing prices. Once the institutions are finished selling, those quality blue chip companies are often left flat on their pants for a week or two, enabling you to pick them up on the cheap."

Occupation: President, The Institutional Strategist
Minneapolis, Minnesota

Birth Date: November 15, 1952

Education: BS, St. Thomas University, 1977
MBA, St. Thomas University, 1989

Biggest Mistake Investors Make: "Not taking a long enough perspective."

Best Investment: Apple Computer (Bought it in the late 1980s and quadrupled his money in less than four years.)

Worst Investment: Computervision (Also purchased in the late 1980s; paid $40 a share and finally sold out for $12 within one year.)

Advice: "Take a long-term global perspective, and know what you own."

Market Outlook: Cautious

KEVIN LANDIS

Firsthand Funds

 Will the recent boom in technology stocks soon come to an abrupt end or keep going on forever? "I think it will be somewhere in between those two extremes," says Kevin Landis, who manages three technology mutual funds. "It's still likely to be a great place to invest for a number of years." In fact, if your investment horizon is 20 years or more, Landis believes most of your money should be in technology stocks. "I would advise you to put all you have the stomach for in this sector," he offers. "Technology in general is such a strong proposition that it just has to keep moving forward. You're creating new ways to make people's life better every day."

Landis was born and raised in California's Silicon Valley, home to many of the world's leading high-tech companies. He studied electrical engineering and computer science in college before getting his MBA and landing a job as a semiconductor analyst for a technology-oriented market research firm. "I learned how to rigorously analyze fast-changing markets," he says. "But I got itchy to dive back into technology. So I went to work for a chip company called S-MOS as their new products marketing manager."

While at S-MOS, Landis began dabbling in stocks on the side and soon realized he was making more money from trading than working for a living. "I determined my true calling was to be investing in technology," he claims. "So I left S-MOS in the summer of 1993, and my partner and I started this new company." His partner, Ken Kam, owned a medical device company and was also new to the investment management business. The two have been friends ever since forming an investment club together in 1987. "Stock picking had been a passion of ours for many years," Landis says. "We sat down over Christmas at the end of 1992 and decided to start an investment firm. It took a while for us to get up and running as neither of us had any direct experience in the industry."

Because the two wanted to make their investment services available to a large number of professionals in the technology field, they decided to launch a mutual fund. Their fledgling company, now called Firsthand Funds, has grown into a family of four funds specializing in both electronic and medical technology. Landis manages those on the electronics side, while Kam is in charge of picking medical stocks. One of Landis's funds is committed to seeking value technology stocks; another, industry leaders; and the third, fast-growing smaller companies.

Unlike most technology managers, who are willing to pay dizzying multiples for fast-growing companies, Landis compares himself to the likes of Warren Buffett and Peter Lynch. "I favor companies with substantial growth prospects but want to avoid paying high multiples for them," he says. In other words, he wants to buy high growth on the cheap. "I look for securities that are mispriced," Landis explains. "I pay attention to all of the normal value statistics, like price-to-earnings, price-to-sales, and the total market capitalizations for companies that aren't making any money. But it's not only the historical PE that I look at. It's price to what earnings I think the company could make in the foreseeable future. In other words, what will this company earn a few quarters out? The standard for a lot of chip stocks is that you can get 30 times next year's earnings."

Management is also important, although Landis contends that when it comes right down to it, customers don't buy managers or PEs—they buy products. "Companies that demonstrate they can come up with the right products at the right price points at the right time are the real winners," he maintains. "I find my favorite companies and then have a patient eye for value, meaning I will only buy when I can get a stock at the right price." He is also willing to give his investments time to make their products successful.

"There are two good reasons to sell a stock," Landis offers. "One is simple outrageous appreciation to where you can't make a case for buying or even holding it anymore. Another is when you are incorrect in your initial analysis and realize a stock is not worth owning in the first place."

As for those hot high-tech IPOs you've read about over the past few years, Landis tends to stay clear of them unless he can get in for a reasonable price up front. "I value IPOs just like any other stock. If it's a good value today, it should be a good value tomorrow. Therefore, I don't think people should buy IPOs if they're trying to make fast money by "flipping" them for a fast buck on their first day of trading," he insists. "That's silly. It's speculating, not investing."

Occupation: Portfolio Manager, Firsthand Funds, Inc.
San Jose, California

Birth Date: April 28, 1961

Education: BS, University of California at Berkeley, 1983
MBA, Santa Clara University, 1988

Biggest Mistake Investors Make: "Chasing hot tech stocks after everyone has turned euphoric and selling into pessimism or panic."

Best Investment: Applied Micro Circuits (Bought as an $8 IPO in November 1997; it now trades above $40.)

Worst Investment: Silicon Valley Research (Purchased in 1996 for $4 to $5, and it dropped down to $1 within a few months.)

Advice: "Expect mood swings in the market, especially with technology stocks, and take advantage of them."

Market Outlook: Bullish

VIVIAN LEWIS

Global Investing

Vivian Lewis once lived a life most journalists dream about. She was a foreign correspondent who covered stories throughout Western Europe during the 1960s and 1970s. During that time, she lived in London, Brussels, and France. Like most who wind up in glamorous jobs like this, she got into the business by accident. After graduating with a history degree from Radcliffe in 1962 at the age of 20, she planned on a career in academia. "I got married to a foreign correspondent while I was working on my PhD thesis, and we ran out of money," she explains. "I didn't think a married woman should ask for tuition assistance from her dad, so I took a job with *Business Week* as an office assistant. A year and a half later, I was bureau chief in Brussels."

When Lewis got pregnant with her first child, the magazine immediately fired her. "When I say this today, people ask why I didn't sue them," she says. "They told me if I sued them I would never get another job in journalism, and I believed them. I was scared to make waves about being treated badly." Fortunately, she managed to land on her feet and went to work for such publications as *The Economist* and the *Institutional Investor,* writing about foreign companies and the financial markets. The magazines were thrilled to have her on retainer because she was stationed overseas, which saved them from paying her travel expenses.

"When my husband was posted back in the United States by his employer, the *New York Times,* 11 years ago, I went sashaying into the *Institutional Investor* offices and said, 'Hi, I'm here.' Their faces dropped. I told them this was their opportunity to make use of my brilliant European connections in the United States. They replied, 'We're not going to send you to Europe and let you run up expense accounts. It was great having you write for us while you were over there and we could get you cheap, but now it's a different story.'" Lewis looked in the mirror and realized she was in her 40s and not immediately employable. "The reason I started *Global Investing* is because I decided there was a niche in the market and I needed a job," she admits. "I was covering this stuff for the institutional market but wanted to cover it for U.S. retail investors who were not, and still are not, being given any information about internationalizing their portfolios."

Global Investing is a monthly newsletter that highlights select foreign stocks that trade as ADRs in the United States. "ADR stands for American depositary receipt," Lewis points out. "These investment vehicles were invented in the period right after the first World War for a specific purpose—for foreign-based companies to raise money on U.S. capital markets. Shares of securities from these overseas companies are deposited in a foreign bank, and a U.S. bank creates a certificate to prove they are there. You then trade the receipts, which settle in the United States under the same system as U.S. stocks." Lewis still takes about ten trips a year to uncover new ideas. She spends most of her time in Europe, which she knows well. She also has a team of freelance stringers from around the world who contribute stories and ideas to her publication.

Although Lewis is a big advocate of foreign investing, she cautions against buying shares directly through overseas markets instead of using ADRs. "Most people do not have custodial accounts on foreign exchanges," she reasons. "If you want to buy foreign stocks rather than ADRs, there are all kinds of obstacles for retail investors. The minimum trades are much higher in foreign markets, and they don't like limit orders. Plus, you don't get 1099s or the same kind of information regarding quarterly and annual results as you do with the ADRs. You're also not treated as well when it comes to rights offerings and stock splits."

Admittedly, it's not easy getting good information about a company in another country when you live thousands of miles away. That's why Lewis, who speaks several foreign languages, calls evaluating ADRs more of an art than a science. "For one thing, you should know more about the country and other stocks in the industry when considering a foreign stock," she advises. But why take such risks? Isn't it a hassle to research and find foreign companies? Wouldn't it be better to just keep your portfolio invested in U.S. stocks that you could keep a close eye on? "No," Lewis insists. "You shouldn't put all of your eggs in one basket. Two-thirds of the stocks in the world are outside the United States. It's idiotic to ignore them. I think people should have one-quarter to one-third of their portfolio invested overseas."

Occupation: Publisher, *Global Investing*
New York, New York

Birth Date: June 19, 1951

Education: BA, Radcliffe College, 1962
MA, University of California at Berkeley, 1963

Biggest Mistake Investors Make: "Being too short term–oriented."

Best Investment: The Japan Fund (Bought it while living in Europe throughout the 1980s. Her earliest investments had returns of some 5,000 percent.)

Worst Investment: Tatneft (It's a Russian oil company; she bought the stock in 1998 for $16. When we spoke, it was trading for around $2.50.)

Advice: "Take a long-term view, especially when it comes to foreign investing."

Market Outlook: Bullish on the United States and Japan but cautious on Europe.

BOB MARKMAN

Markman Capital Management

Bob Markman has had a change of heart. Although he once bought the academic argument that to make the best returns over time you need a diversified portfolio, including exposure to both small and large stocks in the United States and overseas, he no longer believes that. "I think people overdiversify," he says. "The whole financial services industry has blown it by recommending so many asset classes. When you own this much stuff, you have no chance of doing well in a bull market and aren't going to be protected in a bear market."

So this Minnesota investment adviser, who specializes in mutual funds, says he's decided to put all of his clients' money in just one part of the market—large company U.S. growth stocks. "A lot of the advice on asset allocation is based on old data and is flawed," Markman insists. "The world this is based on no longer exists. Things have changed. The market is telegraphing this message to us. That's why large companies have done so well in recent years." Markman doesn't like small-cap funds either, because the premise behind them doesn't make sense to him. "They are, by definition, always selling their most promising companies as they grow larger just because they fall out of a certain range in terms of market capitalization," he says. Markman also thinks investors should avoid international and value-oriented funds. "Value stocks are doomed to underperform," he predicts. "The real action in this economy is in the tech end. Almost by definition, a tech stock is never going to be a value stock. The typical growth portfolio has no technology in it."

Lest you think Markman is hitching a ride on the current hot sector of the moment, he insists he plans to keep all of his money in large U.S. multinational growth stocks for "as far as the eye can see, certainly for the rest of my lifetime." He's also bullish on the market for about that same time span. "This is the world we were too embarrassed to even hope for," he exclaims. "Our planet is going through a productivity and technological explosion with hardly any inflation on a global basis. What's more, we have a regulatory environment that's more benign than ever. And even though Washington is using phony numbers, we've got a budget that's basically in balance and likely to go into surplus. Any one of these things could have been the catalyst for a bull market. But we've got them all together at the same time. I don't think anyone can possibly predict how high this market will go."

If all that weren't enough, Markman also notes that the country's demographic makeup favors a continued rise in equity prices for some time to come. "We have this huge bulge of baby boomers moving through their 50s," he observes. "As everybody knows, that's when most people start saving for retirement more aggressively. This is only adding fuel to an already hot fire."

If things had been different, Markman might be managing the futures of some big Hollywood stars instead of mutual fund portfolios. After graduating from Northwestern University, he worked at the William Morris Agency before leaving to pursue a career in advertising. In 1980 he became fascinated with the financial planning field, which was still in its infancy. He took a job selling load funds with Private Ledger. But the idea of charging his customers a commission each time they purchased a fund never made sense to him, especially after the crash of 1987. "It occurred to me that even if someone had shown me *The Wall Street Journal* two weeks in advance, and I could have known there was a crash coming, I couldn't have done anything about it," he reflects. "I had all my clients' money in load funds and didn't have the discretion." That prompted him to go out on his own, managing money through no-load funds on a fee-only basis.

Today, Markman manages around $460 million in both private accounts and three "fund-of-funds"—mutual funds that invest in other funds. The idea behind these investments is that instead of choosing ten different stock funds on your own, for example, you can simply put your money into a fund-of-funds and let the manager research and select the underlying funds for you.

Markman prefers concentrated funds, which generally own less than 30 stocks. Unlike some of his colleagues, Markman spends little time interviewing individual fund managers, although he concedes the person pulling the trigger is important. "It's rare to find a manager who is a real jerk," he reveals. "The benefits of interviewing managers might be outweighed by the risk of falling for a relationship with them."

Occupation: President, Markman Capital Management
Edina, Minnesota

Birth Date: August 30, 1951

Education: BA, Northwestern University, 1973

Biggest Mistake Investors Make: "Not taking enough risk and overdiversifying."

Best Investment: Rydex OTC (It has more than doubled since bought in 1997.)

Worst Investment: Benham European Government Bond Fund (Purchased in September 1992, 48 hours before the European exchange rate mechanism fell apart.)

Advice: "Simplify, cancel your *Wall Street Journal* subscription, and spend more time with your kids."

Market Outlook: Bullish

CAPPY McGARR

McGarr Capital Management

Cappy McGarr enjoys getting involved in politics. He was appointed by President Clinton to the Kennedy Center Board of Trustees and is chairman of Democratic Senator Tom Daschle's leadership political action committee. But he admits he could never run for an elected office himself. "I like making money too much," he says. McGarr makes plenty for the partners of his Dallas-based hedge fund. Since the $220 million fund's founding some 15 years ago, he has showered investors with an annualized return of 28 percent compared with 17.91 percent for the S&P 500. And he's done it without employing some of the exotic strategies used by some of his colleagues. Not bad for a guy from San Angelo, Texas, who had no career goals growing up, let alone a desire to invest.

McGarr wound up on Wall Street almost by accident. He majored in both journalism and government in college but found the jobs he was qualified for didn't pay much. So he went back to school for an MBA and landed a job with Goldman Sachs after graduation. After spending a year in New York, the firm transferred him to Dallas. Four years later, he decided to go into business for himself. Today, it takes at least $1 million to get into his hedge fund.

When he originally went out on his own, McGarr raised money for various private business deals. He launched his fund in 1984. Despite having the freedom to do whatever he wants, McGarr avoids speculating in currencies, commodities, futures, or derivatives. Instead, he invests his concentrated portfolio of 10 to 15 names primarily in large-cap, household-name stocks, which have an average market capitalization of $11 billion. He likes these big companies because of the liquidity they provide.

The most adventurous thing McGarr does is short anywhere from 5 to 40 percent of the portfolio, although he maintains it always makes sense to have a bias toward the long side. "Over time, managements get up every day to make money for their shareholders," he says. "They may execute a wrong strategy, be in a bad business, or be unintelligent. But if they have integrity and are trying to do what's right, the only goal management should have is to increase shareholder value."

McGarr admits hedge funds have been given a bad rap over the past couple of years, especially after the fiasco with Long-Term Capital Management in 1998. But he claims it hasn't impacted his business one bit. "Whenever you pay someone an incentive fee to manage money, as you do in a hedge fund, there is inherent risk associated with that because the manager is always trying to make more money for himself," McGarr explains. "Another problem with some funds is disclosure. I think it's very important for managers to disclose what positions they hold."

McGarr believes earnings are what ultimately drive stock prices, although the people in charge are also important. That's why he checks to make sure the executives of any potential investment have their own personal wealth on the line. "I spend a lot of time looking at management and what they own of their own company," he says. "I want to see what options they have and how much stock they are mandated to own. That's very important because if management owns stock, they're obviously going to have the same interests as the shareholders because *they* are shareholders." McGarr adds that he invests all of his liquid money in his fund.

In addition, a strong financial standing and reasonable share price are essential. "A solid cash flow and earnings growth rate is very important to me," McGarr explains. "If you can find a company selling below its growth rate, by definition you're buying a stock that's cheap. So I obviously try to purchase stocks that are selling below their growth rate. In other words, their PE sells at a discount to their growth rate."

A final requirement for every stock McGarr owns is that it must be a proven leader. "I like companies that have a dominant market share and are number one or two in the areas they deal in," he says. "I find all of this out by constantly pouring over research, reading periodicals, and running computer screens." On the short side, McGarr does intense research looking for companies that are doing something wrong. "I will only short a company outright if its balance sheet doesn't make sense or management is doing something that I don't consider to be forthright," he shares. "I don't do many outright shorts. When I do, I make sure I've done my homework."

Occupation: President, McGarr Capital Management
Dallas, Texas

Birth Date: August 1, 1951

Education: BA, University of Texas at Austin, 1973–1975
MBA, University of Texas at Austin, 1977

Biggest Mistake Investors Make: "Having a lack of patience and investing for the short term."

Best Investment: Dell Computer (Bought in 1990 for under $10 a share and still owns it.)

Worst Investment: PageNet (Purchased in 1996 for $19 and finally sold out several months later for half that amount.)

Advice: "Invest in good companies with outstanding fundamentals for the long term."

Market Outlook: Bullish

PAUL MERRIMAN

Paul A. Merriman & Associates

Unlike most of the other experts in this book, Paul Merriman believes in market timing. But he readily admits it's not a strategy for everyone. "First of all, it's only appropriate in a tax-deferred account," he cautions. "And it's only for people who don't have the risk tolerance to buy and hold." Merriman acknowledges that it's tough for a timer to beat the market, especially without using leverage. However, he claims timing significantly reduces volatility, and the majority of his clients can't stomach dramatic market moves.

Merriman spends plenty of time following the market and updating his timing systems. "I normally get to the office each morning by 4 AM," he tells me. "I've got about 12 hours of work to do every day. On weekends I get up at 3 AM and work for 4 hours on both Saturday and Sunday. The rest of my time is for my family." Merriman has always been a workaholic. He began this hectic schedule about five years ago, after he and his wife adopted a little girl from a Chinese orphanage. It was Merriman's second crack at fatherhood. He spent little time with his two older kids when they were growing up and vowed to do a better job this time around. "I wanted to make sure our new daughter didn't have to compete with my work," he says.

A lifelong entrepreneur, Merriman started his own small importing business in high school. After college, he became a stockbroker, although he didn't keep that job for very long. "I made a lot of money," he says. "I just couldn't deal with the conflicts of interest. You were really in a position where you had to keep pushing stocks. In 1969 I believed stocks were going to tank, and I was right." He left the brokerage industry that same year to start a distribution business and later took over management of a struggling public company, which he successfully turned around. "As I interviewed investment managers to run the profit-sharing plan for our employees, I was introduced to market timing," he reflects. "When I found out no-load funds would allow you to move in and out of the market without commissions or spreads, it was like magic."

That revelation prompted him to build his own money management firm around the concept of using no-loads to time the market. Today, he runs more than $235 million, both through private accounts and a series of "fund-of-fund" market timing mutual funds. He also publishes a monthly newsletter and operates the Internet site www.fundadvice.com, which gives users free timing advice. Everything he does is based around one simple philosophy: "I believe 100 percent in mechanical systems," he explains. "If you're going to beat the market, you cannot let emotions be part of the decision-making process."

He monitors four different trend-following models and traditional moving averages to decide whether to be in or out of the market. "I look at things like the direction of the Nasdaq, up and down volume, the number of new highs and lows, things like that," he says. "The only thing these mechanical models indicate is that once a trend is broken, the odds are it will continue in that direction long enough for you to either sell out your position at a profit or buy it back at a lower price."

The system isn't perfect. In fact, the performance of Merriman's funds has consistently fallen below that of the S&P 500 in recent years. But he claims his strategy works well over time. "From 1965 to 1982, almost any simple trend-following system knocked the socks off a buy-and-hold strategy," he says.

For his market-timing portfolios, Merriman uses both actively managed and leveraged passive funds. "I am looking for those funds with good relative strength," he notes. "This shows me the manager owns those stocks that are moving with the market. I don't care about ten-year performance because I'm only going to be in the market for maybe six months at a time." But when it comes to his buy-and-hold portfolios, Merriman won't buy anything other than index funds. "I honestly can't come up with one argument in favor of actively managed funds for the long haul," he maintains.

In terms of global diversification, Merriman recommends that buy-and-hold investors keep fully one-half of their portfolio invested overseas. "Academics would say you're crazy to keep all of your money in only one country, including the United States," he reasons. "Just look at the Japanese. Don't you think they felt safe in the 1980s? They questioned why anyone would have money in other countries since they had the strongest banks. Look at what happened."

Lest you think working as many hours as Merriman does running your portfolio will pump up your investment returns, think again. "Working harder does not make you more money in this business," he shares. "In fact, studies show that working harder on your investments tends to hurt more than it helps."

Occupation: President, Paul A. Merriman & Associates
Seattle, Washington

Birth Date: October 18, 1943

Education: BA, Western Washington State University, 1966

Biggest Mistake Investors Make: "Not identifying either their need for return or their tolerance for risk. These two things always go together."

Best Investment: Buying a no-load variable annuity for his grandchildren, which he claims will turn $10,000 into $20 million by the time they reach age 65.

Worst Investment: Purchasing stock in three start-up companies in the 1960s, which ultimately failed.

Advice: "Remember, you don't have to take big risks to make big money."

Market Outlook: Cautious

RONALD MUHLENKAMP

Muhlenkamp & Company

Ron Muhlenkamp says investing is a lot like farming. "I was raised on an 80-acre farm in Ohio," he shares. "My six brothers and sisters and I helped my mom and dad raise hogs, corn, soybeans, wheat, oats, and hay. I may be an investment manager now, but I'm still farming. It's just that I farm stocks and bonds instead of corn and soybeans."

As an engineering student at MIT, Muhlenkamp took a few business courses to broaden his education. By the time he graduated, he was married with two kids. He went on to get an MBA at Harvard, intending to gain a better understanding of the production process for the time when he became an engineer. "My goal was to eventually make enough money so I could retire and farm and live the way I wanted to," he says. "I wound up studying marketing and corporate finance at Harvard." When he graduated in 1968, he decided the job offers that came his way weren't very interesting. Muhlenkamp discovered a few of his classmates planned to start an investment firm in New York, and he decided to join them. "I had never owned a stock or bond, nor had I taken any investment courses," he says. "That turned out to be quite an advantage." By the end of their second year in business, Muhlenkamp and his partners had a modest $3 million in assets. Muhlenkamp felt his future potential at the firm was limited, so he left to join the research arm of an insurance company.

In the early 1970s, stocks went down more frequently than they went up. Muhlenkamp made it his job to find out why. "All of the studies up to this point proved that 4.5 percent was a normal interest rate for bonds and 17 was the normal PE for stocks," he remembers. "As PEs went from 17 to 15 to 7, Wall Street analysts kept telling me about stocks they thought were cheap. I'd ask them what the company was worth, and they couldn't tell me. So I did some basic work to arrive at values for companies. I really wrote another chapter from Ben Graham's book, only my chapter showed how evaluation criteria change with inflation. I've used the same stuff ever since, and it's worked beautifully."

In essence, Muhlenkamp concluded that as inflation changes, there is a lag time before the public realizes it. "When we had high inflation and low interest rates in the 1970s, it was a great time to borrow money," he points out. "That trend reversed in roughly 1981, but all through the 1980s people still believed you could make a lot of money buying a big house with a mortgage. They didn't change their mind about that until 1990. Public fears, if you will, set the attitude of the marketplace. Where a guy like me makes money is by exploiting the difference between these fears and reality." In today's environment of stable inflation and interest rates, Muhlenkamp is convinced that stock prices in the coming years will move solely in line with earnings.

Muhlenkamp began his own investment firm in 1978, running private accounts for individuals. He launched a mutual fund in 1988 and now oversees some $300 million. His goal is to provide clients with the best overall total return, regardless of whether that means investing money in stocks or bonds. "To me, inflation is the rate at which your money is shrinking," he says. "What I'm trying to do is make money after taxes and inflation. I have found over the years that if inflation is 3 percent, I'm not interested in owning bonds unless I can get 3 percent over that, or 6 percent. Similarly, I'm not interested in owning stocks unless it looks like I can get a return of 5 or 6 percent over inflation."

Most of the time, Muhlenkamp's money is in equities. One reason he prefers stocks over bonds is that management works for the shareholder and against the creditor. "You don't know of any company executive who owns bond options," he observes. "Can you name a company you'd rather lend money to than own a piece of?" Muhlenkamp won't buy a stock unless it will give him a return on equity (ROE) greater than 15 percent. And he wants to purchase it for a PE ratio below the ROE. "I say I like to buy Pontiacs and Buicks when they go on sale. I don't want to buy Renaults at any price," he says. "The other thing I'll sometimes do is look for clumps of value. For example, in 1990 all of the banks looked cheap. I concluded any bank that didn't go bankrupt was a buy."

While he's primarily interested in the fundamentals, Muhlenkamp, an avid motorcycle enthusiast, often decides to sell based on technical indicators. "I learned a long time ago that you can't find out the bad news in time for it to do you any good," he says. "So I always set price targets. If one of my stocks gets fully priced or stops performing and I can't figure out why, it's usually best to start selling some."

Occupation: President and Portfolio Manager, Muhlenkamp & Company
Wexford, Pennsylvania

Birth Date: February 9, 1944

Education: BS, Massachusetts Institute of Technology, 1966
MBA, Harvard Business School, 1968

Biggest Mistake Investors Make: "Running with the crowd. In other words, buying based on impulse or the fad of the moment instead of on research."

Best Investment: Green Tree Financial (Bought in 1990 for $1.50 per share. It was acquired in 1998 for more than $40.)

Worst Investment: In high school, he put two summers' worth of work money (about $1,100) in an Ohio savings and loan that went bankrupt.

Advice: "Buy stocks the way you would buy a used car. Do your homework, and get something you plan to own for a while. If you wind up with a lemon, sell out and move on."

Market Outlook: Bullish

LOUIS NAVELLIER

Navellier & Associates

Louis Navellier admits his reputation is changing. He was once known as a premier small-cap specialist. Now he has a publication called the *Louis Navellier's Blue Chip Growth Letter,* which is devoted to large company stocks. And while he used to just manage a handful of small-cap aggressive growth mutual funds, he now oversees value, large-cap, and international portfolios as well. Why the sudden expansion? "We're a big firm now and have specialists in all of these areas," he insists. "There are 55 of us and over time we've added all of these new areas."

Navellier likes to compare his investment strategy to flying a plane. "I'm on autopilot," he says. "I run my computer-based models every weekend and follow them religiously. The best way to think of it is if I were flying an airplane, I wouldn't look out the window. I would just read my instruments."

It's no secret that professional managers have had a difficult time keeping up with the S&P 500 in recent years. Navellier maintains that's because all but 28 of the stocks in the S&P are efficiently priced, making it tough for any one person to gain a competitive edge. "Stocks usually get inefficiently priced because of the flow of funds," he says. "Any time a stock's being discovered or institutionalized for the first time, or when Wall Street hasn't properly discounted the fundamentals, it is inefficiently priced."

The only way you can beat the market, according to Navellier, is by finding and buying those inefficiently priced stocks. That's why he focuses on those small-caps, mid-caps, and large-caps that are most neglected by the major institutions. He determines whether a stock is inefficiently priced by looking at its so-called alpha factor. "A stock's return correlated to the market from week to week over the past year is the beta, and the return uncorrelated to the market is this mysterious alpha factor," he explains. "There are a lot of stocks out there that are totally correlated to the market, and 85 percent of big-cap stocks have alphas at or near zero."

Navellier first began honing his investment skills as a finance student in the late 1970s. He didn't buy the conventional wisdom that the stock market was always efficient. "I knew back then there were money managers beating the market," he recalls. So with the help of two professors, he developed several computer models to prove he was right. It's a system he has refined over the years and still uses today. "I'm continuously testing and monitoring what works on Wall Street and rebuilding my models," he says. "I'm really more of a modeler than anything else."

In other words, Navellier uses his computer to find out which stocks and characteristics the majority of investors are in love with at the present time. His theory is that if you want to beat the market, you must buy stocks that aren't simply moving in tandem with it. He puts his database of 9,000 stocks through several bottom-up screens each week. Predictably, he starts off by calculating each company's alpha factor. "I then take the alpha, divide it by a stock's volatility, and get a reward-risk ratio," he says. "The quantitative screens are designed to stack the odds in my favor, and that's what I try to do. The whole process is automated. There's no subjective judgment to it at all."

The computer puts his entire list of stocks through 36 back-testing models, which check various ratios such as price-to-book, dividend discount, cash flow, and PE, along with earnings momentum. "I'm trying to find what Wall Street likes fundamentally [at any given time], because what it likes does change," Navellier reasons. "I'm overlaying fundamental anomalies on my high alpha stocks to tilt the odds in my favor." Based on the results of this and the risk-reward ratio, the computer sorts each stock in terms of relative attractiveness, and the top 10 percent form Navellier's buy list. Right now, Navellier says, Wall Street likes growth at a reasonable price.

As a final step, he uses an optimization model to determine how to mix and match the final list of stocks to get the highest returns with the least amount of risk. "The model will often say put 5 percent in this stock, 2 percent in this stock, 3 percent in this stock, and so forth," Navellier reveals. "What it's trying to do is find stocks that complement each other and represent different industry groups while attempting to lower the overall volatility."

Navellier is highly diversified and has a strong sell discipline. He keeps his average holding 9 to 11 months. "As a stock moves up in price, it tends to become risky," he says. "My allocation model will tell me to cut back, not because it's a bad stock, but because it's getting increasingly less predictable."

Occupation: President and CEO, Navellier & Associates
Reno, Nevada

Birth Date: November 22, 1957

Education: BA, California State University, Hayward, 1978
MBA, California State University, Hayward, 1979

Biggest Mistake Investors Make: "Putting all of their eggs in one basket."

Best Investment: CMGI (Bought in April 1998 and it jumped almost 1,700 percent in less than one year.)

Worst Investment: Digitran Systems (It suspended trading and ultimately went down to zero.)

Advice: "Sell good stocks to buy better stocks."

Market Outlook: Bullish

VITA NELSON

The Moneypaper

Even though some Internet brokers now execute trades for as little as $5, Vita Nelson pays a better price to buy most of her stocks—nothing. How does she do it? By going directly to the company and investing through what are known as dividend investment plans, or DRIPs. Many of the largest companies offer such programs. To get in, you normally have to buy your first share through a broker. But once you're a shareholder and have signed up for the DRIP, you can both reinvest your dividends and buy additional shares of stock at little or no charge. Granted, some companies are more generous than others. Nelson prefers those that give the most benefits free to DRIP participants. She claims they often turn into the best investments too.

Nelson's rise to becoming queen of the DRIPs was an unconventional one, to say the least. In fact, she owes much of her success to the word *divine.* "When I first graduated from college, I went to work at *Mademoiselle* magazine, which seems as far away from the financial markets as you can get," she concedes. "After being there for about a year, I found myself using the word *divine,* and it was associated with a blouse. I figured that was enough, and it was time to get out of there." In other words, she felt she wanted to do something more substantial with her life. So she began looking through the help-wanted section of the newspaper and was attracted to, of all things, an opening as an apprentice in the municipal bond department at Granger & Company. "I was homesick and kept interviewing over the phone," she remembers. "It was in 1960, and even though the company wasn't expecting to have a woman, I got the job."

She learned the bond business from the ground up at Granger. "My boss had to teach me what an eighth of a point translated to," she admits. "I started out bidding on short-term bonds, and after a while, I was on my own and had millions of dollars that I had to keep busy in the market." Several years later, when Nelson and her family moved to Westchester County, she decided it wasn't practical to keep her job at Granger, even though the company offered to make her manager of municipals. She instead took some time off to raise her three children and decided to reenter the publishing business in 1969, this time founding *Westchester Magazine.* She sold it in 1980 and began what is now known as *The Moneypaper.*

"It was originally called *A Financial Publication for Women,*" she recalls. "I looked for strategies to reduce risk because I knew women were risk averse. But it was very hard to market to women using traditional direct mail. I didn't change the focus, but after realizing everything was equally appropriate for men, I changed the title after four years."

What made her especially popular with subscribers was her reporting on DRIPs. "I'm always looking for ways to diversify and minimize risk," she says. "I first found out about dividend reinvestment plans in 1984 in an article in *The Wall Street Journal*. There was a list of companies you could invest in without going to a broker. I started writing about them immediately. In the next issue, I published a portfolio of companies that had these programs and told people what they had to do to enroll in them. It just kept growing from there." Today she also publishes the biweekly *Direct Investing* newsletter and the regularly updated *Guide to Dividend Reinvestment Plans.*

About 1,100 companies offer DRIP programs today, a number that is quickly growing. Again, the catch is that most plans require you to purchase at least one share of stock through a broker before you can enroll. That's become less of a problem now that you can trade stock for just pennies a share. Nelson also has a service that will get you your first share of stock and register you for the DRIP for around $15. She has even started her own mutual fund of DRIPs for those who don't want to do the direct investing on their own. It is designed to track an index of DRIP stocks she created. The index has bested the performance of the S&P 500 most years going back to 1994. The downside to all this, Nelson says, is that some companies now charge fees for their DRIPs, including McDonald's and Walt Disney. She hastens to add that most DRIPs remain attractive and there is almost always a no-fee alternative in every industry.

"For people with limited resources, in terms of research and finances, DRIPs give you a way to diversify without having to go into a mutual fund," Nelson notes. "Small investors with just $500 can spread their risk among 10 or 20 different companies for only $25 a shot. If you had to pay a commission each time, this would be impossible. DRIPs also encourage people who would not otherwise get into the market to get in, and that's the most wonderful part of it."

Occupation: Publisher and Editor, *The Moneypaper*
Mamaroneck, New York

Birth Date: December 9, 1939

Education: BA, Boston University, 1959

Biggest Mistake Investors Make: "Having a lack of patience and reacting with emotion. Also, not having a strategy."

Best Investment: Phelps Dodge (It's the only stock she has traded frequently.)

Worst Investment: Unocal. (Bought on a hot tip in the early 1980s.)

Advice: "Start investing early. Never do anything unless you're following a rational plan."

Market Outlook: Bullish

JAMES O'SHAUGHNESSY

O'Shaughnessy Capital Management

Jim O'Shaughnessy is the only person in this book who can claim to be a friend of Oprah's. Maybe *friend* is a little strong. But he was a guest on her show in 1998, promoting his book *How To Retire Rich*. "I'd never seen her program before when I found out I was booked to appear," he admits. "It was actually a lot of fun. She was a very warm and open person. She does some pretty amazing things for books. Sales went through the roof after my appearance."

The secret to retiring rich, according to O'Shaughnessy, is pretty simple. "First, you've got to start saving money," he says. "Then you must invest it in the stock market, think long term, and use a proven strategy."

O'Shaughnessy is known for backtesting various investment techniques to see which ones make the most money over time. "Underlying empirical evidence shows certain techniques work very well and others perform poorly," he says. "For example, every strategy that bought high-priced stocks in terms of what you had to pay for sales and earnings underperformed during the period I examined."

Why is it so important to stick with a strategy? For the same reason doctors tell their patients not to smoke, O'Shaughnessy explains. "They know there is underlying empirical evidence that proves smoking is bad for your health. The same is true for investing. If you don't stick with a strategy and just go with the hunch of the moment, you're going to be an accidental investor thinking with your heart rather than your head."

O'Shaughnessy should know. He first learned the perils of investing by using his heart after graduating from college. He had some money in the bank and decided to make a living by trading options, which was a disaster. "I realized how difficult it was to trade well over long periods of time," he shares. "I started doing some research and it indicated that the people who made piles of money were investors, not traders. After coming out whole, I changed my focus and became an investor."

He started his own money management firm in 1988 and now has a series of mutual funds that follow the various strategies he has uncovered doing countless studies with various computerized databases. One strategy follows a version of the popular "Dogs of the Dow" technique, which calls for buying the ten highest-yielding stocks in the Dow Jones Industrial Average and holding them for exactly one year. A more sophisticated technique is what he calls his "price momentum strategy." "Stick with low price-to-sales ratios and high relative strength," he advises. "In other words, buy cheap stocks that have done well on a price appreciation basis. Limit yourself to the stocks in your database with a price-to-sales ratio below 1, PE under 20, or price-to-book ratio below 1, which are all indications a stock is cheap. You then marry that to strong price performance over the previous year. What you're doing is buying a stock the market may have hated but is starting to change its mind about." This strategy turned a $10,000 investment in 1951 into $14 million by the end of 1994. During that same period, a similar investment in the S&P 500 only grew to $1 million. O'Shaughnessy also emphasizes the importance of diversification. For him, this means owning at least 50 different stocks from various industries, although he says individuals with smaller portfolios can do well with around 25 names.

His most conservative strategy is perfect for people in retirement, he says. "It focuses on using the Value Line database," O'Shaughnessy explains. "You take the stocks with the highest safety ranking, which is one, and from that list of about 100, you buy the ten with the highest dividend yield. You'll find they're almost always utility companies, yet the capital appreciation component blows bonds out of the water."

Specific company fundamentals, like management and the current business environment, are worthless to O'Shaughnessy, who now manages around $1 billion. "Study after study proves that when you put too much emphasis on that stuff, you end up doing worse in the end," he insists. "There are two ways to invest: the proud way and the humble way. The proud way is how most of us invest. We think we're smarter and better than everyone else and can make selections on a stock-by-stock basis. That doesn't work, and 80 percent of all managers can't even beat the S&P 500. The humble way recognizes that no one of us is as smart as all of us. So it searches for empirical evidence and sticks with what works. The human forecaster always loses, but models never vary."

Occupation: President, O'Shaughnessy Capital Management
Greenwich, Connecticut

Birth Date: March 24, 1960

Education: BA, University of Minnesota, 1985

Biggest Mistake Investors Make: "Being short-sighted and not focusing on when you will really want and need your money."

Best Investment: Dell Computer (Bought for a split-adjusted $1.75 in 1995 and still owns it.)

Worst Investment: Purchasing an insurance company stock at age 22 because of a takeover rumor. (He lost more than 30 percent of his money in a short time.)

Advice: "Find a strategy that is right for you and stick with it. Also, keep your eye on the long term. Don't focus on short-term performance."

Market Outlook: "I'm a fully invested bear," he says.

L. ROY PAPP

L. Roy Papp & Associates

If Roy Papp is so keen on large, multinational companies, what's he doing starting his own small-cap fund? "The little stocks have been so badly beaten I figured it might be OK to invest in them if I bought the right ones," he offers. "I also can't be sure I'm right about bigger being better." Talk about hedging your bets!

Even though Papp has lived and traveled all around the world, he's most comfortable here at home. After serving in the military, Papp studied economics at Brown University. He went on to get an MBA at the Wharton School before being recruited by the Chicago investment firm Stein, Roe & Farnham. "I started out as an accounting man in training working specifically for Wells Farnham," Papp says. "I was really a glorified clerk, but I worked my way up to becoming a senior partner in the firm."

Along the way, Papp was also involved in politics, which led to an appointment on the Fannie Mae board in 1969. A few years later, he got a personal invitation from President Ford asking him to become the U.S. ambassador to the Asian Development Bank in Manila. "My wife and I decided to accept, and I resigned from both Fannie Mae and Stein Roe."

As a bank director, Papp helped to decide which countries got loans. Although he didn't do any investing as part of this role, he still played the market with his own personal money. "Because I was in Manila, I was never awake when the New York Stock Exchange was open, and I got the *New York Times* about two weeks late," he says. "It was clear to me I could not buy stocks that required quick judgments. So I focused on companies that I felt comfortable owning for three or four years. This was in 1975. Stocks were so cheap at that point, it wasn't hard to find things that were attractive. I learned to just sit with my investments and hold on. As it turned out, I made more money being on the other side of the world using that philosophy than I did actively managing accounts at Stein Roe."

After his term on the Bank ended, Papp and his wife headed for Phoenix, where he started his own investment shop. At first he managed money for friends out of his home. Once his business grew, he recruited son Harry and Harry's wife, Rose, to join him in the firm. Today, L. Roy Papp & Associates manages some $1.3 billion in both private accounts and three mutual funds.

Papp's a big believer in the amazing economic growth that continues to take place around the globe, so much so that he started a fund in 1991 called America-Abroad. But he exploits this potential through buying U.S. multinationals instead of foreign stocks. "I think you're a lot safer that way," he maintains. "You don't expose yourself to currency risk, you avoid having to deal with varying accounting standards, you save on operating expenses, and you don't have to worry about the political instability inherent in some countries. Most important, you have SEC protection. You don't get this when you buy foreign stocks. We've had very few financial scandals in the United States over the last 50 years. That's an enormous plus."

Sticking with American companies, according to Papp, also lets you invest in the future instead of the past. "The big businesses in smaller countries are involved in steel, cement, and infrastructure," he observes. "You can't export this stuff. They're behind the rest of the world, not in front of it like we are in the United States. Our economy is based on technology, which is the future. That's worth a much higher premium."

As for the argument that owning foreign stocks helps to increase the diversification of your portfolio, Papp counters that's nonsense. "World markets tend to move in the same direction," he insists. "There is one major difference. If we catch cold, everyone else gets pneumonia. Conversely, if others catch cold, we usually aren't affected. For example, everyone said that when Japan got into trouble in the 1980s we would too. But we didn't."

When Papp searches for investment ideas in addition to a global business plan, he looks for companies growing at a good rate. "I don't want them doubling every year because that can't be maintained," he notes. "The ideal rate for me is 20 or 25 percent a year, but a good rate is 12 percent. And I want to buy stocks at a multiple at or near that of the overall market." He also prefers monopolies but will settle on leaders in their industry. He'll let go of a holding once it trades for a 50 percent premium over its intrinsic value. "Because that number changes every day, I don't think you're wise setting a specific price," he says. "There are really three good reasons to sell a stock: you screw up, the industry changes, or the company is so successful that it becomes overpriced."

Occupation: Managing Partner, L. Roy Papp & Associates
Phoenix, Arizona

Birth Date: March 18, 1927

Education: AB, Brown University, 1951
MBA, Wharton School, University of Pennsylvania, 1955

Biggest Mistake Investors Make: "Trying to get a high yield or return; you always wind up buying poor quality because high return equals high risk."

Best Investment: Richard Irwin (Bought in 1975 for $10.50 a share; Dow Jones acquired the company a month later for $26.)

Worst Investment: A North Sea oil stock he purchased in the 1960s, on which he lost most of his money.

Advice: "Stick with quality companies, even when it comes to investing in the Internet."

Market Outlook: Bullish

DON PHILLIPS

Morningstar

Don Phillips may be the most influential voice in the mutual fund industry today. As CEO of Morningstar, he has the ear of the press, investors, and mutual fund managers alike. Phillips has been interested in the fund industry since the age of 14, when he used some paper route money to buy shares of the Templeton Growth Fund. "It was magic to me," he remembers. "I was the least important investor on the planet, and John Templeton was my personal money manager. I just thought that was great. I still do. It's part of the magic of funds. You and I can have access to managers that used to be reserved for only the very elite."

Phillips started college as an economics major, but the prospects of working in a bank in the early 1980s weren't very appealing. He wound up getting a literature degree and came to Chicago for graduate school, intent on becoming a professor of literature and an active investor on the side. When he finished his master's program, he had a change of heart. "I was at the point where I had to consider locking myself up in a library for the next seven or eight years to pursue a PhD, and it wasn't very appealing," he admits. "So I asked myself, Why don't I switch this around and see if I can get a job writing about investments and read the great books on the side?"

As crazy as it sounds, his goal was to write about mutual funds even though he wasn't sure such a position even existed. As luck had it, when he looked through the classifieds in 1986, he spotted such a job with a start-up called Morningstar. The company had been formed in the apartment of a 20-something investment analyst named Joe Mansueto just two years earlier. Phillips responded to the ad, immediately hit it off with Mansueto, and became one of the firm's first analysts. Morningstar has since evolved into the most revered name in the mutual fund rating business. The company's focus has shifted from providing written fund reports to delivering this information on the Internet through its Web site, www.morningstar.net.

Morningstar monitors almost 11,000 funds. It lumps them together in terms of asset class (e.g., large-cap growth, international) and gives each one a rating of one to five stars, five being best, based on long-term performance relative to risk. All figures are further adjusted for any and all associated costs, including loads and sales charges. It's a totally objective system based solely on the numbers. "You don't want the rating to be influenced by how cordial the manager is or how well he or she is able to sell the company's story," Phillips notes.

Even though fund companies tend to play up their four-star and five-star funds in advertisements, Phillips warns against using these numbers as a sole determinant of fund selection. "The stars are just a first-stage screen that you might want to use to identify funds that have had success in the recent past," he explains. "Remember, you're looking at the shell of a fund and how the net asset value has changed over time when you're looking at the star ratings. Ultimately, you want to get down further than that to the fundamentals. You want to make sure the people and practices that built the record are still in place. Then you've got to ask yourself how things might be different going forward. To do this, you have to understand what a fund has done to get that success. Has it taken big risks? Has it deviated from its policies? Maybe it follows a very sane policy that has simply been out of favor."

Phillips himself claims he makes a point of avoiding top-performing funds and instead puts his money in middle-of-the-road, consistent performers. "My experience has been that those are the funds that make more money for people as opposed to the ones that shoot way up and then come way down," he offers. "It seems that a lot more people ride those fickle funds down." Despite the recent popularity of index funds, Phillips says he personally doesn't own any. "It's not that indexing is bad. I just believe that active management can be a better solution," he offers. Including his 401(k), Phillips owns about 20 funds and says he seldom sells or switches around. He also owns a few stocks, which he says are more for entertainment than anything else. (Incidentally, Morningstar now offers a stock research and monitoring service as well.)

Phillips expects the fund industry to continue well into the new millennium. "Funds are the investment vehicle of choice for the whole baby boom generation of Americans," he observes. "It's an investment vehicle that makes enormous sense. Funds have several powerful advantages: instant diversification, convenience, and professional management, probably in that order."

Occupation: CEO, Morningstar, Inc.
          Chicago, Illinois

Birth Date: April 10, 1962

Education: BA, University of Texas at Austin, 1985
          MA, University of Chicago, 1986

Biggest Mistake Investors Make: "Identifying good funds but assembling bad portfolios by buying last year's leaders. Almost by definition, you're buying funds that are doing the same thing, so you're not really diversified."

Best Investment: Templeton Growth Fund (Bought at age 14 and still owns it. It taught him he could be an investor at an early age.)

Worst Investment: Cineplex Odeon (Purchased for $12 a share in 1986 and sold it for $4 two years later.)

Advice: "Balance your portfolio. Own both small and large stocks."

Market Outlook: Cautious

MARCUS ROBINS

The Red Chip Review

After years of analyzing small-cap stocks, Marcus Robins has learned that when it comes to evaluating top management, five warning signs indicate trouble ahead: black shirts, great tans, double-breasted suits, hair pieces, and tons of jewelry. "These almost always let you know you're dealing with problem people that you should probably stay away from," says Robins. He publishes *The Red Chip Review,* a newsletter that specializes in analyzing small-cap companies. Robins has lived in Oregon all of his life. Early on, he felt destined to get into medicine. He worked in one hospital or another from the time he was a freshman in high school to the day he graduated from college. But after getting his bachelor's degree, Robins had a change of heart. He decided instead to enroll in graduate school, not to become a doctor, but to get into money management. It was quite a change, though not that far-fetched, as he had been fiddling with the stock market since he was in the fifth grade.

Armed with a master's in administration, Robins went to work as a broker at a small investment boutique in Portland. The year was 1979. "It turned out I wasn't very good at sales, but I was good at analyzing companies," he recalls. "So I was the base foundation of what became our research department. Five years later, I went on to help found another local boutique before moving to the institutional side." In 1988 he got his first shot at money management when he joined Capital Consultants and became primary manager of the WestCap Small-Cap Growth Portfolio. "It was a $100 million western state–based small-cap fund that consisted solely of individually managed accounts," Robins explains. "I wanted to start a public mutual fund, but my boss didn't, so I decided it was time to do something else."

Then two monumental things happened in his life. First, he was about to turn 40 and began rethinking the direction of his career. Then he made a remarkable killing in a small-cap stock called American Pacific. "It's a specialty chemical company, which drew on my background in medicine and chemistry," he says. "In May of 1988, the company's only facility in Henderson, Nevada, blew up, and the stock was crushed down to $2. But American Pacific was an expert at producing ammonium perchlorate, which is used in solid rocket motors to supply oxygen. The U.S. government essentially put the company back in business within 18 months. At the end of 1991, the stock was discovered by two major brokerage companies. It had gone from $2 to $40 when I sold out on February 29, 1992." Although Robins won't say how much he made from his investment, he claims to have owned "a ton" of the stock.

He cashed out, quit his job, and made plans to start his own publication geared toward small-cap company research. He taught a finance course at Portland State University at the time and recruited several of his best students to help analyze companies in the basement of his home. The first edition of *The Red Chip Review* was published on August 2, 1993. "The philosophy behind my business was quite straightforward," Robins confides. "At that time, the institutional research and brokerage arena was concentrating more and more on the biggest 500 or 1,000 companies. But the best performance historically has come from small-cap stocks. I wanted to start the Morningstar of small-cap and micro-cap stocks. It would be a source of unbiased and independent research on these companies, which is something no one else offered."

There are around 11,000 tiny companies trading on the over-the-counter market, although Robins only considers about 4,500 of them to be legitimate. Of those, he's winnowed down the list of the most promising candidates to just 300. Those are the ones he covers and assesses for his readers during the course of the year. For Robins, 20 is a magic number. "My ideal company is one growing earnings by at least 20 percent annually, with a return-on-equity prospect of 20 percent, insider ownership of at least 20 percent, and institutional ownership of less than 20 percent. If I can find that kind of stock and then buy it for a multiple of less than 20, it's probably a pretty good bet." Of course, he believes good management is of utmost importance and avoids what he calls "Slick Willie" executives who own little or none of their company's stock. "I like down-to-earth managers with a lot of their wealth tied up in the business," he discloses.

Contrary to some of the other panelists in this book, Robins insists small-cap stocks should be held for the long haul. "The element of risk declines dramatically with time," he notes. "I tell my subscribers that to make really big money in these stocks, you have to be an investor, not a trader." Nevertheless, he always sets a price target when he goes in, which is always being reevaluated as the stock moves up (or down) in price.

Occupation: Publisher and Editor, *The Red Chip Review*
Portland, Oregon

Birth Date: December 8, 1953

Education: BS, Willamette University, 1976
MAd, Willamette University, 1979

Biggest Mistake Investors Make: "Selling quality companies too soon."

Best Investment: Synthetec (It went from 34¢ to $15 from 1991 to 1996.)

Worst Investment: Boyd's Wheels (Bought in 1997 for $12, got out at $4, and it ultimately went to zero.)

Advice: "Avoid stocks or sectors where there is euphoria or a consensus of opinion."

Market Outlook: Bullish

ROBERT SANBORN

The Oakmark Fund

Although Robert Sanborn has a brilliant long-term track record and was once crowned the nation's number-one fund manager by *Barron's,* money has been bleeding out of his Oakmark Fund over the past year. The problem? Sanborn is a value manager, and until mid-1999, it seemed nobody wanted to own value stocks. Money still isn't flowing into this area very fast. "I've gone from having $9 billion to $6 billion in assets," he laments. "But I feel the almost unanimous view that value is dead is creating an environment that will allow value investors to add more value going forward than ever before." In fact, Sanborn says he's very excited about the prospects for the companies in his portfolio, even though he's cautious about the overall market.

Sanborn has always had a natural bias toward finding cheap stocks. The Boston native grew up in a middle-class family and quickly learned the importance of making every dollar count. "I have a younger brother and sister, and my parents never had a lot of money," he reflects. "We did all of our shopping at discount stores like Filene's Basement. We were always looking for a bargain."

While studying at Dartmouth College, Sanborn was interested in economics and contemplated becoming a professor. But shortly after starting graduate school at the University of Chicago, he decided the lifestyle of an academic wasn't for him. "I found I really enjoyed investing and decided to get an MBA instead of a PhD," he says.

He initially became a securities analyst for the Ohio State Teachers Retirement System pension fund. A few years later, he left to become a portfolio manager at the respected Chicago value investment firm Harris Associates. Back then, Harris managed private accounts only. In 1991 Sanborn convinced company brass to let him launch The Oakmark Fund. Talk about a grand entrance! In its rookie year, Oakmark was up 48 percent compared with a gain of 9 percent for the S&P 500. Oakmark quickly became the number-one fund in the nation, turning Sanborn into a star in the world of personal finance.

While low PEs, reasonable price-to-book ratios, and high dividend yields are the gauges most value investors use to define "value," Sanborn follows a different path. "All of these things are meaningless to me even though I think of myself as a core value investor," he says. "I look at what a business is worth to an owner who owns the whole thing. My view is very eclectic. I can look at a very high-growth company, and if it trades for the right price, I'm interested."

He also wants to make sure every stock he considers is backed by a strong business. "The longer I'm in this field, the more skeptical I am of buying lousy businesses at any price," he says. That's one reason he tends to stick with companies boasting market capitalizations of more than $3 billion while avoiding small-cap upstarts. "I think that larger companies are better positioned," he insists. "Their outperformance over the past several years has been justified by the fundamentals. I think the current environment still favors them." Nevertheless, he's been buying more mid-cap stocks lately because he thinks they are much cheaper.

To determine how much a company is worth, Sanborn examines a multitude of factors. "I look at transactions in the marketplace and try to make sense of them and whether they are reasonable," he explains. "I then try to apply those valuations to comparable companies. I like to buy stocks at 60 percent or less of their true value and sell at 90 percent of value. I am constantly monitoring those numbers. It's a hard-core thing for me." He also pays much more attention to cash flow than PE ratios. "The 'E' is accounting earnings, which I find is often not reflective of a company's true financial situation," he says. "That's why I like to look at cash flow more closely than reported earnings."

Sanborn follows several guidelines in his investment discipline. First, of course, he pays attention to price and value. Next, he wants companies with owner-oriented management. "I will not invest with a lousy management team hoping either someone will take them out or that things will somehow get better," he says. "I always assume the current management team is the one I will be dealing with. If I can't find owner-oriented management, I won't buy the stock." He also believes in portfolio concentration. Sanborn hates to sell a stock. He will only pull the trigger if he has misjudged the management team or if the shares approach that magical number of 90 percent of estimated value. Turnover in The Oakmark Fund averages a meager 20 percent a year.

Occupation: Portfolio Manager, The Oakmark Fund
           Chicago, Illinois

Birth Date: March 8, 1958

Education: BA, Dartmouth College, 1980
           MBA, University of Chicago, 1983

Biggest Mistake Investors Make: "Not knowing why they bought something in the first place."

Best Investment: Liberty Media (He owned the stock from 1991 to 1994 and saw his money multiply more than ten times.)

Worst Investment: Drypers (Bought the stock in 1992 and lost most of his investment.)

Advice: "Be informed, have a long-term program, and stick with it; don't let the inevitable market declines keep you from achieving your investment goals."

Market Outlook: Cautious

STEPHEN SAVAGE
The No-Load Fund Analyst

In the unpredictable world of mutual funds, one thing appears to be certain: "You should keep away from those funds that are ranked poorly," insists Steve Savage, editor and publisher of *The No-Load Fund Analyst.* "It's tough to tell whether a highly rated fund will stay that way. But the bad ones almost always remain dogs." That information is useful because if you eliminate all the stinkers from the list of the 12,000 potential funds competing for your money, you presumably have several thousand fewer names to choose from.

Savage knows a lot about fund ratings. He's devoted most of his career to compiling them. He initially got into the investment area through journalism. In college, Savage was hired by a Canadian newsletter publisher to write for one of its New York–based investment publications. "I got a chance to interview some pretty well-known fund managers," he says. He joined the publisher full-time after graduation and convinced his bosses to let him start a mutual fund research publication, called the *Blue Book of Mutual Fund Reports.* It featured single-page research write-ups on each fund, similar to what Morningstar and Value Line do today. "I went out and bought a computer and learned how to set up my own database and generate my own full-page reports," he says. "I put the whole thing together myself."

The service was marginally successful. However, the publisher faced hard times after a postal strike in Canada and decided to shut the publication down after one year. That was in 1986, right about the time when a then unknown firm called Morningstar launched its first fund research publication. Savage left the company to start his own fund newsletter but had a difficult time building a subscription base. He decided to sell out after just seven months to work as an editor with Wiesenberger, a company known for its meticulous fund research and performance-tracking service. "That job schooled me in the real fine points of mutual fund data and statistics," Savage says.

After being named director of his division, he was charged with modernizing and computerizing Wiesenberger's massive database. "We still had stuff that was being tracked on index cards and hand calculators," Savage notes. "I brought in the resources to build a computerized database and put up a PC network. What used to take 20 hours to calculate now could be done in 30 minutes."

In the winter of 1993, Savage learned that the CEO of Value Line wanted to talk with him about a job. "I called to politely turn her down and we wound up talking for six hours," he remembers. "What they wanted me to do was very exciting. They wanted to build a mutual fund information division from the ground up, applying the Value Line formula to mutual funds, competing head-on with Morningstar." Savage was intrigued by the challenge and accepted the offer.

"The day I started, there was nothing more than a drawing on a page of what Value Line wanted to do," he says. "There were no computers or research analysts, and I was supposed to get the product together in six months." By working late nights and weekends, Savage's team almost met the deadline, and the *Value Line Mutual Fund Survey* was born in 1993. He helped the company to develop both print and online versions of the product. Savage claims there's a clear philosophical difference between Value Line and archrival Morningstar. "I would characterize Morningstar as supporting fundamental research on funds, where as the effort at Value Line is put on finding good funds on an individual basis," he explains.

That focus continues at Savage's new job. In May 1999 he became editor and publisher of *The No-Load Fund Analyst,* an Orinda, California–based monthly publication featuring in-depth research on actively managed funds. "The great thing for me is I no longer have a four-hour commute to and from work each day," Savage points out. Instead, he works out of an office near his home in New Jersey. That gives him more time to spend with his wife and three kids.

While Savage personally has a bias toward active management, he concedes indexing makes a good core holding for many portfolios. He also has no problem with investors owning some individual stocks as well. "My ideal fund is run by a manager with an established track record, a philosophy and discipline that make sense, and a support team of researchers and analysts that will help the manager sustain his or her record," Savage adds. "I honestly don't think there are a lot of managers out there who are able to outperform their benchmarks. But there are some. And if you do the work, you can find them."

Occupation: Editor and Publisher, *The No-Load Fund Analyst*
Orinda, California

Birth Date: June 23, 1961

Education: BA, Hunter College

Biggest Mistake Investors Make: "Chasing fads."

Best Investment: Invesco Technology Fund (Bought in December 1995 and still owns it.)

Worst Investment: Budget Group (Purchased for $29.50 in 1998 and sold for $10.50 a few months later.)

Advice: "Discipline is the single most-rewarded trait in investing."

Market Outlook: Bullish

THURMAN SMITH

Equity Fund Research

Thurman Smith is a changed man. Where he used to believe in buying only actively managed funds, he now includes index funds as core holdings in most of his portfolios. But he's quick to point out that even the S&P 500 is actively managed by a committee. "They make sure companies in the index are representative of the main industry sectors and weed out those that are no longer leaders," he says.

Smith publishes the *Equity Fund Outlook* newsletter, which has a small but loyal subscriber base made up largely of professional financial advisers. He's known for his ability to spot promising new funds before the rest of the crowd, which he especially likes because of their flexibility. "Everything else being equal, a new fund can be much better than an old one, mainly because of the smaller asset base," he says.

Smith views mutual fund research as a bilateral process. "It requires using both sides of the brain," he surmises. "You begin by screening funds using the performance numbers and then you look at the fundamentals." Smith uses various computer programs he developed over the years to examine these statistics. He actually got started in the business as a computer applications programmer for several different investment companies, including State Street Bank and Fidelity Investments. After doing this for awhile, he decided he'd rather be the actual investment manager instead of just creating programs that allowed other people to do it. Since he already had an MBA in finance and investing, he decided to start his own investment firm and immediately began putting money to work for clients using no-load mutual funds.

"I like funds because your universe is under control and you solve the problem of diversification for clients who don't have large accounts," he explains. "An account under $1 million would probably be better off in funds rather than in individually managed stocks, in terms of efficiency, reward-risk, diversification, and expenses."

Smith spends much of his day in front of his computer running screens to uncover tomorrow's top performers. "I realized it was possible to evaluate managers by using some computer tools to generate reward-risk ratios for individual funds. This type of analysis is more useful for evaluating funds and predicting their performance than simply using calendar period figures," he reasons. "I had developed enough software and data to generate a newsletter prototype, and I launched *Equity Fund Outlook* in 1988, figuring if I had all this information, I might as well get something out of it and some national exposure as well."

Smith's custom-built system may sound complicated, but the rationale behind it isn't. "I compare up and down market performance over the past three years," he explains. "During that time, we've had 12 up periods and 6 down ones. That's more useful than looking at beta or standard deviation or anything else I can find. I examine the actual behavior of the funds relative to the Wilshire 5000 index in those up and down periods, which have nothing to do with calendar periods." Smith's database contains 300 funds, which he selects using other computerized products, including Morningstar, and by reading various financial publications.

Once he's run his screens, he gives each fund a grade, which determines whether it winds up on his buy or sell list. To get an "A," a fund must do well in good markets and not fall as much as its peers in bad ones. "Given the same risk level, it would have to have the highest growth potential or reward factors, as measured by its up-market performance," he points out. However, even if a fund is explosive during bull markets, he won't even consider it if it goes into a free fall when the market turns south.

Once Smith finds a fund with good numbers, he moves on to evaluate it more closely, including analyzing the person running the show. "The data are just the initial ABC screening," he admits. "I want to know who's behind the wheel." Smith will sell and replace a fund once its growth and risk numbers start to deteriorate. He's certainly not afraid to pull the trigger. Turnover in his momentum-based tax-deferred portfolios can be as high as 100 percent a year, although he admits he's trying to keep that number down.

Smith notes that one style seems to consistently land on top. "Growth at a reasonable price is a discipline that tends to continually do the best," he reveals. "This technique captures both the growth potential of a stock while paying attention to the price you pay for it."

Smith follows equity funds only. He contends that even the most conservative investor should stay away from bonds. "Bonds just don't return enough, and they don't necessarily offset movements in stocks," he maintains. "If you're nervous, you could use an equity-income or value fund instead."

Occupation: President, Equity Fund Research
Boston, Massachusetts

Birth Date: May 9, 1942

Education: BA, University of North Carolina, 1965
MBA, Babson College, 1976

Biggest Mistake Investors Make: "Not having a properly diversified portfolio."

Best Investment: Oakmark Select (Purchased it in 1996.)

Worst Investment: Oakmark Small Cap (Bought this fund in 1995.)

Market Outlook: Bullish

LOUIS STANASOLOVICH

Legend Financial Advisors

Louis Stanasolovich really believes in diversification, even when it comes to mutual funds. "On a $500,000 portfolio, I might use 13 to 15 funds, depending on the circumstances," he says. Stanasolovich's first rule of mutual fund investing is to buy the manager, not just the fund. "I won't invest in a fund without getting to know the person who is running it," he claims. "I also ask for biographies of all the key analysts and traders, because a lot of turnover among your underlying staff will create chaos in the organization."

Stanasolovich notes that his main reason for getting to know the manager is to make sure the investment approach parlayed on paper and in marketing brochures is accurate. "I send out a questionnaire to each manager I'm considering with about 120 questions on it," he shares. "It covers everything from what they manage privately to how much is in their funds. It also asks about all the members of the management team, how long those people have been around, and how they are compensated [he likes those that get an incentive for good performance]." His favorite funds are run by smaller, boutique investment firms where the manager is also an owner. He also prefers fund companies that don't know how to market as that allows their asset base to remain relatively small. As a result, he tends to avoid families like Fidelity and Putnam.

Stanasolovich has an accounting background and started out as a cost analyst for U.S. Steel Corporation after college. "I was trying to find somewhere to put the extra money I was making, and all I knew about were credit unions, savings bonds, and things like that," he reflects. "A buddy of mine was taking an investment course, and I joined him." Soon after completing the class, he read about the International Association for Financial Planning (IAFP), an industry trade association, and decided to get into the business. He joined a financial planning and asset management firm after receiving his securities license and started his own company, Legend Financial Advisors, six years ago.

"Most of my clients come in with money they've either invested on their own or through a broker who was selling a product," Stanasolovich says. "It's hard to tell whether someone earning a commission is working in your best interest. I would say 97 times out of 100 they aren't. I work strictly on a fee-only basis and believe that's the future of the brokerage industry. It's what the investing public wants. It used to be that half of my clients would start off by asking how I'm compensated. Now I'd say the number is closer to 95 percent."

Stanasolovich builds each portfolio by first figuring out which investment styles and markets he wants to target. Then he puts money to work by buying funds that represent each of those asset classes. "I do it on a valuation basis," he says. "Right now, I think U.S. large-caps are extremely expensive. I'm not out of that area completely, but I've cut back my allocation. I also have between 10 and 15 percent of my clients' money in real estate funds." He prefers funds because they give him more options and have documented performance records. "I believe when you buy a private manager, you're buying sex appeal," he insists. "You can get a huge amount of diversification by using several funds rather than just placing your money with one manager. I believe you need to have all of the major styles covered and it's not practical to do that using individual managers. You have to use funds."

The typical account under Stanasolovich's control contains components of large-cap growth, large-cap value, small-cap growth, small-cap value, two different real estate funds, a hedge fund, a small-cap international fund, and a couple of developing-market funds. He tries to choose one manager for each targeted style.

Although Stanasolovich normally uses actively managed funds, he now buys index funds for the large-cap U.S. growth portion of some client portfolios. "When you're buying big stocks, your universe is maybe 200 securities," he rationalizes. "Therefore, if an active fund is buying 50 or 60 stocks, those stocks aren't going to perform much differently than the S&P 500. So in that case it makes sense. But I don't think it makes sense for small-caps at all. There are about 8,000 small stocks to choose from, so a manager can definitely add value."

Even though Stanasolovich likes to personally get to know each fund manager, he admits that's not easy for the average investor to do. Therefore, he recommends reading the various financial publications and only looking at funds with excellent performance when running your initial screens. "I watch all of my funds very closely to make sure they're keeping up with the indexes for their investment style," he says. "I don't have a lot of turnover, maybe two or three funds a year."

Occupation: Founder and President, Legend Financial Advisors, Inc. Pittsburgh, Pennsylvania

Birth Date: February 5, 1957

Education: BS, Pennsylvania State University, 1979

Biggest Mistake Investors Make: "Reading the news, taking for granted it's correct, and then projecting it into the future."

Best Investment: Caldwell and Orkin Market Opportunity Fund (Bought it in 1997, and it went up about 40 percent in 18 months.)

Worst Investment: An oil and gas penny stock he purchased in the 1980s that went belly-up.

Advice: "Hire a good adviser and/or seek out good sources of information."

Market Outlook: Bullish

ED WALCZAK

Vontobel USA

Ed Walczak is a big believer in portfolio concentration, just like his investment idol, Warren Buffett. For starters, he only keeps around 17 stocks in his $134 million Vontobel US Value fund. What's even more amazing is that he owns only five stocks in his personal portfolio. "I think this kind of concentration makes the most intellectual sense," Walczak insists. "Buffett says you only need three or four investments over your lifetime, so I'm actually pretty diversified. And I would never consider indexing."

As a kid growing up in Norwich, Connecticut, Walczak dreamed of one day becoming a garbage man. "It was neat to see those guys get out there and toss cans into the air," he says. "I thought it was a cool profession as a boy and still do." The only son of a professional baseball player, Walczak decided to study government in college and thought about going to law school. "Instead, I got a graduate degree in international economics before going on for my MBA," he recalls.

His first job was working in the finance department at Ford Motor Company in Ann Arbor, Michigan. "I did that for a little over a year, but it just wasn't as interesting as I thought it would be," he shares. A headhunter then offered him a job in the General Motors Treasury Department in New York. "The most intriguing thing I did was conduct research on why the Japanese could build cars cheaper than us in the late 1970s," he notes. After less than three years at GM, another headhunter offered to bring him to Wall Street.

He landed a job working in institutional sales for Sanford C. Bernstein & Co. in 1982. "I liked the culture there, however I got tired of making the same sales calls over and over again," he admits. "I then decided to switch from sales to junior portfolio manager at Lazard Freres in late 1984." After a few years there, yet another headhunter came with an offer he couldn't refuse—the chance to manage money on his own at Vontobel. "I had never heard of it," Walczak concedes. "I did some research and found out that Vontobel seemed to be a reputable Swiss bank. That was 11 years ago."

Walczak now runs $350 million in various portfolios, including the Vontobel US Value fund. His investment style has evolved over time. At first, he combined both the quantitative and qualitative traits he learned from his first two jobs on Wall Street. "It was more of a Graham and Dodd approach, emphasizing low PE and low price-to-book stocks," he says. "Then I kind of hit the books, and the more I read about Warren Buffett's work, the more I realized how much I agreed with his style." Walczak proceeded to dig up Buffett's old annual reports and became a self-described "Buffett Moonie."

"Just like Buffett, the quality of a company is the most important thing I look for in a potential investment," he says. "I keep my eye on such things as high returns on capital, shareholder-oriented management, elements of a franchise, predictable earnings, and free cash flow. The company should also be involved in an unregulated industry."

After that, he examines whether the company sells for a cheap price. "This involves figuring out its intrinsic value, or what it's really worth," he explains. "I try to go out a number of years in the future and make a reasonable guesstimate about whether the current returns can be sustained for several years into the future. If so, I'll come up with some earnings and free cash flow estimates going forward and discount those numbers back to the present using today's level of interest rates. I usually use the ten-year bond. I look for value in stocks the same way I do for bonds. I am really looking at a company's prospective future returns compared with what I could get in a risk-free 10-year or 30-year government bond. For me to be seduced out of a risk-free investment, a stock has to offer sufficient increments of return."

Walczak has been having a tough time finding stocks that meet his qualifications in recent years. He was holding around 30 percent cash at last check, which has hurt his performance. "If I can't find something that's attractive relative to the risk-free rate, I'll sit on the sidelines," he maintains. "Cash is the residual of my inability to find attractively priced stocks in today's environment."

His sell discipline is equally straightforward. "I'll get rid of a stock for one of two reasons," he notes. "If my thesis for buying has deteriorated, which is a nice way of saying I'm wrong, or if the stock becomes fully valued."

Occupation: Chief Investment Officer, Vontobel USA
New York, New York

Birth Date: September 17, 1953

Education: BA, Colby College, 1975
MA, Columbia University, 1976
MBA, Columbia University, 1978

Biggest Mistake Investors Make: "Chasing historical performance; being too short term–oriented."

Best Investment: Buying regional bank stocks at distressed prices in 1990; many more than doubled in subsequent years.

Worst Investment: Not owning many technology stocks (They don't fit his valuation criteria but have done well in the market.)

Advice: "Be disciplined and, like Buffett says, wait for the pitch. Don't buy unless there's something that's really attractive and undervalued."

Market Outlook: Cautious

MARTIN WHITMAN

Third Avenue Funds

Why have investors been so disinterested in recent years in the cheap stocks Marty Whitman buys? "The inmates are running the insane asylum," he insists. "It's unbelievable." While investors are scooping up shares of the most expensive stocks, the downtrodden issues Whitman focuses on have been getting more and more inexpensive. "I think it's fantastic," he adds. "I haven't been able to find this many bargains since 1974."

As a so-called vulture investor, Whitman loves to read the new low list in the *Wall Street Journal.* "I want to buy what's safe and cheap," he says. Whitman earned his vulture reputation by building a career out of investing in distressed companies that others expected to go out of business. "There's almost nothing I go into where the near-term outlook isn't terrible," he points out. It's a field of expertise he got into almost by accident. "After serving in the Navy, I originally planned to teach economics," he remembers. "But after finishing graduate school, I saw there wasn't much of a future for me as an academic, so I went to work on Wall Street."

He started in research before moving into investment banking, managing private money, and ultimately doing control investing. Whitman first began specializing in distressed companies in the early 1970s, when he decided to start his own firm. "I wanted to do corporate finance, but didn't have a lot of money," he says. "There were two fields that were wide open, where I didn't have to compete with big firms like Morgan Stanley and Goldman Sachs. They were bankruptcy and shareholder litigation. I built quite a reputation in both areas." Originally, Whitman just gave advice to troubled companies. But he soon realized he could make more money by investing in them instead as a portfolio manager. Today, in addition to managing private accounts and two mutual funds, he teaches a course on control investing at Yale.

Whitman invests in both the stocks and bonds of distressed companies. The instrument he uses depends on where he sees the most opportunity. "In all cases, the companies I'm buying have cash well in excess of total book liabilities," he points out. "I also won't pay more than a 60 percent premium over book value and rarely pay more than 12 times what the company's historic net income has been. This is designed to simulate the pricing a first-stage venture capitalist would pay if he were financing a private company."

When it comes to investing in severely troubled companies, Whitman almost always prefers secured debt over common stock because he wants to own the most senior issue available in case of any potential reorganization. "For credit securities, I always assume there will be a credit default," he notes. "Then I figure out how I will come out in the event that happens."

Although Whitman describes what he does as a form of value investing, he pays little attention to traditional indicators of value, like dividend yields and PE ratios. "Graham and Dodd (the two noted authorities on value investing) are all screwed up," he maintains. "I analyze companies just like Warren Buffett does. I examine the values in the business and stop. The basic analysis of all the amateurs, including Graham and Dodd, is to try and determine at which price a stock will sell. You carry an awful lot of excess baggage with that kind of methodology." He also couldn't care less about the overall market. "That's only important to incompetents who want to make a lot of money by charging fees for stuff like asset allocation," he maintains. "For people who know about the companies they invest in, the market is immaterial. There are always bull and bear markets."

Whitman's portfolio turnover averages less than 15 percent a year. "Most of my companies get taken out through mergers and acquisitions," he says. "If I'm doing everything right, there ought to be a lot of takeovers in any six-month or one-year period. I will sell a stock on my own if I conclude I've made a mistake or find out the guy in charge is a crook." Two warning signs are when management starts to "burn" cash or the company has a successive string of bad operating results. Whitman admits that some 20 to 30 percent of his stocks turn out to be total clunkers. However, the gains from his winners more than make up the difference.

As for his own future, Whitman insists he has no immediate plans to retire. "I'd become a tennis pro if I could, but I don't think that's likely to happen," he says.

Occupation: CEO and Chief Investment Officer, Third Avenue Funds
New York, New York

Birth Date: September 30, 1924

Education: BS, Syracuse University, 1949
MA, New School of Social Research, 1956

Biggest Mistake Investors Make: "Not paying attention to fundamentals and not being price conscious."

Best Investment: Nabors Industries (Paid 40¢ a share for the stock in 1987, and it's now worth around $20. He's also a director of the company.)

Worst Investment: Union Federal (Bought for $2 a share in 1993, and it ultimately went to zero.)

Advice: "Buy extremely well-capitalized companies and don't pay more 50¢ for every dollar you think it might be worth presently as a private company."

Market Outlook: Cautious

DAVID WILLIAMS

U.S. Trust

Throughout the early 1990s, David Williams had a record every mutual fund manager envied. His Excelsior Value and Restructuring Fund was the top-performing general equity fund in the nation for a five-year period ending in 1997, returning 27.2 percent annually, 6.9 percent ahead of the S&P 500. Then came 1998, when his fund underperformed along with most others in the value category. He was up around 10 percent compared with the S&P's 28 percent. In most years, that would still be an admirable showing.

And it's the kind of performance Williams thinks investors will be grateful for in the new millennium because he expects stock market returns to become much more "normal" going forward.

Williams majored in art history at Yale in the 1960s and was a Navy pilot for five years. "After that, I went to Harvard Business School and decided I would like to manage money," he recalls. "My first job was working at T. Rowe Price [in 1974] managing private and pension accounts. For the six months I was there, the market went down like clockwork every day. It was an unbelievable period to be exposed to investing." It got so bad that the firm brought in a psychologist to help managers deal with belligerent clients who were furious about getting negative returns. "They kept saying, 'Why should we give money to you when we can get 4 or 5 percent from the bank without taking any risk?' And they were serious," Williams notes. "Now, of course, no one would think of putting their money in a savings account while the market is doing so well."

Nevertheless, Williams isn't apathetic. He has no doubt we'll go through another period like 1974 again. It's just a matter of when. "It all has to do with inflation," he insists. "For the time being, I think inflation's under good control and won't be a problem for the foreseeable future. However, there will come a time when we have higher inflation and the market will take a beating because of it."

Williams spent five years at T. Rowe Price before starting his own investment firm with a partner in New York. They weren't making much money, so Williams took a job with Horizon Trust as chief investment officer in 1981. Six years later, he joined U.S. Trust. "For the first couple of months, I was in charge of a new product that was marketed to smaller accounts of between $250,000 and $2 million," he says. "Most of the proceeds were invested in our mutual funds. Then they asked me to manage larger accounts. My fund was launched in 1993. Today I run about $2 billion altogether."

Like the quirky name of his fund suggests, Williams looks for companies selling at value prices that often are going through some type of restructuring. "I try to find companies that are under a cloud," he explains. "They've disappointed Wall Street for one reason or another. I really like companies that are in difficulty

237

but have done something to indicate they recognize the problem and are addressing it. Often the companies I invest in sell for relatively cheap prices. By that I mean they have low PE or price-to-cash flow ratios. They also often have new CEOs who are changing what the old management botched up."

Finding companies under a cloud and on the bargain table isn't hard. The challenge is separating those that belong there from those that are unduly being punished yet have a lot of promise. Williams concedes you can never be sure about this, although he feels like he improves his chances by scheduling an in-person meeting with management. "It may be psychological, but it does give me more confidence when I hear the story from the horse's mouth rather than secondhand from a Wall Street analyst," he says. "You get a sense of how good members of management are by how they talk. You also learn whether their plan for their company makes sense. If I get a good feeling from management, more often than not it turns out to be a successful investment."

In today's market, Williams prefers to buy companies trading for a below-market multiple. "By mere chance, the stocks in my portfolio have consistently sold at about a 33 percent discount to the S&P 500 since day one," he offers. One way he reduces risk is by maintaining a well-diversified portfolio of some 85 names. "I always have something that's working," he adds. "I have both big and small companies and keep roughly 10 percent overseas."

Going into 2000, he's somewhat cautious on the outlook for stocks but says he'd become more worried if one party wins both the U.S. presidency and Congress this year. "I think that would spell the end to the bull market," Williams predicts. "The market likes gridlock."

Occupation: Managing Director, U.S. Trust
New York, New York

Birth Date: July 4, 1942

Education: BA, Yale University, 1965
MBA, Harvard University, 1974

Biggest Mistake Investors Make: "Listening to other people and taking hot tips. You have to do your own work and at least some simple research."

Best Investment: Donaldson, Lufkin and Jenrette. (Purchased four years ago and it has gone up about sevenfold.)

Worst Investment: Arm Financial Group (Bought two years ago and has lost 50 percent of his investment.)

Advice: "Investing is a puzzle. Listen to all the people you can before making a decision. Don't rely on the advice of any one person. In other words, listen to no one, but listen to everyone."

Market Outlook: Cautious

U PDATE
on *Wall Street's Picks for 1999*

Those of you who read *Wall Street's Picks for 1999* might be wondering, "What should I do with those stocks and mutual funds now?" Well, wonder no more because the answer to that pressing question can be found on the following pages. In most cases, I went back to each of last year's panelists and asked, "How do you feel about your pick from last year going into the new millennium? Do you now consider it to be a buy, sell, or hold?" You'll find their responses on the following pages.

Just so we're clear on definitions, *buy* means they still recommend their pick for purchase in the year 2000; *hold* indicates they suggest holding on if you already own the investment; and *sell* is a sign to take your profits (or losses) and move on to other opportunities.

STOCK	PANELIST	CURRENT ADVICE
Airborne Express	Louis Navellier	Sell
Alcatel Alsthom	David Williams	Buy
APT Satellite	Seth Glickenhaus	Hold
B/E Aerospace	Ronald Muhlenkamp	Buy
Boeing	Joseph Battipaglia	Hold
Carnival Corporation	Alan Bond	Hold
Chubb	Ed Walczak	Buy
FSI International	Martin Whitman	Buy
HBO & Company	Fred Kobrick	Buy[1]
Household International	Cappy McGarr	Buy
INACOM	Philip Carret	Hold[2]
Intel	Vita Nelson	Hold
International Paper	James O'Shaughnessy	Sell
Newmont Mining	Anthony Gallea	Hold
Nike	Robert Sanborn	Hold
Orckit Communications	Robert Kern	Buy
Pagenet	Elizabeth Dater	Hold
Pierce Leahy	Michael DiCarlo	Hold
Powerwave Technologies	Margarita Perez	Hold
Speciality Equipment Companies	John Rogers	Buy
STAAR Surgical	Marcus Robins	Buy
State Street	L. Roy Papp	Buy
Sterling Software	Susan Byrne	Hold
Vitesse	Kevin Landis	Hold
Western Digital	Al Frank	Buy

[1] Company was acquired by McKesson in 1999 and is now called McKesson/HBOC.
[2] Carret called INACOM a long-term hold prior to his death in 1998.

FUND	PANELIST	CURRENT ADVICE
American AAdvantage Int'l	Tricia O. Rothschild	Buy
Baron Small Cap	Michael Stolper	Buy
Barr Rosenberg Market Neutral	Peter Brown	Hold
First Eagle Fund of America	Stephen Savage	Buy
J.P. Morgan Tax-Aware U.S. Eq.	Sheldon Jacobs	Buy
Marsico Growth & Income	Bob Markman	Buy
Rainier Core Equity Portfolio	Larry Chin	Hold
Rydex Nova	Paul Merriman	Buy
Selected American Shares	Michael Hirsch	Buy
T. Rowe Price International	Earl Osborn	Buy
Tweedy, Browne American Value	Janet Brown	Sell

GLOSSARY

of Investment Terms

American depositary receipt (ADR)   Receipt for the shares of a foreign-based stock that are held by a U.S. bank and entitle shareholders to all dividends and capital gains. It's a way for Americans to buy shares in foreign-based companies on a U.S. stock exchange.

annual report   Yearly statement of a corporation's financial condition. It must be distributed to all shareholders of record.

asked or offer price   The lowest amount a seller is willing to take for shares of a stock.

asset allocation   Act of spreading investment funds across various categories of assets, such as stocks, bonds, and cash.

beta   A coefficient measure of a stock's relative volatility in relation to the Standard & Poor's 500 index, which has a beta of 1.

bid price   The highest amount a buyer is willing to pay for shares of a stock.

blue chip   Common stock of a nationally known company with a long record of profit growth, dividend payments, and a reputation for quality products and services.

bond   Any interest-bearing or discounted government or corporate obligation that pays a specified sum of money, usually at regular intervals.

book value   What a company would be worth if all assets were sold (assets minus liabilities). Also, the price at which an asset is carried on a balance sheet.

bottom-up investing   The search for outstanding individual stocks with little regard for overall economic trends.

broker   Person who acts as an intermediary between a buyer and a seller.

buy-and-hold strategy   Technique that calls for accumulating and keeping shares in a company over many years regardless of price swings.

cash ratio   Ratio of cash and marketable securities to current liabilities. Tells the extent to which liabilities could be immediately liquidated.

chief executive officer (CEO)   Individual responsible for the overall operations of a corporation.

contrarian   Investor who does the opposite of the majority at any particular time.

convertible bond   Security that can be exchanged for other securities of the is-
suer (under certain conditions), usually from preferred stock or bonds into
common stock.

current ratio   Current assets divided by current liabilities. Shows a company's
ability to pay current debts from current assets.

debt-to-equity ratio   Long-term debt divided by shareholders' equity. Indicates
how highly leveraged a company is. (A figure greater than 1.5 should raise
a red flag.)

diversification   Spreading risk by putting assets into several different investment categories, like stocks, bonds, and cash.

dividend   Distribution of earnings to shareholders.

dividend yield   The cash dividend paid per share each year divided by the current share price.

dollar cost averaging   The process of accumulating positions in stocks and mutual funds by investing a set amount of money each month, thus buying
more shares when prices are down, less when they are up.

Dow Jones Industrial Average   The oldest and most widely quoted stock market indicator. Represents the price direction of 30 blue chip stocks on the
New York Stock Exchange. (Doesn't always give an accurate view of what's
happening with the market as a whole.)

fair market value   Price at which an asset or service is or can be passed on from
a willing buyer to a willing seller.

Form 10-K   Annual report filed with the Securities and Exchange Commission
showing a company's total sales, revenues, and pretax operating income,
along with sales figures for each of the firm's different lines or businesses
over the past five years.

good-till-canceled order (GTC)   A brokerage order to buy or sell shares of a
security at a given price that remains in effect until executed or canceled.

growth stock   Stock of a corporation that shows greater-than-average gains in
earnings.

institutional investor   Organization that trades a large volume of securities, like
a mutual fund, bank, or insurance company.

intrinsic value   Worth of a company; comparable to the prevailing market price.

limit order   Order to buy or sell a security at a specific price or better.

market capitalization or **market value**   Calculated by multiplying the number
of shares outstanding by the per share price of a stock. One can also cate-
gorize equities into several different classes, including micro-cap, small-
cap, mid-cap, and large-cap. The general guidelines for these classifications
are as follows:

- micro-cap—market capitalizations of $0 to $100 million.
- small-cap—market capitalizations of $100 to $750 million
- mid-cap—market capitalizations of $750 million to $2 billion.
- large-cap—market capitalizations of $2 billion or more.

market order   Order to buy or sell a security at the best available price.

mutual fund   An investment company that raises money from shareholders and puts it to work in stocks, options, bonds, or money market securities. Offers investors diversification and professional management.

Nasdaq Composite   An index of the National Association of Securities Dealers weighted by market value and representing domestic companies that are sold over the counter.

net current assets   Assets calculated by taking current assets minus current liabilities. Also referred to as working capital.

price-earnings ratio (PE)   Price of a stock divided by its earnings per share.

price-to-book ratio (PB)   Ratio calculated by dividing shareholders' equity by the number of outstanding shares. If under 1, it means a stock is selling for less than the price the company paid for its assets, though this is not necessarily indicative of a good value.

Standard & Poor's Composite Index of 500 Stocks (S&P 500)   An index that tracks the performance of 500 stocks, mostly blue chips, and represents almost two-thirds of the U.S. stock market's total value. It is weighted by market value. (As an equity investor, your goal should be to beat the return of the S&P 500. This is not an easy task, and roughly 75 percent of all mutual fund managers fail to do so.)

stock   Represents ownership in a corporation. Usually listed in terms of shares.

INDEX

ABOUT THE AUTHOR

Kirk Kazanjian is a nationally recognized investment expert, stock and mutual fund analyst, best-selling author, and lifelong entrepreneur. He is also the director of research and investment strategy for one of the nation's largest fee-only investment management and financial planning firms. Mr. Kazanjian previously spent several years as an award-winning television news anchor and business reporter. He now appears regularly as a guest on radio and TV stations across the country, including CNBC, CNNfn, and Bloomberg. In addition, he is a popular teacher and speaker on investment topics.

The author welcomes your comments and feedback. You also can register to receive his quarterly e-mail newsletter, Wall Street Insider, which is offered complimentary to readers of *Wall Street's Picks for 2000*. Send your comments and requests to <WallStreetsPicks@aol.com>.